KU-247-406

THE LOST COMMAND

The
Lost
Command

ALASTAIR REVIE

Military Book Society

© 1971 Alastair Revie

This edition published by
THE MILITARY BOOK SOCIETY
St. Giles House, 49/50 Poland Street, London W1A 2LG
by arrangement with
David Bruce & Watson Ltd.

Printed in Great Britain by
The Garden City Press Limited
Letchworth, Hertfordshire
SG6 1JS

List of Illustrations

Acknowledgement

The photographs are acknowledged to the following sources:

Crown copyright numbers 1, 2, 3, 4, 6 and 15
Sport and general number 5; Keystone 7, 17, 19 and 20
Photographic News Agencies Limited number 8; Sekker number 9
Associated Press number 10; Fox Photos number 14; Illustrated number 16
Odhams Press numbers 11, 12, 22, 25, 26 and 28
BIPPA numbers 18, 21, 23 and 24
Planet News number 27

Preface

Group Captain Leonard Cheshire,
V.C., D.S.O., D.F.C.

Written by an Army Officer who himself served in World War II, this book has the unmistakable ring of authenticity and truth. To all who may be interested in the story it relates I warmly commend it. Especially to those of the younger generation so concerned with the needs of humanity; so anxious to rectify the man-made imperfections of this world and to make it a better place to spend those fleeting years we call a lifetime. Though the story it relates is over and done with, as are the young lives of so many who took part, it nevertheless has relevance to the present day and to the hopes and longings that flower in every human heart. Moreover it sheds light upon the nature of those men who made up the crews of Bomber Command, and perhaps also upon the lessons and mistakes of the past.

These crews were all volunteers and many of them, especially the Pathfinders, volunteers within a voluntary force. Though mostly from Britain they came also in large numbers from every country of the Commonwealth and Empire as it was then constituted. They came from the occupied countries of Europe—Poland, Czecho-slovakia, France and Norway—and more than a few from Eire. In some cases, as with Canada, they contributed a complete Bomber Group, in others entire Squadrons; for the rest they comprised a stream of individuals of widely differing colour and creed. Many came from countries not then threatened by Hitler, but in order to stand by us in our hour of need and because freedom and justice were at stake. Their backgrounds varied from that of an English Public School to that of the back streets of Glasgow, as represented by

Sergeant Hannah, VC. We soon discovered that the best welded and most efficient squadrons were those containing members from these different countries and dissimilar backgrounds.

But what of the moral issues underlying the task which it befell Bomber Command to attempt and which has been so often discussed? That war is inherently evil no one can deny; the younger generation of 1939 longed no less than the present one for the opportunity to live out their lives in freedom and peace. But like every single individual, no one excepted, the world is a mixture of good and evil; each struggling to overcome the other. At times in our lives we find that there is no option open to us other than to choose the lesser of two evils. Regarded solely in itself the action which we take may appear wrong, perhaps even brutal, but taken in its full context and weighed against the consequences of inaction, or whatever the alternative might be, it may well be seen to operate for the greater good of our fellow men. What for instance if one should be confronted with an assassin in the process of wiping out an entire family? For such, translated into individual terms, was the situation in 1938. Fanatically and deliberately Hitler set out to destroy everyone who stood in the way of his evil dreams. Before war was declared he had decreed that all Jews, all Poles, and all gypsies should be exterminated, and in 1933 had established Dachau, his first concentration camp. In the twelve years between then and the end of the war, he methodically liquidated 20 million men, women and children in these camps; not as a necessity of war but as a matter of predetermined policy. With the exception of a small, and therefore the more courageous, underground movement, whether knowingly or otherwise, the entire nation was behind him. One single resolute stand by Britain at any point on his diabolical march would have been enough to halt him. But despite the many individual voices proclaiming the danger, that stand was not forthcoming. In consequence Hitler was able to pick us off one by one; free to committ his total forces against each individual country successively; and leaving Britain in 1940 as the sole guardian of freedom. Given this situation, given the fact that everything would be lost unless some inroad could be made into their frightening and ever expanding armoury; given all that would follow if Hitler were to break free, what could the crews of Bomber Command do but slam their young bodies against the Nazi fortresses of Europe, as Alastair Revie so vividly puts it in this book. In World War I, in a comparable effort to stem the fearful casualties at the front, Germany was blockaded with a resultant death toll of three quarters of a million, half as many again as those who died under the allied bombing offensive of 1939-45. The irony is that having launched Bomber Command upon its flight path, having given it a precise directive, and having reaped the fruits of its labours such as these were, the politicians then denied its Commander-in-Chief the public honour that his achievements would normally have merited; one almost feels because he was too successful because the politicians of the time recognised the danger of identifying themselves too closely with their own policies which he had implemented to such effect.

For all that it may be that the whole campaign of area bombing, and the way in which it was conducted, did not produce results proportionate to its cost. Those who read this book will form their own judgment. For me these pages that follow depict in a most real and vivid fashion the life and the character of the Command that today is in two senses lost. They reveal its weaknesses, its problems and its mistakes, as well as the spirit which inspired its members, the motives which led them to act as they did, and the odds against which they had to operate.

We were of course, as all well know, a very small part of an infinitely greater whole, so many of whom suffered far greater privations and dangers than we, and who have not received the public honour that we have. But it is my hope that this book will serve to remind that to us who have been privileged to survive, whatever our nationality, has been entrusted the task, each according to our own means, of striving to attain that priceless goal of justice and peace. The goal for which in six years of war 55 million gave their lives.

In the poet Housman's words:

> Here dead lie we because we did not choose
> To live and shame the land from which we sprung
> Life, to be sure, is nothing much to lose,
> But young men think it is and we were young.

Cavendish,   LEONARD CHESHIRE
17 July, 1971.

Chapter One

In the beginning, they stood poised, tensile, with a wide-eyed eagerness for their first take-off. At the end it was all too clear that Bomber Command had suffered a rate of loss never before borne by a military force of comparable size in the history of the world. The price paid in human terms for the strategic and tactical bombing of Germany—*the* major innovation of World War II—was almost unthinkable. In all, more bomber crewmen died between 1939 and 1945 than infantry officers in the slaughter of the trenches of World War. I. It was small comfort that they had been granted, in the process, more awards and decorations than the men of any other arm.

Certainly, no one can set it all down adequately now—least of all those who were close to it. Too much of the deeply-felt detail perished with the few who understood what they were doing; most were too young and too inarticulate even to comprehend the reasons for their deaths. The bare bones of the story are in this book.

The important few who survived to tell the tale have never managed adequately to do so, and probably never will. Adjustment to civilian life is in many cases difficult still. A slamming door can set flak-happy nerves jangling anew. Many still sweat in the night as memories crowd in from the few short years of hell . . . so long ago, and yet too close to bear; some still experience physical nightmares in which their planes are hurtling to certain destruction . . . in which they cannot believe that they survived, when all about them died . . . and in which they cry out in guilt because their error of judgement may have sent following crews to their doom.

Bombers came and went in fifty years. There was only one such force as Bomber Command and there can never be another in history.

Were its efforts and its sacrifices worthwhile? There is no doubt that German war production increased steadily, despite the bombing, between mid-1942 and mid-1944. But it was only in that period that Bomber Command was to get into its stride. Again, the German war economy was never stretched in the early days and only began to expand in 1942. Until that time few women were employed, and industry was operating largely on a single-shift basis. Even in 1944 it had a lot of slack to take up, compared to Britain. At the end of the war there were still a million domestic servants employed by the wives of the 'master race'—the same number as at the beginning. Let us not keep alive the legend that the Nazis were all-efficient as well as all-powerful.

The Allies' bombing offensives eventually brought the German war economy to its knees and hastened its collapse. The infamous '10 year rule' had crippled the inter-war RAF. It had proved impossible to repair its deficiencies in the time available. Alas, had the improvement in operating techniques (through better planes, bombs, devices and aids) taken place earlier, things would probably have gone very differently.

Probably.... No one knows. The imponderables are too numerous and the facts too much wrapped in misrecollection or fantasy. That air power made major contributions to the course of World War II in other roles is not to be argued. That, although the V-2, the submarine, the tank, radar, and a multitude of other advanced ideas, influenced the course of the war, none had a more dominating influence than the heavy bomber, is probably also a fair assessment. But whether the attendant demands made on aircrew, and the sacrifices asked of them, were justified is another matter. They gave more than anyone, but how many people really cared then or now?

The war ended; the leaders retired; the vast fleets of bombers rotted on their hardstandings; the surviving crews went home to their families and to rationing. Only the weather continued its battle in the air, which man can never decisively win.

In all the gloom of the profit and loss accounting of the lost command, there were some miracles to be recorded. 'It can never happen to me' had been the phrase that had kept many thousands of men flying . . . until it did. But among the prisoners of war who returned to Britain in time for the dancing in the streets on VE day were two rank and file aircrew who had lived to tell miraculous tales of how they had been done for and yet had survived. It is to be hoped that they are both drinking out on their incredible stories to this day.

One was Sergeant N. S. Alkamade, who had been tail-gunner in a Lancaster on a raid against Stuttgart in mid-March, 1944. As they were leaving the target, an 88 mm ack-ack shell tore into a fuel tank and flaming petrol engulfed the fuselage. Almost at once the huge plane heeled over in agony, and Alkamade reached for his parachute, which he had hung on a hook by his side. To his horror, it was already a mass of flames and was too far gone to be of any use. The fire was belching around him and his boots were already burning, so he decided to jump anyway, preferring sudden death on the ground to the inferno around him. He jerked open the blistering door and threw himself into the night . . . 18,000 feet over Germany.

Next morning, Sergeant Alkamade woke up, believing himself to be dead, and was surprised to see the sun shining from a cloudless sky overhead. After contemplating this phenomenon for a few minutes, he stirred himself and felt around his body. He had no apparent aches or pains. Then he noticed that he was lying in snow in a pine forest. On standing up, he found he had no boots and his flying suit was in shreds. Broken branches in the trees above him showed where he had plunged to earth. The indications could only add up to the fact that the big trees had reduced his speed and the deep snow had done the rest.

Later in the day, Alkamade was taken prisoner by the local German soldiery, who were disinclined to believe his story. But he kept on about it to the point that an official German investigation was carried out. And when he was eventually released, and flown home, he carried in his pocket a certificate, signed by a German colonel, attesting to the fact that he had fallen three-and-a-half miles without a parachute—surely the greatest plunge of its kind in history.

Jack Worsfold had an equally bizarre story to tell. On the night of 3-4 May, 1944, then a nineteen-year-old, he was also a tail-gunner in a Lanc, and flew with 101 Squadron from Ludford Magna, Lincs, to bomb German tank concentrations in France in preparation for the D-day landings.

It was one of the precision raids of the period, led by 617 Squadron, and Leonard Cheshire was the marker. The moon was high, and a swarm of German fighters took a heavy toll of the 300 Lancasters taking part as they left the target, after bombing it successfully. Worsfold's Lancaster was hit in several places by cannon, and 'brewed-up' at once. He tried to climb through from the tail to see if the others were all right, but the entire fuselage was alight, so he slammed the bulkhead door shut.

The next thing young Worsfold knew was that he was on terra firma in France after having had 'no sensation of falling . . . nothing'. Just after he had closed the bulkhead door, the Lanc had blown up, killing the rest of the crew instantly. The tail-section, with the gunner inside, had been seen by French villagers to fall 7,500 feet, hit some high-tension wires, bounce on to a fir tree and then on to the ground. And a woman in the fields had fainted to see him crawl out with a broken thigh, a broken finger and rib fractures.

The village was Aubeterre. Local Resistance fighters rushed to his assistance, hid him in the woods, and treated his wounds. Eventually he was captured by a German patrol and spent a year in prison camps. In the chaotic days towards the end of the war, while being marched across country, away from the advancing British, he slipped into a ditch, waited and then walked in the opposite direction. It worked. British troops found him hiding in the chimney of an empty house and he was flown home.

Today, Jack Worsfold runs a coal business at Chilworth, near Guildford, Surrey. 'If I ever win the pools,' he says, 'I'll go back to Aubeterre and plant an English oak where I landed.'

He was lucky, and he knows it. But he still broods somewhat unhappily about his short, 'teenage life as an airman'. 'Somehow, none of it seems real. Sometimes I can't believe the war ever happened,' he says. Immediately after his safe return, he visited some of the relatives of the crew who had died in his Lancaster ... 'but only once', he says. 'It was awful. They tried to talk to me, but there was no communication, really. I felt antagonism, as if they were saying, "Why him, and not our boy ...?" '

Why, indeed?

Chapter Two

More has happened to the tempo of transport this century than in a thousand generations gone before. Life on earth has quickened to match the pace of technology. In several bold moves, in a handful of decades, man has stepped from a horse's back to a staging-post on a route to the stars.

Most of this progress has been made since, and by the grace of, concentrated experience in the Hitler war. In less than half-a-lifetime, most of us have taken to the air and have gone on to become blasé about flying. In the context of regular rockets to the moon, flips around the earth's slight sky seem less than adventurous. The safety record of civil flying has taken the thrills out of the aeroplane. Alas, most of the wonder at being aloft seems to have drained away, too. We are cosseted in the womb of a flight plan. Jet travel is as uninspiring as it is uneventful because computers have taken care of every detail in advance. The terrors of the heavens are hidden from us.

It was not always so. When RAF fliers took to the air 'on a wing and a prayer' in 1939, the wing was shaky and the prayer heartfelt. They had many enemies to face in the sky and Nazi planes were often the least of them. The primitive, elemental, mysterious sky was still a dark stranger to be faced and feared.

There had been a certain amount of civil flying in the 'thirties, with scheduled airlines averaging 5.3 passengers per aircraft in 1937-8, but most of it was restricted to flying boats on safe and simple routes in good weather. Airlines relied principally on weather-wise pilots and navigators, except for the few highly-skilled 'air explorers' who were cautiously pioneering

• •

new air-paths towards possible future schedules. In spite of flying a million commercial miles a year Britain had less than a thousand commercial pilots, and not more than a dozen of them had explored any of the higher or more remote paths of the sky in anything but perfect flying conditions.

In the late 'thirties, too, ordinary people were much more naïve and untutored about travel. There were still social backwaters which had never been touched by progress in transport or communications. Even in the British Isles, many country children knew nothing of towns; many town children could not comprehend a cow. That both these backward social areas would throw up their quotas of youths capable of adjusting almost instantly to the skills of aviation was to be one of the wonders of the decade.

Before the recruiting campaigns, of 1938, and the subsequent introduction of conscription in 1939, the RAF had developed a certain mature professionalism in its bearing. Established in 1918 as an independent arm, it had proudly attained its majority in the late 'thirties. Its thoroughbred officer corps now spanned a generation, and it was assiduously building its own toplofty traditions.

Inevitably, the professionalism of the fliers had a soft and stuffy English edge to it. The RAF was considered, throughout the 'thirties, to be the best 'flying club' in the world, with its oak-panelled, leather-perfumed anterooms; its silver trophies and oil paintings; its well-stocked bars and obsequious servants; its tennis courts and cricket teas; its beaten-up Bugattis and languid, debbie ornaments. 'Shop' was never talked in the messes and war was remote from flying 'games'. 'One's' heroes were World War I flying aces, cricketing giants, Brooklands racing drivers and the like. Airfields tended luckily to be established near county towns with good hotels, pubs and rugby clubs. Streams stocked with fat brown trout were fished in the spring and wild fowling was practised in the golden autumn.

Hangar doors were often closed by teatime, to be reopened by about 10 a.m. on fair-weather days. Dashing cross-country flights were made to other squadrons for drinks and a meal.

There *were* dedicated squadrons, No 58, for instance, had night

2—TLC * *

flying exercises four time a week, weather permitting and took only Wednesday and Saturday afternoons off.

Generally, tactical lectures were few; instrument flying was known to be the coming thing, but there was no hurry to embrace it; if you lost your way, or if the weather suddenly turned menacing, there was always the last resort of landing on a sports field or in a meadow; aerobatics in light biplanes was the most important aspect of flying, with occasional target practice to keep the brain ticking. Once in a while, a sortie over France was undertaken to show the flag to our ally. Flying over a girl-friend's house, with red 'kerchief fluttering from the tail plane for recognition, was considered the thing to do. Preparation for the Hendon display, at which twin-winged bombers would trail coloured smoke across the sky, before knocking over giant skittles, was the peak of hard work in each year. At other times, Oxford bags, plus-fours, Norfolk jackets and heavy golf bags were the order of the day.

The auxiliary and territorial units had begun to expand fairly fast after Munich. The young men of the RAF Volunteer Reserve, sworn in for evening classes and week-end flying, came from every walk of life, but all entrants were restricted to other-rank categories, with only a selected number gaining commissions when they won their wings. The universities were considered suitable breeding-grounds for RAF VR squadrons.

The Volunteer Reserve was not the *corps d'élite* the socially-orientated Auxiliary Air Force had long been, but it was creating a much-needed pool of flying young men, to be called on if required. The RAF, in all its aspects, was very relaxed and English, even in the shadow of Hitler's threats. The Germans were already a nation apprenticed in arms. Our apprenticeships were still random, slap-dash and characteristically unhurried.

Perhaps the best story about how things were just before the war is the one recounted in *Wing Leader* by Johnnie Johnson, who was to become top-scoring Allied fighter pilot of World War II and one of the greatest professional airmen of the post-war years. In 1938, Johnson was mad about flying, so he applied to join the Auxiliary Air Force. In due course he was called before a recruiting officer who, having asked the usual questions about family background, school, profession (he had just qualified as a civil engineer) and sports, appeared unimpressed until he learned that the applicant's home was at Melton Mowbray.

'The interviewer's flagging enthusiasm revived a little when he heard this,' Johnson recalls.

'That's a jolly good thing,' he drawled. 'I know Lincolnshire well. I hunt there quite a lot. Tell me, which pack do you follow?'

Johnson replied that he was learning to fly at his own expense and that, although he could ride a horse, he had no money to spare for hunting.

'The interview was then speedily concluded,' he remembers ruefully, 'and my services with an Auxiliary squadron were not required until the shooting war had begun.' He was also turned down by the Volunteer Reserve at about the same time because 'there were more candidates than vacancies'. Fortunately he persevered, or Britain might have lost an ace of aces, for his was a 'reserved' occupation.

It was altogether a frustrating time for young men who felt they were born to fly That anomalies existed was perhaps inevitable. From their well-regulated grooves, staff officers resisted change and fussed over old-fashioned drills. Memos were sent to squadrons asking for the views of officers commanding about such things as whether Personal Assistants should be permitted to wear aiguillettes. As an aiguillette or 'aglet' is a metal tag of lace hanging over the breast of a uniform from the shoulder, and has cavalry connotations to do with the tethering of horses, it may have been thought that the Air Ministry staff should have had better things to do, with Hitler about to rape Czechoslovakia, but that's how it was in Kingsway, London. And, despite such well-known goings-on, Prime Minister Neville Chamberlain rejected RAF-inspired requests for an enquiry into the administration of the Air Ministry, and in the same speech announced that, as he saw it, Britain had absolutely no need for a Ministry of Supply.

Fortunately, the principal commanders had made their careers in the RAF. They were experienced, energetic and unflappable. They fought ferociously for the well-being of the service they loved.

Fortunately, also, the 'shadow factory' scheme was now well

under way. This was an arrangement by which leading manufacturing companies in Britain had agreed to run shadow factories to produce aircraft and aero engines for the RAF. As well as capital expenditure laid out on building the factories, the Government had agreed to pay the net costs of manufacture, and the firms were receiving £200-£225 for each aircraft produced or £75 for each engine, in addition to management fees. By 1939, the quantitative results of this unique scheme were dramatic in the extreme, proving once more that Government money can act as a spur for manufacturers and workers alike, war or no war. That vast profits were made and distributed in armaments (while some of those who were to die nobly to free us from Fascism were earning a shilling a day) let no one deny or forget.

Air Commodore A. T. Harris, later to be Commander-in-Chief of Bomber Command, worried at the quality of some British planes available or likely to be available early in 1939, went on a one-man mission to the United States to see for himself if there were any suitable types of American aircraft the RAF could rapidly obtain. The result was an immediate order for 200 Lockheed Hudsons for reconnaissance and 200 North American Harvards for training, to be supplied by the late summer of 1939 at a cost of over £5 million, and to be budgeted for in record British Air Estimates of £205 million, and the initiation of the Air Training Scheme in Canada. There were no American bombers available to him at that time. The US Government had embarked on its own intensive programme to build up an air arm (part of the Army, as it was to remain throughout the war) capable of Douhet-style strategic strikes at the heart of an enemy. They could not therefore spare us any bombing planes. But Harris succeeded in arranging for Canada to build British bombers under licence. He also arranged the purchase of a quantity of ·5 mm guns. The dominion, by the way, had an air force at that time of a mere 225 officers and 1,826 men, compared with Britain's total of 69,500 officers and men.

Germany, meanwhile, was still pursuing an airship programme (additional to her mass-production of all-metal planes) and had launched the supposedly-revolutionary Graf Zeppelin at Friedrichshaven—regretfully using hydrogen in the bag because America was refusing to supply non-inflammable helium.

The summer of 1939 was the finest anyone could remember. Day after day the sun shone out of clear blue skies and there were cheap strawberries with cream for all. Early in August the annual defence exercises in south-east England took place, together with a practice 'black-out' throughout the area. Almost 1,300 aircraft of all categories took part, together with 110 guns, 700 searchlights and 100 barrage balloons. Something of the order of 33,000 men and women were involved. It was, nevertheless, a bit of a shambles and unhappily underlined Britain's continuing unpreparedness in the air as late in the day as a month before the war. Fighter planes failed to intercept 'enemy' bombers sweeping in from the direction of Holland and anti-aircraft guns tended to go off half-cock. As the happy-go-lucky days of flying faded and a grim do-or-die mood closed in, morale never the less remained high.

Conscription had been introduced in April, and the RAF was changing as fast as it was growing. Recruits were still screened for quality, but they now came from a much wider social bracket. New schools for pilots, wireless operators, gunners and navigators were springing up throughout the home counties. Training methods were rather rough and ready. Radio was making great strides forward, but its air applications were being directed to defence rather than offence, to fighters rather than bombers. Navigation was still the poor relation. Only a navigator could train navigators and there were very few with any sort of worthwhile experience.

By August, 1939, the first Harvard Trainers were arriving from America to join the little Tiger Moths that had been the mainstay of the schools up to then. Pressed into training service straight from their packing cases, these hundred or so Harvards were an absolute godsend. Featuring such sophisticated 'innovations' as a retractable undercarriage, a constant-speed propellor and American instrumentation, they were 'hot' aircraft, even to the instructors. The latter now had to be very much on their toes as well as stamping on those of their pupils.

The marvellous Empire Air Training Plan had not yet come into being and a growing worry was that most of the flying schools were around south-eastern England, within convenient reach of German aircraft.

Flying instructors while all qualified at Central Flying School were mainly short-service pilots called back hastily to pass on their skills. Inevitably, in the haphazard nature of the training programme, recruits were having to learn to fly and navigate 'by the seat of their pants'. This was a phrase handed down by pioneer fliers who were wont to judge the degree of skid in a turn by the tightness they felt in their trousers, as they acted on honest-to-goodness hunches in difficulties. In terms of navigation, the phrase implied looking out of the cockpit and following roads, canals, railways and prominent geographical features. More advanced learners plotted simple courses for students to follow, using an old-fashioned system of navigational pilotage based on point-to-point landmarks. The drills taught took little account of bad weather.

Private flying clubs had been roped in as auxiliary schools and did much stalwart work. Instructors in the clubs were carefully screened. Only those who were fully qualified were employed, and they were themselves subjected to periodical examination. The Central Flying School was responsible for passing recruits by means of travelling Examination Boards, and their standards were high. But inevitably the tempo of recruitment caused crack-ups all round. In the weeks before the war, training crashes increased alarmingly, and it seemed that trainees were destroying more aircraft than were in the pipeline. One important reason for these losses of planes, pupils and instructors was that intensive flying training was now going on from dawn to dusk, seven days a week.

The end of August, 1939, came with the Flying Training Organisation still trying to multiply itself a hundred times over to meet the demanded expansion of the service, and, with the war obviously only days or even hours away, under-strength squadrons had to make ready with whatever extra pilots they could whistle up from the schools. Some units prepared to go to France with half their strength raw and inexperienced militiamen, and other squadrons dug in to play vital roles of defence and attack from British airfields with equivalent weaknesses. Some training squadrons were even turned into operational half-squadrons.

On 1 September, when complete mobilisation was ordered, and the black-out was enforced, our strength in planes looked reasonable on paper. The theoretical order of battle in Bomber Command showed six groups, made up of ten squadrons of Wellingtons, ten of Hampdens, ten of Blenheims, eight of Whitleys and fifteen of single-engined Battles. At the normal establishment of sixteen planes per squadron, this should have added up to 848 first-line bomber aircraft. In fact the Bomber Command strength on that day, as listed in the Official History, was 272.

This discrepancy between generally-believed fiction and necessary-to-be-faced reality was brought about by the facts that (a) many of the recently manufactured Wellingtons, Whitleys and Hampdens still had inbuilt 'bugs' which had to be ironed out, or were inadequately worked up to be ready for action; (b) ten squadrons of the anachronistic Fairey Battle single-engined day-bomber had been hived off to become the Advanced Air Striking Force in France and Belgium; and (c) some twenty miscellaneous squadrons were non-operational, or had been given a general purpose role.

Against our 272 first-line planes ready for the fray, Germany boasted 1,180 strategic bombers on all fronts at this moment in time, plus 366 dive bombers, of which we had none.

The RAF Battles in France were soon to be proved death-traps for their crews, and the two squadrons of Blenheims which were due to join them would be little better. Both types were too old in conception and too lacking in range and lifting capacity to be counted in the ranks of strategic bombers: yet both were still being mass-produced in enormous numbers in shadow factories by Austin and Rootes respectively. Thus, there were in fact and in truth only seventeen squadrons in Bomber Command when the war started which could be considered ready for their operational roles. All these squadrons were equipped with twin-engined Wellingtons, Whitleys and Hampdens—the so-called heavy bombers of the day. Also operational under the cloak of Bomber Command, but less relevant to its tasks, were four squadrons of Blenheim day-bombers.

Any fool possessed of these facts knew that the total force was completely inadequate to carry through the Western Air Plans. It was obvious that Sir Edgar Ludlow-Hewitt, now fortuitously AOC-in-C of Bomber Command, had been more foresighted and realistic than the whole Air Staff put together in his estimate that Britain could not hope to deal any severe tactical blows from the air before 1941, when the first four-engined true 'heavies' were expected, and then only by steady build up. Clearly, the wise thing to do was for Bomber Command to 'go to ground' as far as it could and conserve itself until the crews could be self-multiplied in an enormous training scheme and given modern aircraft to fly. There was also the ever-present consideration that it would be foolish to provoke the Luftwaffe into heavy attacks on the cities of Britain.

Fears were strongly held in the UK that the war could be over almost before it began, like a snap checkmate early on in a game of chess. Hitler had been successfully blackmailing Britain and France for eighteen months with threats that his Luftwaffe would deliver sudden knock-out blows from the air. There were few so bold as to say we could call the Nazi leader's bluff. The bloody demoralising bombing of Warsaw and other cities in his latest blitzkrieg (which included the wiping out of Poland's air force—as large as that of France—in a matter of hours) seemed warning enough that he meant what he said.

So it was that the Air Plans were so decimated as to be almost unrecognisable, in the RAF's latest change in policy. When war came, Bomber Command was to restrict itself initially to a narrow field of limited objectives by modest forces. There could be no heavy strategic bombing at least until late 1940 or early 1941.

This reasoning was coincidentally linked to new thinking among the free nations on the moral issues involved in strategic bombing. On 1 September, Britain had accepted an appeal to all European nations from Franklin D. Roosevelt to refrain from 'unrestricted aerial warfare on civilian populations or unfortified towns'. Our immediate reply to the American President had included the promise, to be kept only for a time, that 'indiscriminate attack on civilian populations as such will never form part of our policy'.

Despite the limitations these policies imposed, there were still certain lines of action open to Bomber Command which would neither incur moral criticism nor the risk of heavy casualties.

These were mainly thought to be attacks on the German fleet wherever civilian casualties could be avoided, and long-range leaflet raids on German cities.

Bomber Command's aircraft were dispersed at this time in four groups in three main geographical areas. Groups Nos. 2 and 3 were based in East Anglia, with four squadrons of Mark IV Blenheims and six squadrons of Marks I and IA Wellingtons respectively. Group 4 was in Yorkshire with five squadrons of Whitleys, Marks III and IV. No. 5 Group was in Lincolnshire with six squadrons of Hampdens.

All these bomber aircraft had been lauded after their prototype flights as the finest in the world, but there was now some disquiet in the squadrons over their performances and handling.

The ubiquitous Bristol Blenheim light bomber had been hailed, at its debut in the summer of 1936, as a major advance in the design of combat aircraft, denoting a new modern approach to bomber construction. It was the first British all-metal cantilever monoplane, of stressed-skin construction, built around powerful nine-cylinder engines, and as such had sounded the final death knell of the offensive biplane. At its birth, it had been faster than most fighters of the time, but by 1939 it was no longer so, and there were doubts about its likely fighting properties. The Blenheim IVs, of No. 2 Group with Bristol Mercury XV engines, rated at 920 hp for take-off, were capable of 266 mph at 11,800 feet, and could carry 1,000 pounds of bombs for 1,460 miles; but initially their sole defensive armament was a single Vickers 'K' gun in a turret, plus a forward firing Browning ·303—giving totally inadequate protection.

The superior Vickers Wellingtons had also flown for the first time in 1936, and the Marks I and 1A in service with 3 Group at the outbreak of war were powered by Pegasus engines. They were immensely strong aircraft, featuring, in construction, the 'basket-work' designs of the brilliant Barnes Wallis. Armed with six machine-guns (four of them in power-operated turrets) they had a top speed of 255 mph at 12,500 feet. They could carry 4,500 pounds of bombs for 1,200 miles, or 1,000 pounds of bombs for 2,550 miles, and were sufficiently ahead of their time to remain in front-line service throughout the war.

Eldest of the standard RAF twin-engined bombers in service at the outbreak of World War II, the Mark III and IV Armstrong Whitworth Whitleys of Group 4 were virtually obsolete before they ever went to war and were to be withdrawn from combat in 1942. Angularly ugly, and unpopularly known as 'the flying barn doors' or 'the old ladies', the earlier versions lumbered along at a speed of only 185 mph; the Merlin engines were difficult to synchronise, giving the planes an unmistakable recognition signal of note-variation, which the Germans soon came to recognise. The Whitley also had a characteristic nose-down flying attitude, a slab-sided fuselage, and thick, broad wings. The Mark IIIs had 920 hp Armstrong Siddeley air-cooled Tiger VIII engines and a retractable, ventral turret, aft of the wing trailing-edge. The Mark IVs featured more powerful liquid-cooled Rolls-Royce Merlin IV engines with constant-speed airscrews giving a 60 mph improvement in speed, to a maximum of 245 mph at 16,250 feet. Ugly, though they were, the box-shaped fuselages were strong when shot at, which was to endear them to their crews. The Mark IIIs had a powered nose turret and a manually-operated tail turret. The Mark IV had progressed to all-powered turrets, with four or five ·303 Brownings—the last word then in defensive armament.

The Handley Page Hampdens of No. 5 Group were faster, with a top speed of 265 mph at 15,500 feet, and could carry 2,000 pounds of bombs for a distance of 1,900 miles. But their distinctive tapered wings and slim fuselage (which led to their being nicknamed 'flying tadpoles') while aerodynamically ahead of their time, were responsible for extremely cramped conditions for the crew. The guns were not mounted in turrets, with the result that the gunners suffered from a number of blind spots in their fields of fire, which the Hampden's excellent manoeuvrability could only partially offset. Hampdens were produced in large numbers in 1939, thanks to a revolutionary idea of mass-production in which each fuselage was built in two halves, like a split-lobster, and mated at the last moment. Although named as a heavy bomber, the Hampden was in truth a medium one.

Indeed, the concept of a heavy bomber was due for drastic revision within a few years, as will be realised when you consider that the Whitley, the heaviest of the four types just described, had

a normal gross weight of 28,200 pounds, with a defensive armament of five machine guns of rifle calibre, whereas the American
Superfortress, to be introduced towards the end of the war,
normally weighed-in at 120,000 pounds and carried twelve half-
inch guns plus a 20 mm cannon. The relative bomb loads carried
are even more startling, the Superforts being capable of dropping
bombs to a total weight of two-thirds that of the Whitley bomber
itself, fully-laden. Ammunition and bombs were also to become
much more efficient and effective.

As the fliers of the early bombing planes were about to embark
as the ancient mariners in the new ocean of the sky, it may be
interesting also to compare the lengths, nose to tail, of the main
British bombers of 1939 with those of sailing ships which pioneered the sea lanes in equally brave fashion. The Blenheims,
Hampdens, Wellingtons and Whitleys measured 42, 53, 64 and 70
feet respectively.

Among famous early ships, the *Bounty* was 90 feet long, as was
the *Mayflower*, with the *Santa Maria* about 3 feet more.

The bombers which were first to see action in 1939 would fight
and flounder through impossible weather and incredible hardship,
ill-equipped for their pioneering jobs, just as the sailing ships had
been and had done 200-300 years before. The main differences
were that the bombers were flying at 200 or 300 miles an hour, as
against 2 or 3 knots, and that the crews knew that, unlike those on
the sea, if their craft were to slow down or stop when flying, their
deaths were certain.

The boys in blue of the RAF were fairly regarded as something
akin to supermen in 1939 as they droned over English towns and
villages, trying out their new bomber aircraft. And much was
added to this image by the colourful imaginations of propagan-
dists in the press and on the radio in the last days of peace. But in
truth the brave crews of Bomber Command were mainly apprehensive novices, as uncertain of the intrinsic qualities of their
aircraft as they were of the elements through which they would
soon have to fly blindly almost every day.

On the morning of Sunday, 3 September, within a few moments
of Neville Chamberlain finishing his historic 'this country is at war
with Germany' speech, the sirens wailed their mournful warning in

the English capital. It seemed that the experience the good people of London had been told to expect had arrived. Devastation was to be their burden from the first.

The war was less than half-an-hour old, the alarm having originated at 11.20 a.m. in the Headquarters of Fighter Command. The officer on watch in the secret Filter Room, into which information from all radar stations was fed, had received a buzz that at least one unidentified aircraft was heading towards the south coast from France. This seemed to be 'it'. He instantly alerted the nearby Operations' Room, whence the air raid alarm was sounded without delay. By 11.25 a.m. the people of London and south-east England were pouring into shelters in their millions.

Meanwhile, over the Channel, in a private light plane bound for Croydon, a young Frenchman was singing of the land of his birth. An assistant air attache at the Embassy in London, he had been on a week-end social trip to Le Touquet and was returning cheerfully to duty, totally unaware that he was responsible for driving half the population of England molelike into holes and tunnels in the ground, as well as for alerting guns, fighter planes and balloon units over a wide area. So it was that the 'raid', very much a false alarm, was soon over.

A subsequent thorough investigation by Robert Watson-Watt, fearful that something was basically wrong with his RDF system, was to reveal the two factors that had set off the sirens unnecessarily. The first was that the French pilot of the private plane had inadvertently omitted to file a flight plan in the approved manner and there was therefore no pre-knowledge of the plane in the operations' room. The second was that, as it was a civil aircraft, it was not equipped to put out an IFF (identification, friend or foe) signal, which would have cleared it. These were the simple reasons for it appearing on the map table as hostile. The system had been right, but the human element had fooled it.

At least the 'warning' had the effect of bringing home to the British people right away that they were indeed at war. And at least our radar defences around the coasts had picked up the tiniest of signals, with a consequent speedy response from the defence arm.

We were, in fact, far ahead of the enemy at this point in the development and use of radar. Germany was working on very primitive types of radar scanners, known variously as 'Freya' and 'Wuerzburg', but none were yet reliably in use; and they had not devised any jamming or other effective counter-measures against the British chain by the start of the war.

Before the sirens screamed the end of the first alert, Bomber Command had pressed the button for its initial planned mission. At one minute after noon on 3 September, a solitary Mark IV Blenheim, of 139 Squadron, code number N6215, had taken off from an airfield at Wyton in Huntingdonshire on a top-secret reconnaissance sortie. Piloted by Flying Officer A. McPherson, with a naval observer as passenger, the specially-prepared plane's aim was not even known to the other members of the squadron who had shared stand-by with it since the day before.

It was a fine afternoon and within two hours the Blenheim had become the first British warplane to cross the enemy's frontier, when it flew unopposed, at its maximum height of 24,000 feet, over Wilhelmshaven, Prussia, the fortified German North Sea naval station. As the two men peered down on the seaport, they could see several heavy warships moving slowly out into sheltered waters of the Schillig Roads. McPherson circled steadily and the observer took seventy-five photographs of the ships.

As soon as they had set course for home, the pilot picked up his microphone and called his base to pass on the information that the ships were far enough from the town to be attacked without fear of civilian casualties—the object of his sortie. But there was no response. His radio had frozen-up in the intense cold of the atmosphere. This was to be a fault that was to plague Blenheims well into the war; and their crews, too, were to suffer greatly from the cold on future missions.

The most serious consequences in McPherson's case were that his news had to await his return to Wyton, four hours and forty-nine minutes after he had taken off, and it would then be passed on to Bomber Command headquarters too late for any action to be taken that day.

The reconnaissance sortie, and the first raid of the war that was supposed to follow immediately, had actually been planned on the basis of information received the day before. On the morning of Saturday, 2 September, a nonchalant young Australian had dropped several cans of film into the Air Ministry building in Bloomsbury, London. His name was Sidney Cotton and he was ostensibly in the colour film business. In fact, he had been recruited by British Intelligence some nine months earlier and was one of the most dramatically successful spies of the period. The owner of a splendid pale green Lockheed 12A transport plane, the only one of its kind in Europe, Cotton had succeeded in ingratiating himself with senior officers of the Luftwaffe by offering them flights in his unique aircraft. With their blessing, he had been able to fly around restricted areas of the Rhine. But, unknown to his distinguished passengers, the Lockheed featured a secret panel under the fuselage. On each flight, Cotton would press a switch, whereupon the panel would slide back, permitting three concealed cameras in the belly of the plane to film factories, airfields and installations beneath. Over the months, his films had been analysed by British service experts and much useful information had been amassed therefrom.

Cotton's official business was to fly between Berlin and London with cargoes of German colour film. On 2 September he had taken a chance, at the urgent request of his Intelligence bosses, and had made an unscheduled detour via Wilhelmshaven, in the north of Europe, on his way to London. Thanks to photographs taken over the naval base, Admiralty and RAF experts knew by noon on Saturday, 2 September, exactly which units of the German fleet were assembled there. And McPherson's flight on the 3rd was to confirm that they had not dispersed.

The temporary stand-down, caused by the failure of McPherson's radio on the Sunday, meant that the first actual raid of the war did not take place until the night of 3-4 September and was a much less dramatic hors d'oeuvres than Bomber Command had intended.

As soon as it was dark that night, ten Whitleys of 51 and 58 Squadrons of No. 4 Bomber Group, had their bomb-bays fully loaded at Leconfield, in Yorkshire, and took off into the broody darkness, setting course for the Ruhr. But when they reached Germany's greatest industrial complex, and opened their bomb doors, it was merely to release 13 tons of leaflets over the munitions plants and the cities of Hamburg and Bremen.

So, instead of an aggressive raid by the RAF, the war started with a 'bumph-mission', as the Whitley crews were to dub these sorties. In a way, this was appropriate, because leaflet-raids were to characterise the 'phoney war' for many months thereafter.

Ironically, when the crews returned safely to base, they, too, were handed propaganda sheets, designed to bamboozle their own hearts and spirits. These bore 'a patriotic message from King George VI' which read, in part:

> The Royal Air Force has behind it a tradition no less inspiring than those of the older Services, and in the campaign which we have now been compelled to undertake you will have to assume responsibilities far greater than those which your service had to shoulder in the last war. One of the greatest of them will be the safeguarding of these Islands from the menace of the air. I can assure all ranks of the Air Force of my supreme confidence in their skill and courage, and in their ability to meet whatever calls may be made upon them.

Several 'calls' were in fact to be made on the skill and courage of Bomber Command units within twelve hours. At breakfast, on 4 September, for instance, at Wyton, Hunts, and at nearby Wattisham, Suffolk, bleary Blenheim crews were still standing-by for the delayed raid on Wilhelmshaven. Five planes had been chosen from each of three squadrons of No. 2 Group and routine checks were taking place on the selected aircraft as Flying Officer McPherson again took off for Germany to check the latest naval situation.

As luck would have it, the weather, which had been glorious all summer, had turned nasty and by the time he reached the German naval base, he had to descend to 300 feet, to avoid low cloud and heavy rain, before he could see that the ships were still where they had been the previous day. No pictures were necessary this time, so he hot-footed for home without delay, only to find that his radio had again packed up, this time for no accountable reason. There was therefore again a two-hour delay before his message could be got through to headquarters, but it was not so serious this time because he had set out much earlier than he had the day before.

Meanwhile, back at the two airfields, engineers were fussing over the Blenheims like mother hens with their first clutches of eggs. It was now known to everyone that the initial British bombing raid of the war was about to take place, and the honour that Nos. 107, 110 and 139 Squadrons had been chosen for the job was deeply felt. This was the real thing at last and everyone tried to show it in his bearing, from Commanding Officer to the humblest aircraft hand.

Not that the stations at Wyton and Wattisham were in themselves ship-shape. Everything had happened so quickly over the week-end that, simultaneously with the Blenheims being readied for action, general war-readiness was still being worked up. Sandbagged gun-emplacements were being dug around perimeters; surplus planes were being hauled by tractors to dispersal points in nearby fields or woods; gas-officers were fussing around with yellow detectors; and petrol bowsers were queueing to unload their high-octane fuel into underground tanks still smelling of new paint.

The all-important air-crew chosen for the raid were squatting around the messes, their flying kit strewn on the grass nearby, nervously smoking and keeping up their accustomed banter about 'popsies' and beer. They were restless as stallions in a cloud of flies, bored by the delays and anxious to be 'blooded' by the foxes of war.

The briefing, when it came in the late-morning, was casual in the extreme. The changed weather situation meant low-level instead of high-level bombing. The bombs had to be changed in the Blenheims to 500-pounders (four to a plane) each with a delayed action of $11\frac{1}{2}$ seconds. These fuses were new and had had to be brought into use because of a number of disasters in the summer exercises in which planes flying at a few hundred feet had been destroyed by their own bombs. The simple plan was to attack as low as possible, allowing a margin only for barrage balloons. 'Try to pop one down the nearest funnel', was the laconic last command.

Over a snatched lunch at Wattisham, Flight Lieutenant K. C. Doran quietly explained the drills he wanted his ten crews from 107 and 110 Squadrons to follow en route. And when they reached the target area, they were to spread out to about 600 yards behind and on either side of him, attacking in a shallow dive to about 500 feet before releasing their bombs on the nearest suitable target. Togetherness was all. They had to remain within visual distance on the way and they had to attack together so that surprise was used if possible .'That way,' he concluded, 'we may knock them out and be on the way home before they know what's happening.'

Alas, it was not to be quite like that. The signal to board came through as they finished their snack lunch. The crews, consisting of pilot, navigator-bombardier and gunner-radio operator, beat all known records for mounting their Blenheims, so keen were they to do something other than standing around. Take-off was immaculate—each pilot being all-too-conscious of the fact that the 'erks' were lined up, watching open-mouthed—and in a moment the ten planes were headed for the coast on the course and at the speed they had been given, their pilots fussing over the somewhat complicated controls that were a feature of Blenheims.

Over the sea, they descended to about 1,000 feet, where clouds could be avoided and visibility was fairly clear. As the time passed slowly, Flight Lieutenant Doran was concentrating on the course instructions and corrections his navigator was feeding him, and his young pilots were keeping straight on at their practised distances, watching his head, almost hypnotically, through the grated portholes of the almost panoramic cockpit windows. 'Poor buggers,' he thought, as he looked across and back at them. 'They're very green. But at least they understand the bombers' main aim is to get straight there together and straight home again. I only hope I can keep them with me through and back.'

Two hours after take-off, within about fifty miles of Wilhelmshaven, thunderous anvils of cloud suddenly appeared, their bases descending to about 600 feet. Doran signalled to close formation; even so, several of his pilots had to open their windows to keep him in view.

Twelve minutes later the ten planes began their slow dive from just over 500 feet, with heavy rain cascading over their aircraft's Allclad stressed-skins, and it seemed to the crews that hell had suddenly opened up beneath them. Somehow the Germans had been alerted. Ship and shore anti-aircraft batteries opened up together, throwing up every kind of shot and shell they possessed.

Even machine guns were rattling and spitting from the battleships. It had to be every man for himself. Flight Lieutenant Doran made straight for the largest target, the battleship *Admiral von Scheer*, and had the chagrin of seeing several of his bombs, released from about 200 feet, bounce and ricochet off her armoured decks. The 11½-second-delay fuses were far too slow and useless. All this hell, he thought bitterly, and no end result.

As Doran turned for home, there was a tremendous flash from the cruiser *Emden* and fires elsewhere in the waters of the bay. But the weather was worsening and he could not look back. In the clouds he gathered together the only four aircraft that were responding to his signals and together they flew home at maximum speed.

Back at Wattisham he reported what he had seen and done and his crews did likewise. The picture that emerged was appalling. The five Blenheims he had failed to bring home (one from 110 Squadron and four from 107) had been seen by other crews to be shot down as they dived. One of them, crippled and in flames, had plunged straight into the cruiser, *Emden,* and it was the fire from this he had seen. The other conflagrations had been caused by blazing Blenheims. The twenty tons of bombs carried all that way had done no damage whatsoever, his own having exploded uselessly in the depths of the sea.

Equally disquieting was the news of 139 Squadron at Wyton. Their five planes had also had radio as well as weather problems, and navigation in their case had been so bad that they had flown for nearly three hours without ever finding the target. They had then dropped their bombs aimlessly in the North Sea and had returned to base almost out of fuel. So, in truth, 50 per cent of the bomber force that had reached the Schillig Roads had been wiped out. It was a dreadful beginning. That Flight Lieutenant K. C. Doran was to be awarded the first DFC of the war was only just. He himself was to remark unhappily that it should have been awarded to the young men who died.

As the various reports were being processed, Bomber Command's Plan 2, Day 2, was swinging into operation. This was for six Hampdens of 83 Squadron, No. 5 Group, from Scampton,

Lincolnshire, to attack the same target in two flights. Apart from Squadron-Commander Leonard Snaith (noted as a Schneider Trophy pilot) who was to lead A Flight, the fliers involved were even less practised in the arts of flying, navigating, bombing and communicating than their East Anglian colleagues. Indeed, not one of the pilots had ever taken off before with a bomb-load aboard. They had to be told at briefing how to ease the Hampdens off the grass by working the tail trimming tabs after the tail had come up. If this failed to give them height, they were to use the emergency boost override. It emerged at this point that no one in the squadron knew for certain that a Hampden could leave the ground with the 2,000-pound bomb load they were to carry on this their first mission, so haphazard were the plannings of those days.

Take-off was scheduled for 1430 hours, but because no signals were being received at Wattisham or Wyton from the Blenheims, it was delayed until 1600 hours and then again until 1700. By this time, news had come through of Flight Lieutenant Doran's bombs bouncing off the armoured decks, and the Station Armament Officer was hastily summoned to give advice on this happening, as the Hampdens were loaded up with similar $11\frac{1}{2}$-second delayed-fuse bombs. 'Try to lodge your bombs in the superstructure, where they can go off after you have passed safely over,' was his considered advice. 'And Irish pigs can fly,' muttered Flying Officer Allen Mulligan, as the crews filed out to the lorries that were to take them to their aircraft.

The difficulties of taking off with a 2,000-pound bomb load had been exaggerated, and all the Hampdens got away safely, albeit sluggishly, and set course over Lincoln Cathedral, heading for Skegness. One hour later they passed a German Dornier 18 flying boat, which ignored them completely, as they did it. The war was young and nobody on either side (especially the still-polite English) knew quite what to do in such circumstances.

After ninety minutes' flying, the weather closed in completely and as the Hampdens flew on blindly and reached what should have been the target area there were furious arguments going on in the leading plane, between the pilot and the navigator. And, as the first flak was bursting around the planes, the order was given, loud and clear, to return to base. Puzzled, the young pilots closed in on their leader, duly jettisoned their bombs over the sea, and flew home to Scampton.

'That was a bloody awful show, sir,' said one of the A Flight pilot officers to Snaith when they got back to the mess. 'What in hell happened?'

'The instrument went crazy and we were over Heligoland instead of Wilhelmshaven,' the Squadron-Commander explained ruefully. 'Don't worry, Guy; we'll get it right next time.'

'Guy' was Flying Officer Guy Gibson, who was later, as Wing Commander Guy Gibson, VC, DSO, DFC, to become leader of the Dambusters and certainly one of the greatest bomber pilots of the war.

As the frustrated Hampden crews of 83 Squadron were drowning their disappointments in the Scampton messes, Bomber Command was having one more bite at the German naval cherry. A force of fourteen Wellingtons from Nos. 9 and 149 Squadrons of 3 Group had flown late in the day to Brunsbuttel (in the same general area as Wilhelmshaven, but at the entrance to the Kiel Canal) to attack shipping in open waters. Like all fliers that day, they had been warned to avoid the German mainland like the plague and not to take any chance that could lead to civilian casualties. In fact, they ran into extremely heavy anti-aircraft fire before they reached their target. As a result, two Wellingtons were shot down and the others made for home in considerable disarray, only one crew having claimed even a possible hit on a ship.

The Germans immediately broadcast propaganda reports on each of the raids, claiming that a total of thirty British bombers had been shot down in the act of attacking 'the civilian populations of several seaside towns in North Sea areas'. Goebels went on the air to threaten immediate reprisals, and Goering said that 100 bombers would be sent over London to do ten times the damage. In fact, the Germans had bigger problems to tackle that week and Hitler decided that the Luftwaffe would have to stay its eager hands. But this was not known in London at the time.

At the Air Ministry and at the Admiralty (which had requested the North Sea raids) it was immediately decided that there would be no more RAF attacks on naval bases. It was too risky, as a possible instrument of provocation at a time when reprisals from the

Luftwaffe were most highly feared; it was obviously not worthwhile in terms of successful bombing; and flying over heavily defended bases had taken a higher toll than we could afford in aircraft and crews.

It was announced therefore that in future attacks should only be made against ships at sea.

At Bomber Command headquarters, Ludlow-Hewitt was presented with the appalling task of reappraising the realities of air war in the light of hard experience. He was also faced with problems of radio that did not work, of heavy bombs that were about as effectively explosive as a child's stink bomb, of the difficulties of target-finding in bad weather and of how to catch up with decades of neglect of navigation as a science. He had still to find out, because his bombers had not yet met their first fighter foes, that he had another enormous problem in terms of the defensive weapons his crews had been given as emergency life-savers.

There was one other factor the AOC-in-C of Bomber Command could not possibly guess at, and it was as well he could not do so. This was that the thousands of crews under his command on that September day were doomed. Their chances of ever reaching middle age were as near nil as made no matter. St. Peter had their names set in type for his book at that very moment. In no time at all they would be queueing pink-faced at his gates—the first sacrificial lambs slaughtered on the ill-constructed altar of the air war.

Not one in five hundred of the crewmen then in service, from the legendary Guy Gibson to the bumbling Joe Smith, would see the end of the war. As 1939 became 1940 . . . 1941 . . . 1942 . . . 1943 . . . they would be urged, as their numbers diminished, to risk more and more, until they, too, had offered up the last thing they had to give. The grim reaper came nearer and nearer, but the melodrama was reality.

So, they were the first few of the command; so, the many would follow them in 1943, 1944 and 1945. And who would assess the relative sacrifices—delayed, but certain, or sudden and sure?

Walking the plank was walking the plank. The drop was equally final, whether you did it in small numbers over a long period or in large numbers and quickly. All their cries as they died can still be heard by those with an ear to hear. But the official history has no doubts. In vol. III, p. 310, it says '. . . strategic bombing made a contribution to victory which was decisive. Those who claim that the Bomber Command contribution to the War was less than this are factually in error.'

Chapter Three

The breathing space granted to Britain in the first nine months of the war was miraculous. It was also to prove tedious for many. The workers and the home-based Services had been told to expect a fierce onslaught from the air. The come-down was confusing and depressing. Initiatives appeared to have ceased on both sides.

Leaflet raids were Bomber Command's chief contribution to the war; the Luftwaffe laid mines and made two minor attacks on shipping in Scotland. Loudspeakers slung on poles on both sides of the French Maginot Line fought wordy battles, and British soldiers sang half-heartedly of hanging out their washing on the German Siegfried Line. The navy fired a few shells at distant targets.

At home, daily doses of false-sounding propaganda were spooned out. It all seemed so bogus and rudderless that people felt deflatedly empty of purpose. It was a funny war, a static war. Inevitably, Britons found a word for it—the phoney war.

After the ill-starred raids of the first week-end of September, Bomber Command apparently did nothing. The sole exception was one ill-planned, unhappy raid on 29 September, in which eleven Hampdens, in two sections, found and attacked two enemy destroyers near Heligoland, did no damage, and lost five of their number. The lesson was that the Hampdens went in too low, while the destroyers proved to be highly manoeuvrable and packed a hefty ack-ack punch. The air staff responsible for such operations then sat back licking its wounds and panting its perplexity for nearly two months before daring another move.

One reason for the general lethargy was that France, our

deeply-divided and jittery ally, was daily urging us to play for time. If our bombing planes were somewhat elderly in design and only one-third as strong in numbers as Germany's, the French were immeasurably weaker. Their air force was positively decrepit and their bombers useless. Touchily aware that they could not offer any sort of retaliation in the event of Hitler being provoked into playing his trump card, their air staff worried the life out of their British opposite numbers lest we got out of line. Their cities and their munitions-producing plants, being nearer the German airfields, had no chance if Hitler started a bombing blitz ... such was the gist of their messages.

This undoubtedly affected all Air Council and Bomber Command thinking throughout the phoney war phase, and it was certainly used as an excuse for our bombers rarely bombing in anger, and *never* strategically, during the entire nine month period.

The steam-rollering of Poland's large air force brought further gloom to the Air Ministry and caused various emergency measures, including the temporary evacuation of some bomber squadrons from east coast bases to hastily-prepared airfields and civilian airports in the western counties—Lancashire instead of Lincolnshire, for example—thus dubiously reducing the range of the aircraft, should they be called upon suddenly to counter-bomb Germany.

Meanwhile, the front-line crews, conscious of the heavy losses that had characterised the only raids that had taken place, and not knowing when their turn would come, threw themselves into spasms of merry-making that were to lead to crew members generally being labelled wild womanising boozers. Inevitably there were retaliatory outbursts of unctious rectitude from some of their civilian neighbours, but there was also a great deal of hero-worship for them, especially from young country girls who had never seen such goings-on.

The fact was that the crews had far too little to do. The only regular daily routine on most stations in the September-October, 1939, period was on check and test their aircraft. This generally consisted of half-an-hour's cockpit drill followed by up to an hour spent on 'circuits and bumps'. The remainder of each day was invariably devoted to lazing around the huts, messes and offices until the 'pub-crawl' transport arrived at about five p.m.

WAAFs had begun to join up in considerable numbers, and most of them were spirited girls who really wanted to be involved in RAF work and life. They wore civilian clothes at this time and made marvellous efforts to be gay. They gained the sort of reputations that air-hostesses have today—much sought-after super-type girls. In general, frivolous affairs were preferred to serious ones among crewmen, but smooching to Glenn Miller and strolling sentimentally in the moonlight were desirable activities.

There were also frequent civilian parties, at which the boys in blue were very welcome, in the emotional mood of the time, and at which the hospitality (in terms of girls as well as drink) was almost embarrassingly plentiful. Outwardly carefree, the now comparatively well-paid crews were frustrated at not being able to do anything positive for their money.

Although there were occasional stand-bys in some squadrons, everyone soon got brassed off hanging around the wireless room by day waiting for a dramatic message, when all that passed was the odd signal about missing laundry or an urgent advance request from a 'visiting fireman' for a girl friend to be provided on arrival.

The general news, too, continued to be uninspiring. South Africa and Canada belatedly declared war on Germany. Australia offered Britain the personnel for six air squadrons. Statistics about the 'bumph raids' were issued weekly, as if they were important to the course of the war. The Anglo-French-Turkish treaty of alliance was signed in Ankara; a Heinkel forced-landed near Dalkeith; and two Blenheims were shot down in the Thames Estuary . . . by our own guns. It was all rather small beer.

The one high spot of October was the setting up of an Empire Air Training Scheme, in which Canada, Rhodesia, New Zealand and Australia were to co-operate. Training schools were to be established at once in the Dominions to train crews from Britain and other countries for service in the RAF and in the fledgling air forces of the Empire. This had been initiated by Harris on his purchasing mission to America and Canada a few weeks before. Advanced training was also to be organised in Canada. Before it was closed down, in March, 1945, this splendid scheme would have given birth to 360 training units in Canada alone, and these would have turned out 137,739 members of air crews, including 54,098 pilots, mainly for the RAF.

But the Scheme would mainly be of benefit in the future. In the remaining months of 1939, although the needs were urgent, crew training in Britain was proceeding rather slowly and clumsily. In the squadrons, a certain amount of instrument flying by night was begun, but only when the moon was shining or when there was little cloud. Indeed, when fog descended on Britain in October, night training was cancelled instantly for a time.

Flying schools had multiplied and some pupils now rated the rank of officer-cadet. Many of these were public school types, brought up to 'play up, play up and play the game', and not quite knowing now what the game was. It was still a period when patriotic slogans were all. Young men joined up in response to appeals to 'help preserve all that is best in the British way of life' and they truly believed that such was to be their mission.

Recruits learned basic flying in Moths or Miles Magisters with 'old school' instructors and recalled ex-instructors, many of them middle-aged men who had themselves learned to fly in Avro 504s and who knew little of the sophistications fast flying would soon demand. Pupils graduated to advanced trainers, instructed by men little older than themselves and using principally the light-bomber-sized North American Harvard, the banshee-like screams of which, sometimes by night as well as by day, soon became familiar to villagers in many parts of Britain. Final training for probationary pilots who had not failed to make the grades with the powerful Harvard, before joining or not joining bomber squadrons, was usually either in the single-engined Fairey Battle, or in the twin-engined Bristol Blenheim, or very occasionally in Hampdens, at operational training units. They had to be fairly good at this stage, as dual instruction was not possible except in a very small number of the planes, although when the Battles (of which 2,000 were to be built in all) were later withdrawn from front-line service, many were to be converted into dual trainers and shipped to Canadian schools. The Blenheims were also later to be given a primitive dual-instruction arrangement in the spare right-front seat.

When young pilots were called upon to take up Battles, some-times an aircraftsman had to be carried in the back seat—as ballast —and it was said that these were among the most fright-ened men in the wartime RAF ... which was saying something.

Cockpit, take-off and other drills had now been devised and were more or less standard throughout the service. Through these, almost any plane could be mastered quickly, so the theory went, on the principle that all aeroplanes were aero-planes, however different they might seem superficially. Only the mnemonics varied from school to school. These drills were practised by the hour on the ground and had to be known backwards before any actual take-offs, circuits and landings.

The take-off drill, for instance, was HTMPFFG (for which a popular mnemonic was How To Make Potty F—— Fuhrer Growl). These 'drill' letters stood for Hydraulics, Trimmers, Mixture, Propellor pitch, Flaps, Fuel cocks, and Gills. The landing drill was the same, except for the substitution of 'U' for 'T' (the second letter), 'U' being Undercarriage.

Before they finally left school, pupils even learned the totally new drill of flying a Blenheim with one engine cut, the tech-nique of engine-failure safety speed having recently been devised.

So the new young pilots were taught to fly strange and relatively complicated aircraft, but the time that could be allocated to them—with hundreds pushing forward in the queue—was all too short, and when they finally reached their squadrons, most were relatively inexperienced. The result was than many were made second pilots for a time, with the useful bonus that they had to learn some navigation.

'Some' navigation was all that anyone possessed, even in the squadrons, in those unsophisticated days. Airspeed indicators and altimeters had been added to the maps, crayons, compasses, watches and sextants of earlier fliers. But most air crew were frightened of the whole subject and shied away from all but its simplest aspects.

It may be true that navigators are born rather than made, and that the selection process was at fault in 1939. But it is also true, and has been proved to be so in the proliferation of navigators in recent years, that a large number of suitable types *are* born and can be made masters of navigational skills. Accuracy, not higher mathematics, is the navigator's star quality. Indeed, there have been many girls over the years who have made excellent navigators—girls who would equally well have made top class secretaries and who could readily have operated complicated telephone switchboards. Their gifts were unflappable efficiency allied to accuracy. These are the qualities that should have been looked for in RAF navigators in 1939. Alas, there was no one of sufficient standing in the air staff who understood what navigation was about sufficiently well to see that it was taught simply and properly. And the result was that, for a time, as many planes were lost through faulty navigation as from any other cause.

Fortunately, most of the navigational errors led only to the loss of single planes, or two or three at the most, but much alarm was caused in Lincolnshire and at Bomber Command in November, 1939, when several squadrons of Hampdens had failed to show up ten hours after they had set out on an armed mission. There were understandable fears, in view of recent patterns of off-course crashes, that a navigational error might have occurred, bringing with it an unthinkable tragedy, the truth of which might never be known.

The crisis came about in this way. Sir Edgar Ludlow-Hewitt, as Air Officer-in-Chief of Bomber Command, had been very conscious for weeks of the fact that very few of his first-line squadrons had had any experience in battle. And, although he was being urged to exercise every possible restraint, as well as avoiding any repetition of the losses sustained in the first raids of the war, he was forced to the conclusion that further attacks against ships at sea should be hazarded in the form of armed bomber reconnaissances in force. His decision was speeded by the growing impatience of the First Lord of the Admiralty, Winston Churchill, who was fuming at our lack of success against the German navy at a time when British shipping losses to U-boats and aircraft-laid mines were mounting.

Orders were therefore issued that stand-by bomber squadrons should take the earliest possible opportunity to carry out a medium altitude attack in good weather on any important enemy warships that could be located in open waters. This was easier ordered than done. Any ships spotted by recce planes were invariably near enough the coast to make for port before the bombers could possibly get there. The Germans were aware of our fears of bombing near towns and cunningly played their shipping moves accordingly.

The crisis-mission was preceded by an abortive one. One day in mid-November, the 'hot' telephone rang at 5 Group headquarters in Lincolnshire. It bore the all-important news that three German destroyers had been sighted within a few miles of Newcastle. This was the sort of opportunity Ludlow-Hewitt and Churchill had been watching for, and seemed too good to be true. The enemy ships could not possibly reach their bases, towards which they were said to be steaming, before they would be attacked. The chances of bombing them in the open waters of the North Sea were ideal.

Without delay, 83 Squadron took off from Scampton, on an armed reconnaissance, with orders to carry out a medium-level attack on sight of the destroyers. When they reached the area, however, there was no sign of anything remotely resembling a German destroyer anywhere near the north-east coast, and after a fruitless search lasting an hour, the Hampdens returned to Scampton.

A few days later, the German pocket battleship, *Deutschland,* which had been sinking Allied ships in the Atlantic, was spotted leaving Kiel and heading for open waters off the Norwegian coast just south of Stavanger. There was no doubt about the report this time, so Ludlow-Hewitt decided on a major show of force. No. 5 Group was again on stand-by and, as soon as it was light forty-eight Hampdens, from several squadrons, took off with orders to attack the battleship in Flights of three.

It was to be the largest bomber strike of the war so far. In the event of fighter attack, the Hampdens were to fly in close formation and help each other as best they could, this being the defensive day-bombing philosophy of the time. The raid was led by Wing Commander J. Sheen, who commanded 49 Squadron. And his aircraft carried a naval expert with powerful binoculars, whose job it was to identify the *Deutschland* and so obviate any danger of a British cruiser being attacked by mistake; for British naval units from Scapa Flow were already on their way to intercept the pocket battleship.

Sheen's force, despite the comparatively slow speed of the Hampdens, reached Norway in just over two hours, thanks to a powerful tail-wind. Flying a few miles off the coast in perfect weather at about 10,000 feet, they swept the sea, towards the Arctic Circle, as far as they dared and then, after nearly five hours' flying, turned west into the wind towards Scotland, having seen no sign of any German battleship. The stiff breeze that had to be faced all the way home was now nearing gale force. After some hours of this, buffeted into flying at a much reduced speed, it became obvious that something was wrong with the course. Land should have been in sight, but only mountainous, white capped waves could be seen.

The navigator chosen to lead the force was urgently asked to check his figures, but while he was doing so, with fear in his belly, the observer grimly pronounced that, in his considered view: 'We've missed the north of Scotland and we're heading out into the Atlantic.'

While the navigator continued to scribble, Sheen thought it best to heed the observer and set a course due south-east. There being no inter-plane radio for bombers at this stage in the war, he signalled his intention by coloured Verey light to the others, who had been puzzled as well as worried by not having seen a coastline.

Fortunately, before long, the navigator came up with what he was sure was a correct position in the North Sea and not the Atlantic, so the forty-eight planes again turned and headed west. As they had now been flying for almost ten hours and were extremely short of petrol, Sheen signalled that they should land the moment they saw a suitable airfield, wherever it was. They had taken off at about 6 a.m. and it was now late afternoon, with nothing but sea around them and about ninety gallons of fuel left per plane. All Sheen could think of, as he prayed his navigator was right, was the appalling and unforgivable tragedy of having to ditch nearly fifty valuable aircraft in the sea.

Ten minutes later he suddenly saw a trawler in the fading light. Signalling the others to circle at height, he dived his Hampden to 200 feet and told his operator to flash a lamp at the small ship. When no signal came back, he flew lower and began a pantomime of hand signals. At first, all the anxious men in the Hampden got back from the trawler crew was a sequence of cheery waves and thumbs-up signals. But something of Sheen's worry must have communicated itself, because the fishermen at last pointed vigorously in the direction of their home port. The leader then quickly rejoined the other planes and after flying for another fifteen minutes they all had the fantastic relief of seeing the mottled sea breaking on a rugged coastline.

By a miracle, Sheen's operator, although he had been unable to contact his base, was able to raise a coastguard station on an emergency wavelength on his radio, and learned that they were over the Peninsula of Long Craig, Angus. A quick glance at the map showed that there was a naval aerodrome a few minutes away, at Montrose. So it was that, to the amazement of the small staff at the RN Air Station, a cloud of Hampdens swept in low out of the twilight at about 5 p.m. on a grim November evening requesting immediate landing permission. Ironically it is in the graveyard at Montrose that dozens of World War I trainee pilots are buried, for the place was one of the original RFC Training Schools.

In they went, two by two, on all-too-short parallel runways, with Sheen circling overhead like a father eagle. Only one Hampden did not quite make it, and crashed in a graveyard three miles from the airfield, completely out of petrol; and even so, the Sergeant-pilot and his crew of two stepped out, alive and well if somewhat pale.

Sheen's navigator had the last word. As the crews queued for the cup of tea they had feared they might never enjoy again, he turned to the Wing Commander and said cheerfully: 'I told you land was over that way somewhere, Skip.'

Telephones were rather random instruments in those days so that the relief at 5 Group headquarters when Sheen eventually got through on a trunk line late in the evening was only matched by that at Bomber Command itself, where Churchill had grimly joined Ludlow-Hewitt for the expected disastrously-bad news. Much drinking punctuated the prayers of thanks all round until very late that night.

Fog was by this time blanketing much of southern England, helped as much by factory chimneys belching smoke by day and night as by prevailing maritime-tropical air masses sweeping in from the south-west, and it was quickly decided that this was a good excuse to postpone, until conditions improved, any further strikes at enemy warships.

Air staff, indeed, were much worried by this time about the continuing inaccuracy of meteorological forecasting. Planes were frequently setting out on training flights in the security of a favourable forecast, only to have to dive back to base when faced with fast-worsening conditions.

There were no real guide-lines. Hundreds of planes were taking-off and landing throughout the British Isles every day, and also, when weather permitted, at night. Such widespread air traffic had never been known before, so there was no organisation in existence for putting out reliable reports in each of the many varied geographical areas of Britain. And the first winter of the war was certainly bringing this weakness to light. While a regional meteorological network was being devised, and established, many planes and crews, even in areas which were fog-free, were finding grim graves in hillsides, in the sea, and even in towns and villages, with attendant civilian casualties.

Several interim drills were introduced hastily to help pilots in difficulty. One was the 'square search', designed to pin-point a known landmark, or a dim night flare-path, when fliers were lost in the general vicinity of their bases. The drill was to fly for two minutes on each of four courses—north, south, east and west—which formed the square in which the landmark was believed to be. This was, at the same time, a good discipline and a fairly successful method of finding 'home', and it undoubtedly reduced the number of panicky balings-out that had been taking place, apart altogether from manned-crashes.

Another drill belatedly introduced was to furnish all crews with details of alternate airfields on which they could land in case their destination was closed by fog, high-winds, snow, flood, fire or accident. Thereafter, every navigator, as well as knowing his point of no return on a flight, had his map well marked with suitable emergency landing spots en route. These drills represented progress, but they had come, as did so many advances in the war, as the outcome of experience.

Fog was still the great imponderable and it gravely restricted flying training in November and parts of December, 1939. Like alto-stratus cloud (which is ground fog raised a few thousand feet) it frightened pilots almost to death . . . and their superiors did not know how to cope with it either. Such instrumentation as there was gave little confidence to crews when faced with occasional swirling blankets of the stuff, let alone when confronted with the blinding four-foot visibility walls of the grey-black advection fog, known as the 'London particular', which had settled on parts of England that winter. People died in their sleep from its fumes and vehicles were reluctant to start in its smelly, dirty vapours, even planes undergoing engine tests on the ground. Ground crews even found difficulty in finding their way from breakfast in the mess to work in the hangers a few hundred feet away.

Altogether, fog set back flying training and exercises for the RAF by weeks, and this at a time when every moment counted. The one good thing about the unhappy winter weather of 1939 was that it provoked scientists to find ways of improving the devices coming into use for instrument flying and landing earlier and with greater vigour than they might otherwise have done. To be fair to the scientists, this was a period in which scores of allegedly war-winning ideas had to be examined, in case there was a pearl in the rubbish. Mr. Churchill himself had an obsession with scientific 'gimmicks', and with his well-known 'midnight follies' he wasted a lot of the time of Air Ministry and other scientists in the examination of proposed inventions straight out of Jules Verne.

Caught equally in fogs of unreality and reality, crews on bomber stations were becoming increasingly irritated with life. They were finding, initially to their surprise, that nightly mess parties could become infinitely boring after a time. They retired more and more to their huts to read, write letters and listen to the radio, rather than put on yet another drink-aided neurosis-disguising act in the bar. Before long, this too became boring, and much was the moping and homesickness that descended on the still-adolescent young bloods on many a station, as the phoney war dragged on.

Whenever there was a fog-free day, everyone would be clamouring to fly. Squadron commanders would hastily arrange landing competitions, bombing competitions and simple navigational competitions. It was a change from darts and brag.

December opened without fog and again there was talk of action. It was back to stand-by, stand-to and stand down, with only three-day breaks to look forward to—and even then there was no real escape, except to the nearest town, with a 'twelve-hour recall' rule strictly enforced.

As soon as there had been two fog-free days, Churchill bombarded Bomber Command with demands for strikes against the Nazi naval vessels that were harrying our convoys, and Ludlow-Hewitt decided to put into operation a planned series of raids involving Wellington bombers. When 3 December dawned bright and fair, the signal was given at once for the first in the series to proceed. This was to be an attack on a cluster of enemy ships in the vicinity of Heligoland, the North Sea island off the west coast of Schleswig-Holstein. Wellingtons, Mark I and IA, from 3 Group, had been chosen for the job and twenty-four of them, from Nos. 38, 115 and 149 Squadrons, took off north-east immediately after breakfast.

Flying through cloud at about 3,000 feet, they mainly avoided attack from German flak batteries on the coast, dropped some bombs, and got home intact. The 500-pounders selected this time were set to explode on contact, but they again proved to be damp-squibs. Indeed, the only success claimed was the sinking of one small minesweeper. Ironically, this was achieved by a bomb which failed to explode. Its heavy casing passed right through the decks and out through the hull.

For various reasons, about half the planes had failed to press home their attack and returned to base with their bombs still aboard.

Modest and largely negative though this success had been, it encouraged air staff to believe that a substantial force of Wellingtons could operate unescorted in daylight, provided it maintained formation. The second anti-warship raid was therefore given the go-ahead on 14 December.

This time, twelve Wellingtons from No. 99 Squadron had been chosen to make a reconnaissance in force over the Schillig Roads. The weather was extremely bad and, due to inexpert navigation, the planes were forced to circle over the German mainland for forty minutes before they found their target. As a result, German fighters had plenty of time to locate the raiding force. Five Wellingtons were shot down over Wilhelmshaven and a sixth, pursued by fighters on the way home, decided to jettison its bombs in the Channel from 200 feet to gain a few miles an hour. The bomb doors opened and when the pilot pressed the bomb-release button, it was the last thing he ever did. For once, the ghastly British cargo exploded to order on contact with the waves and blew the plane to bits.

Despite this serious set-back, the third raid in the series was proceeded with four days later, on 18 December, when twenty-four Wellingtons (two of which 'went spare' after sortie-ing and took no further part) from Nos. 9, 37 and 149 Squadrons, were sent to attack shipping at the Jade Roads and Wilhelmshaven. Flying at 10,000 feet in mutually supporting Flights of three, they found that all ships had gone into harbour near the town, so no bombs could be dropped. They were flying without fighter screen or escort, and as they were leaving the target area the twenty-two remaining Wellingtons were pounced upon by a strong force of Me 109 and Me 110 fighters.

Attacked by cannon fire on the beam from above (to which the Wellington had no answer) and from the rear, they fought back as valiantly as they could with their relatively ineffective .303 machine guns. But the odds were impossible. In one of the most one-sided battles ever, ten woefully weak Wellingtons went down in flames over the target area, petrol streaming from their punctured tanks; two more had to ditch in the sea; and three were lost subsequently in forced-landings, having previously been crippled by cannon-fire.

Self-sealing fuel tanks had been invented some time before this, but no one had been intelligent or foresighted enough to apply the principle to bombers.

It also emerged later that the Messerschmitt fighters had been ready for the Wellingtons because German Freya early-warning radar, still in its experimental stages, was in use in the area for the first time, unknown to British Intelligence.

The consequences of the 18 December raid were too serious to be avoided. There could be no excuses this time and no prolonged white-washing post-mortem. The appalling facts were that two-thirds of our raiding force had dropped out of the sky or perished subsequently, picked off at will like sitting ducks by superior and better-armed German planes; and fifty highly-trained young crewmen had died agonising deaths for no well-thought-out purpose. With commendable speed, the Air Ministry announced, a few hours after details of the tragedy reached them, that daylight formation raids, by Wellingtons, Hampdens or Whitleys, were suspended until further notice.

In fact, they were never again to be a feature of British policy. Within a few days, decisions were taken that were to have a major and binding influence on the yet-to-come strategic air offensive of Bomber Command. Operational policy was switched completely from day to night bombing. The theory that heavy bombers could offer mutual defence in close formation against day-interceptor-fighters was abandoned once and for all.

Meanwhile, priority orders were passed down from the top for the fitting of beam machine-guns, extra armour plating, and self-sealing fuel tanks to all Wellingtons in service or in the pipeline; and production of the improved Mark 1C version was speeded. Protests were made to the Armament Directorate over the inadequacy of its bombs.

It was obvious that, there having been too little night training for Wellington and Hampden squadrons, the change-over from so-called precision day bombing to hoped-for precision night bombing would take time. So nothing at all happened for a few weeks, the weather again being made the scapegoat, which was rather unfair as it was merely offering the usual miserable mixture of an average English winter.

Everywhere, bomber men had been shattered at the news of the burnt offerings of Wellingtons and crews made to the gods of war over Wilhelmshaven, but nowhere more so than at Hemswell, near Gainsborough, Lincs, whence the ill-fated planes had taken off. The survivors could scarcely comprehend what had taken place. They little knew that they were the first of a legion of young men who would similarly mourn their comrades yet to be lost equally unthinkably and damnably in the five and a half years of war that had still to be faced. Some wanted to take off again, with or without permission, and beat hell out of the Hun—any Hun. Others chose to find what escape they could in drink.

Christmas Day, the first of the war, fell just a week after the raid. It found widows and families still inconsolable, and grown men staggered by the nightmare they had brought back with them.

The traditional peacetime RAF drill of officers serving Christmas dinner in the airmen's mess was got through, somehow, but the cheers were muted and the ceremony short. Likewise in the sergeants' mess, where strong potions were awaiting the officers' afternoon visit, the drinking was serious rather than riotous. Everyone was all-too-conscious that in quarters and village houses, fatherless children and their mothers were trying to adjust to the emptiness of loss that was already engulfing them.

Two hundred miles away, in the Ridings of Yorkshire, the night-trained Whitley crews were still flying, Christmas or no Christmas. The Air Ministry was being allowed to persevere in its view that the more leaflets that were dropped over Germany, the sooner the war would be over. The 200 ton mark for these officially-named 'Nickel' raids had been passed the week before. But the real value was in experience gained.

Nightly, the 4 Group Whitleys were ignoring fog and frost to range far and wide over enemy territory, from the Ruhr to Hamburg, Berlin, Nurenberg, and even, with lighter loads, as far as Vienna, Prague and Warsaw. To celebrate the festive season, water closets were ripped from huts as presents for Hitler, to be dropped with the 'bumph'.

Casualties for Whitley crews in the four months of war had been surprisingly light, and the opposition encountered had been much less than expected. Of course, the great advantages of leaflet raiding were that unless they were dropped tied up in heavy, skull-cracking bundles they offered no real threat to the enemy, and should they not be dropped in exactly the spot ordered, for reasons of heavy flak or faulty navigation, it did not greatly matter.

In truth, though, there *were* severe hardships and dangers Whitley aircrews had to contend with in 1939. These stemmed from lack of foresight by experts who had failed to provide suitable technical equipment and other necessary refinements either before or after the bombers had been designed and built. Principally, the deficiencies added up to lack of interior heating, inadequate oxygen, de-icing gear, and electrically-heated clothing. Apart from related discomforts, several planes of 51 Squadron, flying at maximum height in severe winter weather, had crashed in France on their way back from southern Germany because weighty ice had formed on the wings.

Nevertheless, with Whitley losses reported at less than 6 per cent for the first three months of the war, no one worried too much at the Ministry about 'minor' inconveniences to crews.

The Whitley bombers of 4 Group were themselves somewhat unsophisticated and self-willed planes, particularly the Mark IIIs that still had Tiger radial engines, with two-position propellors, demanding a fixed, fine-pitch setting for take-off and a fixed coarse-pitch setting for cruising speeds. This and the nose down attitude it adopted, due to its curious wing-fuselage design (in which it seemed to be scraping the grass on take-off and landing) could often prove unnerving for young pilots, and this led to occasional fatal misjudgements.

Whitleys had to be handled with a sort of rough firmness that came with experience. The Rolls-Royce Merlin-engined version, introduced in a few Mark IIIs and in all Mark IVs, offered different but equally unnerving problems to their crews. In particular, they were very inclined to drift inordinately to port during take-off, resulting at best in rather untidy, crab-like 'scrambles' by the squadrons involved.

All these hazards (together with the discomforts of the actual missions) the crews put up with fairly cheerfully, but the fact that there were no direct results, maybe no results at all, from their missions depressed them greatly. The 'urgent messages to the German people' their leaflets bore seemed no more urgent and less appropriate than toilet rolls would have been. Why should the Germans, who had deified Hitler for nearly a decade suddenly overthrow him because we demanded it—in writing?

But there were plusses for Whitley crews the value of which was not fully realised at the time. Chief among these was that, by practice and experience, navigation improved in 4 Group in a way that put them miles ahead of all other bomber units. Their ideas and suggestions, plucked from difficulties, led to many improvements in instrumentation, layout, navigational aids, emergency drills and devices that made high-flying tolerable.

Observations made by Whitley crews en route, of such things as radar stations, activity at enemy airfields, the location of anti-aircraft units and the construction of dummy factories, were all processed and were to prove useful in due course.

As an interim step, and a sensible one, the Ministry decided, just after the final ill-fated Wellington raid of December, that 5 Group's Hampdens and 3 Group's Wellingtons would join 4 Group's Whitleys in leaflet raids from January, 1940, so that they could gain much-needed experience of night flying, navigating and aiming before any bombed-up raids were hazarded again.

There was of course the inevitable Achilles heel hidden in this otherwise-admirable step forward. No one had thought deeply on the fact that there was virtually no accurate target-finding or aiming involved in such missions. The new dream was of spot-on bombing of small targets (with ships still top priority) by night. That there were no bomb-sights, not even the new American ones, that could offer such accuracy was ignored. That navigators, even in Whitleys, could rarely pin-point such targets was apparently not known outside the squadrons. Manfully sticking his head in the thickest fog available, the Air Officer Commanding-in-Chief, Bomber Command, pronounced bravely on the prospects for the immediate future: 'I see no reason,' he pontificated, 'why the major destructive part of our plans cannot take place in the form of precision bombing by night.'

All over Britain, in January, 1940, many young fliers prepared to adjust to the new demands to be made of them ... and to prove with their lives in the air that others more highly placed on the ground had been wrong.

Chapter Four

The new decade opened to a winter wonderland of snow, the like of which had not been seen in England for many a year. All flying was again suspended. Granted, the feathers of white had parachuted down in tons per acre rather than pounds, but snow had been prominent in the lists of flying hazards for so many years that its effects and dangers should have been anticipated.

There is always snow falling somewhere in the world; it has its own home in the upper sky, where it is permanently present, whether it also descends on the earth or not. Fliers had at that time been facing its challenges for nearly fifty years, and there were on record endless cases of pilots being caught with their defences down in blurry rushes of the stuff. Best of these was probably the tale of the Canadian plane that, in 1939, had flown unexpectedly into a particularly heavy blizzard of fresh snow. Within minutes, the crew thought they were still flying, although their popping-out eyes could see that the airspeed needle had slipped back steadily to zero. In truth, the pitot head had choked for a measurable period of time. For a moment, the propellors fought a losing battle to clear tunnels in the onrushing snow before the plane dropped earthwards exhaustedly and fortunately kept its balance to recover its momentum sufficiently in less fierce conditions nearer the ground.

Judging by the call to panic stations, however, nobody at the Ministry in London had previously seen or heard of the white stuff which began to cover the face of England on 1 January, 1940. There were no snow ploughs available to bomber stations, no regulations to cover the situation, no emergency procedures for obtaining supplies, and no rule books on how individual aeroplanes would react if they did have to fly in such conditions.

By the second of January, snow blocked all runways in the entire Bomber Command area, from Suffolk to Yorkshire; it piled itself vigorously against hangar doors; it balanced such a tonnage of weight on delicate telephone wires that the foot-thick poles holding them up collapsed; it buried aircraft at their dispersal points; and it cut off remote air stations completely from the outside world. Food ran out and beer ran dry, with no news of how stocks were to be replenished.

After a week of this, someone got a rough emergency plan going. A runway was cleared by tractors at a maintenance unit in Wiltshire and three old long-range Wellesley bombers, manned by veteran crews who were unafraid of snow, made flight after flight dropping by parachute what supplies they could muster to their grateful bomber squadron colleagues.

The absolute altimeter, which radar eventually made possible, had not yet emerged from the research establishment, so the Wellesleys dropped their bundles from a considerable height, with only fair accuracy in rather poor visibility. They were right in this because, without an exact height reading from their instruments, the higher they were the better. Snow makes it almost impossible to judge height or distance accurately, when flying above an unbroken whiteness, and planes had been lured to their doom by the deceptive condition known as 'whiteout', which can make objects appear hundreds of yards away when they may only be fifty feet distant.

Another little-realised danger in 1940 was damage to aircraft from slushy ice. Several squadrons, when cut off, cleared part of a runway and sent up any light aircraft they had to forage for food and beer. In most cases these planes returned temporarily unserviceable because flying slush had punctured their flaps.

Lessons were being learned all round that winter, most of them the hard way. Roared sing-songs around a roaring fire were the most popular form of energetic activity, as, week after week, snow continued to descend and ascend to the wind's whim in flurries of flakes, penetrating ever-deeper into corners of machinery or buildings, and building therein new feathery frostings of ephemeral ice cakes.

During this period, while Churchill fumed and the air chiefs shrugged their regrets at being able to do nothing, Germany's sea power was being used to its utmost in support of Hitler's theory that the easiest way to defeat Britain was to cut her sea supply routes and equally to starve her industry and people into submission.

In the last week of January, the wayward snow vanished almost as quickly as it had come, and by the time the resultant floods had died down, and work was able to proceed normally, the planned conversion of day bombers to night bombers was under way. As their aircraft were returned to them, strengthened in protective armour and in defensive armament, and with the latest night-flying devices fitted, Wellington and Hampden squadrons took turns of flying over Germany by night together with experienced Whitley squadrons, both on reconnaissance and on leaflet raids. These were particularly useful in 'hardening' inexperienced crews. The first raid over enemy territory was invariably the most terrifying. The leaflet raids were a useful way of 'blooding' crews and showing them what the procedures should be on the real thing.

Squadron take-offs and formation-flying by daylight were also practised by the hour. And landing on a beam from a radio signal was introduced in Bomber Command for the first time, with the result that crashes at bases were eventually cut down considerably.

At about the same time the Luftwaffe resumed its raids on the east coast of England, sometimes making brief attacks on airfields but mainly concentrating on unarmed merchant shipping or trawlers in open waters. Neither side had yet indulged in any strategic bombing, as such, and Germany appeared to be paralleling our 'wait and see' philosophy.

At home, civilians were becoming blasé about the war, which, except at sea, was very different to what people had been led to expect, and many had taken to relieving their boredom by devising ever-new ways of fiddling or black-marketeering; munitions manufacturers, too, were growing fat and lazy, as long mass-production runs of the same old rubbish piled up the profits. What matter if someone had forgotten to stop an order for bombers that were slow and inefficient, and that their manufacture was using up materials that could have gone into new planes: at least the production figures (minus spares) would look good. . . . So it was that hundreds of Battles and other antiquated aircraft—proven failures in combat—continued to roll off the production-line, to waste the valuable time of ferry pilots, and to pile up around the RAF maintenance units, unloved and unwanted . . . while operational squadrons were screaming for later marks of Wellingtons, Whitleys and Hampdens (let alone for the four-engined true heavies which had been promised for so long but which were still not in production).

Meanwhile, new squadrons were being formed, some re-equipment was proceeding in existing squadrons and night training was at last being taken very seriously indeed. Hundreds of Hampdens and Wellingtons flew west from East Anglia and Lincolnshire night after night, like schoolboys on a paper-chase following map clues and moonlit landmarks from about 2,000 feet. There were a few crashes, most of them stupid collisions, and a few near-disasters. But on the whole, standards of blind flying and navigation improved dramatically.

Schools were being set up even within operational units and three-hour lectures on navigation, armament and meteorology became the daily rule for all crews not on 'general duties' or stand-by. Rather tiresome but probably useful disciplines were introduced, such as morning roll-calls, in units that had previously got by on a minimum of orders.

On the night of 16 March, 1940, German bombers again took the initiative when they made a mass attack on units of the British fleet at Scapa Flow. This was not apparently intended to be a strategic raid in any sense, but some of the German bombs landed on Orkney islands causing the first British air-raid casualties of the war. Little damage was done to our warships but at Bridge of Waith in the island of Hoy one civilian was killed, five were injured, and four cottages were destroyed. This incident, minor compared to what was to follow, was the subject of an immediate Cabinet meeting at which it was decided that an escalation of the war in the air had taken place.

Bomber Command was at once told to take the brakes off a bit and three nights later, on 19 March, the first major night raid of the war by British bombers took place. The target was to be the German seaplane base at Hornum on the island of Sylt. A mixed force of thirty Whitleys and twenty Hampdens was chosen for the job, comprising 'experienced crews and those with particular knowledge of the area in which the target was situated'.

It should have been a model raid. It was nothing of the sort. In effect, it was the first Bomber Command attack against a land target and strict accuracy was demanded. Nine of the planes failed to reach the target area for various reasons; the remaining forty-one claimed to have attacked the base, at heights of around 2,000 feet, with standard 500-pounders and new 250-pound high-explosive bombs. Only one aircraft failed to return.

According to the Official History, at de-briefing 'all the bomb-aimers reported that the target was easily recognisable and could be seen through the bomb-sight. They said they had experienced no difficulty in aiming their bombs', although they found the powerful searchlights in the area troublesome.

But something was very wrong. The Germans went on the air at breakfast time to say that no damage of any sort had been done to their base, although several bombs had landed on the Danish island of Bornholm. And they took a party of American and other neutral journalists around the area to prove the point.

A few days later, when one of the RAF's new photo-reconnaissance unit's Spitfires flew over Sylt and Hornum it was forced to report that all buildings and hangars around the base appeared to be outwardly intact. This was the writing on the wall, for all who could see it, that Bomber Command was embarking on a policy of so-called precision night bombing when it had not yet the accuracy or the material or the crew disciplines to do so But then there was no alternative.

Ludlow-Hewitt was said to be 'furious' at the poor results, but keen to prove that this was a dummy-run for greater things. He was being pressed to do more by Churchill and others, with good reason. Germany had introduced its new secret weapon—the magnetic mine—and these were being sown in British sea lanes by seaplanes, flying from bases between Hornum and Borkum. Secret night patrols, by relays of Whitley bombers, were then begun over the area. The crews' orders were to circle all night long and drop bombs every time a flare-path was lit in the sea. This mine-patrol proved very successful for some weeks, there being no German night fighters at the time, and only ceased because the Luftwaffe was forced to convert Heinkel 111s to do the job from bases well inside the Reich.

Nor were we all that far behind Germany in this particular advance. A month later, a squadron of Hampdens had its bomb-bays converted to carry British 1,700-pound 'vegetable' magnetic mines, and these were dropped around the Danish and Norwegian coast, as well as in German waters, with some successes.

Before he could get another major night raid organised, Sir Edgar Ludlow-Hewitt was replaced, as AOC-in-C Bomber Command, by Air Marshal Sir Charles Portal, and the first thing the latter did, very sensibly as it turned out, was to cancel all leaflet-dropping operations so that 4 Group Whitleys could be used instead in night bombing offensives. By this date, 6 April, Bomber Command had unloaded about 65 million leaflets over the Reich. Reaction had been nil.

Three days later, Germany attacked and began to overrun Denmark and Norway. The phoney war was almost over and six of the most incredibly action-packed months of the war were about to begin.

On 15 April, Stavenger airfield was attacked by eleven Blenheims in the first Bomber Command attack on an inland target; and on 20 April, Aalborg airfield in Denmark was bombed by a small mixed force of Hampdens and Wellingtons. The pace was hotting up and the crews were generally relieved to be getting on with the job.

The Aalborg raid was of deadly importance because it was from this field that the Luftwaffe was ferrying men and materials into southern Norway in giant Junkers 52 transports, 200 planes at a time.

Improved bombs were coming forward by this time and each Hampden and Wellington involved carried thirty small fragmentation bombs, weighing about 40 pounds each, plus a few incendiaries, with all of which they were to attack the transport planes, and one 250-pounder to demolish the hangars. The plan was to sweep in at 1,000 feet at dawn and away again immediately the mixed bombs had been dropped.

It turned out to be a foul night, with heavy rain and low cloud. More than half the force mistook their pin-point and found themselves over the Copenhagen region instead of Aalborg. Scattered and battered by gale-force winds, they were only able to get safely home from having to fly for 200 miles over enemy territory in daylight because a fog bank swept over them from the sea to cover their nakedness; and thanks to recent instrument training they all managed to navigate their way home through the fog.

The five planes that had reached Aalborg at dawn had met with tough reception from flak batteries as they broke cloud at 800 feet. Although all were holed and damaged they had managed to struggle back to the nearest airfield at Lossiemouth in Scotland. Reconnaissance subsequently showed that only three Junkers transports had been hit, out of 200 parked around the field, and no damage had been done to the hangars.

Portal had meanwhile been studying the much-revised Air Plans and had come to the conclusion that we were deferring too much to the French. In his view, up to now we had only been nibbling at targets; civilian casualties were unavoidable if we were to do an adequate job of night bombing. As he saw it, the best objectives were oil plants, with their self-destructive incendiary element, night-lit railway marshalling yards, and aircraft factories. There was new justification for such a view in the fact that the Germans had been systematically bombing Rotterdam, killing nearly 1,000 people, while negotiation for surrender of the city were going on.

Portal was greatly encouraged in his planning for the weeks ahead by the fact that under the Churchill coalition Government which had taken over from that of the demoralised Chamberlain on 10 May, 1940, a Ministry of Aircraft Production had been quickly set up, under Churchill's great friend, Lord Beaverbrook, and had absorbed the Air Ministry's research and production departments. This meant less interference in future for Bomber Command.

Beaverbrook knew what life and business were about. The night he took over, he was on the telephone to managing directors of every leading aircraft firm and to the bosses of subsidiary shadow factories. It happened to be between 3 and 4 a.m. when he got round to this, but if he found he had to get any of them out of bed, he gave them 'bloody hell' for daring to sleep when bomber crews were over the Reich risking their lives to keep the factory bosses in luxury. It was a good beginning and his 'larger than life' lordship's continuing direct shock-treatment of bosses was exactly what was needed. He also took the trouble to ask Portal at once what he wanted in the way of improved equipment instead of telling him what he could or should have.

Indeed, Beaverbrook's drive and energy had much to do with the speeding of the heavy-bomber programme, and with the improvement in bomber 'fixtures and fittings', let alone the even more urgent production of hundreds of Spitfires in time for the Battle of Britain. Whatever harm his subsequent political bickerings may have brought, Beaverbrook was (like Portal) the right man in the right place at the right time ... and only just in time to help save England.

If, as philosopher Isaiah Berlin has it, British thinkers can be divided into Hedgehogs and Foxes (with the hedgehog bounding his territory, reducing it to a unity and, having started with his own terms, squeezing everything inside these terms ... while the fox roams wide searching for ever-new scents) then Beaverbrook was the Hedgehog and Portal the Fox in relation to the RAF at that time.

Initially, they worked well together. One of the first things Portal sniffed out was the fact that one of many things the Air Ministry research and development branch had neglected to do was to fit a simple toilet for the pilots of Hampden bombers. In these planes, the cockpit is so narrow the pilot cannot move out of it in flight. The result was that on flights of ten hours and more, Hampden skippers had to improvise their own evacuation arrangements—an unhappy state of affairs. The usual drill was to take along beer bottles or empty Verey light cases for one function and to try and avoid the other function altogether. There were of course accidents—with the usual accusations of 'yellow cowardice' and worse—and altogether it was a crazy state of affairs nine months after the start of the war. It had got to the point that some pilots had devised a sort of garden hose which led from the cockpit to a hole in the tail, whence the liquid was appropriately sprayed over Germany. But it was said that ground crews who were niggled about something were wont to tie knots in the hose before a flight, with alarming results. Anyway, no sooner had Beaverbrook heard about this than a chamber-pot-style loo was added for Hampden

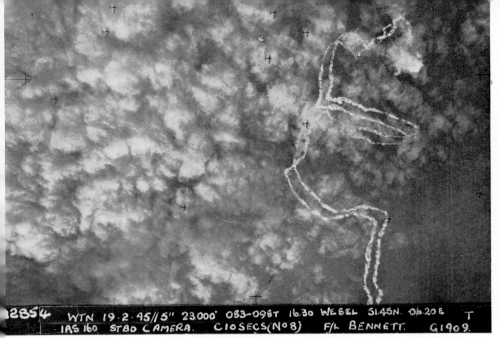

2854 WTN 19.2.45//5" 23000' 083-098T 16.30 WESEL 51.45N. 06.20E T IAS 160 STBD CAMERA. C10 SECS (N°8) F/L BENNETT. G1909.

2856 WTN 19.2.45//5" 23000' 083-098T 16.30 WESEL 51.45N. 06.20E T IAS 160 STBD CAMERA. C10 SECS (N°8) F/L BENNETT. G1908

1,2. *First picture shows the downward spiral of a stricken Lancaster . . .*
. . . before it explodes, the victim of enemy anti-aircraft fire.

3. *Human error is about to bring about the destruction of this attacking Lancaster. The bomb-aimer of the upper aircraft has not seen his comrade immediately below.*

4. *Heavy anti-aircraft fire confounding the main force in an attack on Pforzheim.*

pilots, later to be improved in the course of production. It was a small thing, perhaps, but it was the neglect of many small things by the Air Ministry in the past that had added up to a lot of troubles and difficulties for bomber crews.

Immediately following the destruction of Rotterdam, with the French lines breached at Sedan and Belgium about to fall, Portal sought and obtained permission to extend Bomber Command's operations from naval and battlefield targets to attacks on the heart of Germany. It was a major decision—the all-important switch from tactical to strategic bombing—and Portal wasted no time in implementing it.

Only twelve hours after the Dutch capitulation, Portal gave the go-ahead for the first of a series of watered-down Ruhr raids. He had extracted these from the Western Air Plans and had adjusted them to suit his limited forces. They mainly featured oil plants and railheads. With the Battle of France about to begin, heralding the first major crisis of the Second World War, it was obvious that Britain had to waste no time in trying everything, including strikes against vital German supplies, to check the coming German advance against Paris and the Channel ports.

While our ill-starred, inadequate Battle and Blenheim light bombers in France were seeking the destruction of bridges and other immediate battlefield targets, Portal unleashed a mixed force of ninety-nine home-based bombers in an effort to sap the strength of the German war machine. It was the night of 15-16 May.

It is a measure of Portal's foxy instincts that he let the pack run free while he watched for points. It is too little realised or remembered that in those earliest days of night bombing, squadron commanders were allowed a great deal of freedom within the general scope of a mission. There were few German night fighters. Ground defences were the main enemy. So formation flying was not necessary. The result was that crews chosen for a night raid were told to take off any time that suited them within a period of two or three hours, proceeding on their own to the target and back. These staggered departures had the advantage of maintaining a state of air-raid-alarm in Germany for lengthy night periods with consequent disruption of sleep-work schedules, and they suited the crews.

5—TLC * *

The briefing would take place the day before and they would then be free to work out a sequence of timed departures with their colleagues, according to whether they wanted to go to the cinema before departure, or get some sleep in, or whatever. They could work out their own routes. To some extent they could decide on their own bomb loads. And, again within the framework of the briefing, individual crews were given a fair amount of latitude in the matter of the actual bombing, with many of the more experienced skippers having worked out pet techniques all their own, in which their crews were well versed.

Such were the drills in the series of raids begun immediately after Holland had fallen.

The main targets were in the Hamburg area—refineries and oil tanks around the docks. Half the force was directed there. Other oil targets in the Ruhr were also to be hit, as well as a number of rail-heads. Four Hampdens, with previous experience of the area, were singled out for a special mission, aimed at blocking the Kiel Canal.

Six of the ninety-nine returned almost immediately with various troubles, including the notorious one—attributed to crews 'lacking moral fibre'—of 'intercom not working'. The other ninety-three pressed on at their own speeds and did their best in difficult circumstances. The old troubles dogged them. Bombs failed to release, or did not explode, or fell far from their targets. The moon was in the south-west over Hamburg and as the bombers flew in from the north-east, the better to see it reflected in the waters of the harbour, they ran straight into immensely heavy flak and blinding searchlights. Under orders not to bomb the town itself and to bring back their bombs if they could not strike at the chosen targets, many crews gave up. Some fires were reported by planes that managed to 'do' the docks. Anti-railway raiders also reported some damage.

Meanwhile, the four Hampdens had run into low cloud and, unable to find the Kiel Canal, had also returned to base with their new mine-type bombs still aboard. Most aircraft were punctured or damaged by flak, but all got home. It was neither a success nor a failure, as was to be the case with the other raids in the series.

But ten days later astonishing news got through to the Cabinet, via American Intelligence contacts. This was to the effect that these first ever attacks in force on the German fatherland had had a traumatic psychological effect on the Fuehrer.

His apoplectic response had been to draft an official directive on 24 May. On this date, the Battle of France was approaching its climax. Hitler should have been concentrating on exploiting his successes by destroying the encircled Allied armies. Instead, he became obsessed with the 'insult' of the comparatively-paltry Bomber Command raids on the Ruhr. He temporarily withdrew his attentions from the main battlefield and prepared an emotional order which was to alter completely the nature and purpose of proposed air operations against Britain.

In his impulsive and ill-considered directive (issued without any research or consultation) the furious Fuehrer ordered that a large-scale strategic air attack should be mounted against Britain, as a 'crushing' retaliation to the Bomber Command raids. This was something the Luftwaffe was not ready for, with its hands tied in air battles and raids in France and over the Channel. But 'god' had spoken. Hermann Goering at once got to work, with his young Chief of Air Staff, Hans Jeschonnek, and within a few days they had produced detailed plans for a series of probing attacks along the southern coast of England, to be followed by major attacks on London. To make these possible, it was ordered that, as soon as the fighting came to an end in France, the Luftwaffe bomber squadrons were to be redeployed at new bases along the Channel coast. This was Hitler's demand and it was therefore given highest priority at a time when German crews were deeply involved in battles and weary of daily sorties.

Dunkirk did not make things easier for the German air force. They had been given a false impression of the strength of the RAF as an antagonist by the badly-equipped Air Striking Force and BEF Air Component. Although bravery far beyond the call to duty had been shown by British bomber crews in France, their slow and vulnerable aircraft had been decimated by Luftwaffe fighters. Examples were: 10 May when five crews from No. 11 Squadron flew their Battles to certain death to destroy a bridge (and won the first two, albeit posthumous, RAF VCs of the war) ... 11 May when one out of eight Battles returned from an attack on German troop columns . . . 11-12 May, when 114 and 139 Blenheim squadrons lost all their planes except two. . . .

In three days of May, in fact, the strength of Advanced Air Strike Force bombers had been cut by half; and subsequently, in an all-out effort on 14 May to halt the break-out from the bulge at Sedan, only forty aircraft returned from a mixed force of seventy-one Blenheims and Battles—the RAF's heaviest loss in a single battle up to that date.

Desperate appeals were flung across the Channel for reinforcements from Bomber Command, but the futility of hopes of holding out on the Continent had been clearly read from the latest situation reports and Portal wisely resisted the temptation to send over further squadrons. Instead, he threw everything he had into cross-Channel sorties and helped the hard-pressed evacuation forces to snatch survival from defeat.

During the nine days of Dunkirk, to 4 June, 1940, the RAF flew 651 bomber sorties, 171 reconnaissance sorties and 2,739 fighter sorties in direct support of the evacuation. The operations of May and June, 1940 cost the RAF a total of 959 aircraft. It was a terrible toll which greatly helped to save Britain; and it led Winston Churchill to say after Dunkirk that 'there was a victory inside this deliverance which should be noted. It was gained by the Royal Air Force.'

Only Britain now stood between Hitler and complete victory. As he prepared to gloat while the Luftwaffe threw everything at our cities and factories, in what was to become a frenzy of terror-bombing, only one weapon remained to us capable of hitting back. It was Bomber Command.

Chapter Five

The miracle of Dunkirk was immediately followed by the capitulation of France on 17 June, 1940, when Hitler's mood was euphoric. He told Alfred Jodl, his Chief of Operations' Staff: 'The English have lost the war, but they haven't yet noticed it; one must give them time, but they will soon come around to accepting it.'

The English, in fact, plus the Scots, Welsh and Northern Irish, were having very different thoughts, and these were being expressed for them pungently by Winston Spenser Churchill. Immediately after Petain's armistice plea, Churchill verbally took Hitler to pieces as only he could and bade everyone here 'be of good heart'. In an angry, defiant and utterly resolved voice, and offering, in winged words, only 'blood, sweat and tears', he called for volunteers to defend their nearest beaches, streets and villages, armed with shotguns, pikes, maces and broom handles; he demanded that factory workers should strive as never before to produce planes and armaments; he warned of the coming air-raids, but said that 'the people should be accustomed to treat [them] as a matter of ordinary routine'; and in Parliament on 18 June he was first to give a name to the Battle of Britain: 'What General Weygand called the Battle of France,' he said, 'is over. I expect that the Battle of Britain is about to begin. Upon this battle depends the survival of Christian civilisation. Let us therefore brace ourselves to our duties, and so bear ourselves that, if the British Empire and its Commonwealth last for a thousand years, men will still say: "This was their finest hour". '

In fact, the preliminaries to the battle had begun. That night,

100 German bombers raided southern England, and from then on Luftwaffe operations against Britain were to continue without interruption, save for the weather, with increasing intensity, until the Luftwaffe would itself be put on the defensive by October 1940.

In all the circumstances, Churchill's words in June, and the uplifting response to them by the British people, bespoke perhaps the greatest act of unreasonable (but characteristic) defiance in history. We were utterly alone and totally unready for a fight. The Navy could no longer hold our island seas unless the air above was made secure (and in that connection all but three of our fighter squadrons had been thrown into the battle over northern France and Dunkirk, with stunning losses in planes and men). The Army was totally disorganised and had lost nearly all its military equipment in France. Sensing victory, Italy had jumped on the Nazi bandwaggon to add radius to our troubles. Britain was at her weakest and the Axis was at its strongest. To Hitler, it seemed that peace was likely to come the moment the first bombs were dropped on London, if not sooner. 'Surrender or face total destruction' was his 'magnanimous' offer to the British people. The French High Command opined that 'in three weeks England will have her neck wrung like a chicken'. America's Service chiefs believed we were doomed.

But we did not believe it, not any of it, and that was what mattered.

On the well-tried principle that, no matter how bad things may seem, 'the best method of defence is attack', Churchill decided that Bomber Command should attack, attack and attack again, with the ultimate object of undermining Germany from within. It did not matter that bombers could not yet be used with rapier accuracy; it was a time to '*bludgeon*' the bloody Nazis. Indeed, it was the *only* alternative to yielding all initiative to the Axis. Without our strategic bombing weapon we would have had to be entirely on the defensive, which would have been disastrous for the maintenance of Britain's toughening spirit, described by Churchill as our 'will and faith'.

There are many ways of measuring the comparative strengths of two or more air forces. On paper, it did not seem that

Bomber Command, with less than 500 medium bombers, could do much harm to Germany, especially compared to the Luftwaffe's undoubted capacity for blitzing us. The facts were that they outnumbered us three to one. But numbers and types of aircraft are meaningless when considered aside from the quality of the crews that fly them. Britain had found a small and growing band of gladiators, with flair and guts, who chose to ignore the odds against them and would not know when they were beaten.

Our gladiators had hope, too, in a way that their German opposite numbers could not have. They had been through the worst with aircraft developed years before. In this respect, at least, things could only get better. And the omens were seen to be good for a change. Beaverbrook was transforming the aircraft industry. Already we were producing more planes than Germany, in numbers at least. More importantly, at long last the four-engined bombers, specified as far back as 1935 and 1936, were more than gleams in their designers' eyes. Production of them had begun, and although it would yet be some time before they would be in service, the fact that they were on the way was a great boost for morale. The War Cabinet, on the basis of information from the Air Staff, claimed that 4,000 front-line would be built within three years—a forecast that was never to be fulfilled. But at least we had true 'heavies' in the pipeline (essential for the major strategic offensive Churchill was demanding) whereas the Luftwaffe had no four-engined bombers of any description in fact or in prospect.

Bomber Command also had an important new source of fresh blood. London was teeming by this time with refugee foreigners from every country in western Europe. Among them were Poles, Czechs, Belgians, Dutch, French, Norwegians, Danes and Finns, some of whom were highly-trained aircrew with battle experience and fire in their bellies. Many talked their way into Bomber Command and into flying or crewing planes almost before they had learned a word of English. They were different from our boys, but they were welcome, they were good, and they knew how to fight.

With the Battle of Britain beginning, there was an inevitable switch in priorities for Bomber Command. Anything that could clip the wings of the Luftwaffe at this stage was vital. So the first choice of targets, day by day and night by night, became airfields along the Channel coast and aircraft factories in Germany. The latter were by no means as easy to find and to hit as were the former, being comparatively small in size and located at considerable ranges from British bases. But a beginning was made at once and, in addition to night sorties by Wellingtons, Whitleys and Hampdens, some daylight attacks were made by Blenheims whenever there was sufficient cloud to give them cover. The Blenheims mainly went for aerodromes in Germany and the occupied territories, but as there were over 400 of them, it was a token effort rather than a serious campaign.

Sometimes a night mission by Whitleys to a distant airfield or factory would take eleven or twelve hours, and a new factor crept into the reports of accidents to aircraft. This was the sleep phenomenon. Generally, when a medical hypnotist goes to work on a subject, he puts him in a comfortable chair in a darkened room, and makes him look steadily at a lighted object while listening to a droning voice. All these conditions are reproduced in a cockpit when pilots are flying on instruments. And longer hours were demanded of bomber pilots in wartime than any *two* pilots are asked to share in civil flying. So there were unexplained accidents, and it was only when survivors' experiences were collated that the hypnotic sleep explanation was half-understood. Crews worked out a part-solution of their own. This was to take an occasional whiff from their oxygen tubes to clear the head, even when not flying high. But the real explanation was that everyone was flying too often and too long.

Synthetic oil plants and storage depots were next in priority for our bombers, with railway tunnels, signal boxes and marshalling yards third in the list; and soon an important new category was to be added—invasion barges. Furious that Britain was ignoring his overtures and spitting in his face, Hitler had decided 'to prepare for and if necessary carry out an invasion'. This was 'Operation Sea Lion', and his first moves were to assemble large numbers of generally-suitable craft in French ports. Bomber Command sought them out the moment they began arriving and attacked them with a will.

An immediate rap on the knuckles had also been dealt to Mussolini, when thirty-six Whitleys from Nos. 10, 51, 58, 77 and 102 Squadrons of 4 Group, with extra petrol tanks aboard, had flown from Yorkshire to northern Italy and bombed the Fiat works at Turin, plus targets in Genoa. They were able to do this by refuelling in the Channel Islands. Although the bomb loads the Whitleys could carry were light, and only thirteen of them won through to the target after facing heavy storms and severe icing, this was a prestigiously dramatic sortie. Alas, before it could be repeated, Germany occupied Guernsey on 30 June, and Jersey soon after.

Bombing was very much a matter of individual technique in those days and varied enormously even within squadrons. There was always the odd skipper who was mad enough to risk his life, and those of his crew, by going in at such a low height that even 500-pounders could scarcely miss the target, and risking the balloons which, by now, were to be found floating every 300 metres or so over important targets. By contrast, there was invariably a colleague who would fly at such an altitude that his bomb-aimer could see nothing and would have to take pot luck. Between the two extremes were various degrees of wavering or of skill and dash. But the strange thing was that as many of the play-safe high-flying bombers were picked off as of the do-or-diers. In all cases, pilots really tried to get to the target every time because only if such action was confirmed did the trip count towards a crew's total of tour missions.

At this period, bombsights and bombs remained major headaches for crews. Modified but still inaccurate, World War I bombsights were still in use, and would be until the first reliable new one, the Mark XIV—the 'tactically free' sight—would be introduced in two years' time. Similarly, the 250- and 500-pound bombs that had been used since 1918 continued to be the main projectiles available. Aerodynamically, these were undependable and liable to soar waywardly in the wrong direction, sometimes falling the wrong way round or see-sawing alarmingly. Fusing was equally unreliable, with large numbers of bombs failing to detonate. And explosively these old weapons remained largely impotent.

On 2 July, 1940, however, the first 2,000-pounder, with an armour-piercing capability, made its appearance, when three were dropped by a Flight of Hampdens of 83 Squadron in an attack on the battleship *Scharnhorst,* in dry-dock at Kiel Harbour.

The Hampdens used a new dive-bombing technique, devised partly to avoid flak and searchlights, and partly to improve accuracy, in which they zoomed from 6,000 feet in a 60-degree dive and pulled out at 2,000 feet. One of the ancient Hampdens attained such a frame-shaking speed in the pull-out, with its engines literally red-hot, that its glass nose shattered and the bomb-aimer therein blacked-out, making it impossible for him to pull on his 'cheese-cutter' device (it being before the days of automatic stick-droppers) and release his AP load. And, as the pilot pulled it upwards, making emergency use of his tail-trimming tabs, and giving the twin Pegasus engines the gun, one wing was nicked by a balloon cable and partly-crumpled. Shaking, rattling and rolling, the damaged plane headed for home and a difficult laden-landing.

Meanwhile the other two Hampdens had controlled their dives better but not their aiming. Their armoured-piercing 2,000-pounders missed the battleship by a mile and landed in the streets of Kiel, so nothing was proved at this stage about the new bomb except that, as reconnaissance showed the next day, it could demolish houses.

In fact, although bigger, this first 2,000-pound bomb was still to prove unsatisfactory. As with the others, it had a poor ratio of explosive charge to casing, contained the comparatively useless Amatol explosive, and was too lacking in stability for an armour-piercing function.

That it could have been much more effective is a matter of history. A British scientist had stumbled on the fact, early in 1940, that a simple aluminium additive, fed to existing explosive mixtures, would improve their power by as much as 100 per cent. But because of aluminium shortages, the modest tonnage required was refused and the Armament Research Department at

Boscombe Down was told to discontinue the experiments. Germany, having made the same discovery, was already producing bombs twice as powerful, weight for weight, as ours.

We were still muddling through in this and many other technical respects. Nor were the brave 'supporting cast' of Bomber Command being given the rank, let alone the credit or the money they deserved. Few aircrew members were NCOs in the 1939-40 period. Wireless operators were ACs and gunners were AC2s. They got 25p. per week 'danger money' for flying. Many of them had been ground crews who had shown keenness and aptitude within the squadron and who mainly picked up their skills on active missions. Even target practice for gunners generally took place within the units rather than at gunnery schools. Improvisation was a necessary evil, although navigators had to put in longer hours to gain experience and many of them had to know the rudiments of flying, in case the pilot was knocked out. Radio communication was still very much a hit-or-miss affair and it was the exception rather than the rule if a plane was able to get through to base when in difficulties to be 'fixed' for rescue . . . the Air Sea Rescue branch of launches and Lysanders having been formed to retrieve crews from the Channel.

There was one famous occasion about this time when even the best operators could do nothing. A squadron of Hampdens had been over Bremen and shortly before they were due back a morse SOS was heard briefly at 5 Group HQ near Grantham. Before the plane's position could be fixed, the signal suddenly ceased and all wavelengths in use by the group went equally dead. Simultaneously, telephone conversations became unintelligible. Everyone on duty was thrown into a panic. Could this be Hitler's much-talked-about secret weapon? Nobody had ever experienced anything like it. The AOC-in-C was called out but he could offer no explanation either . . . which was understandable because the area had been hit by a rare magnetic storm, of the sort that nature puts together only every twenty years or so. Fortunately, the Hampden in trouble managed to struggle home safely and land unaided.

Parties were rare for bomber aircrew in the Battle of Britain period. They worked at maximum effort with very little sleep. It was a question of bombing every night the weather was good, and there was little time for pleasure or even relaxation. Pecking away at Germany, the crews built up formidable tour totals, those that survived, as Bomber Command's 500 aircraft put up a nightly average of 100 solo sorties over Germany and the invasion coasts.

It had been decided that there would be no fighter cover for our bombers, by day or by night, in order that the entire Fighter Command could be employed to repel German attacks, with the result that the Luftwaffe had to hold back some of its fighters for defence against Bomber Command's unescorted raids. In effect, this was a major added contribution to the balance of the Battle of Britain, although it meant a much harder life for bomber crews.

Airborne radar had been developed by this time, and the RAF was again ahead of the enemy, but it was sensibly being fitted to night fighter planes. Bomber adaptations had to wait. It was largely employed to track down invading aircraft earlier than they could be picked up on the limited-range Chain Home ground stations. A few coastal patrol aircraft, Hudsons and Blenheims, were also fitted with a device known as ASV, which had been fathered by the original A1 airborne 'red box', and which could track down ships at up to five miles' range.

Across the Channel, the Germans were engaged in building a chain of Freya scanning stations, and these were giving an increasing amount of trouble to Bomber Command planes. But in quickly processing data and alerting fighter planes to intercept incoming bombers, the RAF was away ahead of the Luftwaffe.

Britain's defence arm had also rumbled that the Luftwaffe was taking a leaf out of Bomber Command's book in night raids by sending single aircraft over before and after the main attack. This was designed to impose protracted air raid alarms, which would interrupt night production as well as seriously interfering with sleep for day workers. The sensible British answer was to risk occasional unheralded bombs and sound the siren only when radar indicated that the main attack was on its way.

Lessons were being quickly learned on both sides. As June became July, the Germans reduced their night bomber losses by flying at heights that took them above the power of our search-lights (which up to then had been 'finding' bombers for night fighter pilots) and the nightly average of British 'kills' dropped to about two German bombers out of each main force. During the early experimental raids (before the 'official' start of the Battle of Britain on 8 August) the Luftwaffe also tried out a crude but effective device, known as Knickebein, which consisted of two radio signals beamed to intersect over a chosen target area. The existence of this direction-finder was quickly detected by a scientist at the Air Ministry, Dr. R. V. Jones, one of Churchill's 'wizards', and after a number of secret experiments, he was able, by the end of July, to 'bend' the German beams, to the consequent puzzle-ment of Luftwaffe pilots and the delight of our night fighters, who were only beginning to flex their muscles.

Knickebein had been introduced for the very good reason that German bomber pilots were having as much difficulty as ours with navigation. Perhaps the most astonishing case of this had been the bombing, by three Heinkel 111s, of the old German university city of Freiburg in mistake for the French town of Dijon—a naviga-tional error of more than 150 miles as the Heinkel flies.

Also, thanks to bad Luftwaffe navigation, the RAF had cap-tured a number of German planes intact (to test and learn from at Farnborough and Boscombe) because the German pilots had forced-landed in bad weather on British fields thinking they were in France. But, of course, there were also reverse cases, including several of Bomber Command crews burning their valuable aircraft on English aerodromes because they thought they had landed on enemy territory.

Another constant source of worry on both sides was failure by gunners to recognise friend from foe. And in this respect, the Italians had succeeded in Libya in putting up the biggest 'black' of the season, so to speak. Alerted by British bombers passing overhead, a company of Italian anti-aircraft gunners had excitedly shot down in flames the next plane to come along . . . killing the Governor of Libya, Marshall Balbo, previously Minister for Air in Rome, who happened to be its Very Important Passenger.

Bomber Command was having surprisingly few losses in its night operations, although damage from 'light flak' was a major factor. (The much-used abbreviation flak, by the way, had been curiously derived from the German Flugabwehrkanone anti-aircraft gun, which was extremely efficient and accurate.) Whereas in Britain, anti-aircraft units were Army artillery batteries temporarily under Fighter Command control, in Germany the Flakartillerie had been part of the Luftwaffe since 1935, and had a fantastic understanding of bomber techniques, which it used to full effect.

Below 10,000 feet flak was generally intense over important targets. Bomber Command pilots, caught in the coning of supporting searchlights would watch, terrified as they were enthralled, as shells came shooting and hissing upwards like colourful showers of fireworks—green, white, yellow and red—bock-bocking when distant, and roaring like thunder when close to the plane. Already efficient and well-equipped in 1940, the Flakartillerie corps were to be the nightmare that would not go away for Bomber Command fliers throughout the long war.

Fortunately, thanks to advanced ideas on aircraft construction, our bombers were strong from the start. It became an astonishment, as experience increased of night flying through flak, that Wellingtons, Whitleys and Hampdens could take so much punishment from shells and still get home. The light but extremely resilient frames and skins the aircraft factories were turning out were proving to be increasingly reliable, even when smashed, torn and punctured again and again.

This reliability was also true in respect of the general construction of the latest Blenheims. One afternoon, late in July, 1940, a Mark IV Blenheim of 2 Group dived out of low cloud to attack a German destroyer in the North Sea. Weaving violently on its second run to avoid heavy cannon fire from the ship, the Blenheim actually struck the water with such force that one engine was ripped completely out of its mounting and the airscrew of the other was badly bent. Nevertheless the airframe suffered only negligible damage, and the pilot managed to nurse the remaining engine for nearly 200 miles to a Scottish coastal airfield, where he made a rough but successful emergency landing before dark.

Putting down a damaged aircraft by night was infinitely more difficult. Like the birds before them, most pilots slightly misjudge the occasional landing and, when tired, can seriously miscalculate one. Nowadays this is allowed for by the fact that runways are wide, long and well lit. Landing gear, too, has been greatly improved to cushion bumpy arrivals. But in 1940 things were much more limited and landing accidents were the most common of flying mishaps, especially after dark. Undershootings, overshootings, skewshootings and Chinese landings (with one wing low) were a constant worry to Station Commanders, and inability, by reason of shot and shell, to lower or lock landing wheels took a heavy toll.

Errors and misjudgements in take-off were also prevalent, mainly when heavily-laden planes were straining to achieve utmost speed and lift. There were even cases of crashes through carelessness or inexperience of pilots in raising their landing gear a little too soon on take-off.

The Luftwaffe had meanwhile decided not to make things any easier by indulging in methodical attacks on bomber airfields, especially when our planes were taking off or landing, with the result that Station Commanders tended to allow their fears of being bombed to overcome their fears of landing losses. They would douse all normal lights and substitute a couple of dim red lights instead of a flarepath on nights that seemed likely to be favoured by Luftwaffe bombers. This certainly did not make landings softer, even for undamaged aircraft.

It did not always work quite that way, however. On the night of 1 August, 1940, a formation of Dornier 17s crossed the Yorkshire coast at Barnston and attacked the big Whitley bomber base near York, while the flarepath was temporarily lit to guide back a plane in distress. This field was less well defended than those in the south and considerable destruction was done to the four hangars, the workshops and other buildings. Only the sergeants' mess escaped, but few of the Whitleys dispersed around the perimeter were hit. All the German planes got away safely because raids elsewhere had tied up the night fighters, which was not surprising when you consider that their sparse squadrons had a total of 800 miles of assailable coast to defend—a frontage twice as long as that which the joint French, British and Belgian forces had failed to hold in May.

The following morning a German recce plane was seen flying

high above York and Fighter Command, although alerted, knew the drill for this phenomenon by now and allowed it to go home. Sure enough, that night the twelve Dorniers again droned over Barnston to finish the job they had begun the night before. And sure enough, Fighter Command was free and ready this time. Not one of the German bombers got home to tell the tale. All were picked off by night fighters over the North Sea. It was a major success and raised many a cheer around Bomber Command messes.

Cheers were needed in those grim days and nights. The Axis was growing ever stronger from Narvik to Biarritz. Mussolini's hundred or so divisions were ready to march into Somaliland and Egypt. Soon the Japanese would enter the conflict. The Luftwaffe now had 1,400 first-line medium bombers and 1,300 modern fighters concentrated in the airfields of northern France and the Low Countries. Processions of barges were floating down the rivers and canals of Europe towards the Channel ports, their crews singing the latest German hit song, 'We March Against England'. Powerful shore batteries were seen to be being built at Cap Gris Nez, France, to shell the areas behind the invasion beaches of England.

Early in August, reconnaissance of Wilhelmshaven revealed the battleships *Admiral Scheer* (in Austrustungshaven) and *Tirpitz* (in Banhaven) obviously getting ready to give support to 'Sea Lion'. Large concentrations of barges in the Belgian canals were observed, as were gathering merchant shipping, miscellaneous light naval forces and a barge-borne balloon barrage unit at Kiel. Wellingtons and Whitleys of Bomber Command had a go at all these targets, map-reading their way carefully from canal to canal in the moonlight, while Hampdens carried out mine-laying operations and bombed sea-plane bases in the general area.

Blenheims were also active by day when cloud cover permitted, but when a force of twelve was caught out in suddenly-improved weather conditions over Stavanger airfield, only five, all damaged, got back to Britain, the others having been picked off one by one by thirty-six German fighters.

The Luftwaffe's technique against day bombers, as exemplified on this occasion, seldom varied; but so effective was it, it did not

5. *These Wellington bombers were flying at the outbreak of war. Blooded from the second day of the war, the remarkable 'Wimpey' as it was affectionately nicknamed, would carry the main burden of night bombing until the first of the true 'heavies' would come forward two years later . . . and it would still be first-line equipment at the end of the war.*

6. *The Mosquito, one of the most superbly versatile aircraft ever built.*

7. *The ubiquitous Lancaster bomber.*

8. *This picture, first published in September, 1942, was one of the earliest released of the Lancaster. It shows bomber crews and ground staff in front of a spanking-new Lanc just prior to a night raid on Dusseldorf.*

have to. In the Stavanger case, the Blenheims had made their attack and were heading at full tilt for the safety of cloud over the sea. They were flying, as instructed, in a tight self-defending formation. But they were attacked by Me 110s which had sideways-firing guns, so that all the German pilots had to do was fly in formation with the Blenheims fifty yards or so out and to the front, whence they could pick off the outer planes one by one by aiming no-deflection shots at the pilots. The Blenheim crews had no answer to this. If they broke away they were immediately pounced upon by three or more Messerschmitts waiting above for just such a move. If they stayed where they were, they could be sure their turn would come, as one by one they were picked off, from the wingman inwards. Thus, on this occasion seven were hacked down and the five others sprayed with machine gun fire before they found low cloud and staggered home. They had lived through a 'sitting duck' mission . . . which was more than a majority of Blenheim day-bomber crews would be able to say in months to come.

Day-bombers were now only a small part of a growingly complex bombing picture, with their losses causing the odd 'tut-tut' and 'too bad' at the most. It was from the medium bombers that morale-boosting successes were expected. Altogether, in the first week of August, Bomber Command pecked at priority targets at Hamburg, Bremen, Wilhelmshaven, Emden, Hamburg, Hamm, Essen, Kiel, Evere, Gelsenkirchen and Monheim, as well as at barge concentrations throughout Belgium and Holland. Maybe only small forces attacked each target, but the distance and variety of these made good reading next day for the beleaguered British public.

The pre-invasion Adlerangriff or Eagle Attack by the Luftwaffe on England was now in full flight, with heavy raids on British convoys and harbours in the south, as well as on radar stations, factories and airfields throughout the country, involving hundreds of bombers in six or seven major operations each twenty-four hours. Even Junkers 87 dive-bombers were used in this opening phase of the battle, flown from bases just across the Channel and supported by the equally-limited-ranging Messerschmitt Bf 109s.

Day after day the new fast eight-gun Spitfires and slightly slower Hurricanes were shooting down more raiders and their supporting fighters than they were losing themselves in ever-more-daring battles in fine summer skies. But a major and successful bombing counter-attack was now needed for reasons of prestige, as well as to rap the German nose and make it draw back instinctively. This was achieved dramatically on the night of 12-13 August when five of the most experienced Hampden crews from 49 and 83 Squadrons were sent to bomb the Dortmund-Ems canal. It proved that numbers of aircraft were not necessarily the criteria for inflicting maximum tactical damage on the enemy.

The prestige Dortmund-Ems raid—one of the most famous of the war—had come about this way. Early in August, twenty-four Hampdens from 49 Squadron at Gainsborough, Lincs, had pressed home a successful mass attack on a minor bridge on the Ems canal. On return, they had reported that the area was only lightly defended, and it was immediately decided that a further raid should be hazarded on an all-important aqueduct nearby which carried the Dortmund canal over the River Ems. Absolute precision would be vital on this mission, so ten of the most experienced crews were selected from the two best squadrons in 5 Group—49 Squadron and 83 Squadron. Tirelessly, they trained every day for a week. They dived by moonlight on canals in the east midlands of England which were judged to be the same width as the Dortmund. They dropped practice bombs over and under mocked-up bridges, created for them by a local theatre workshop. Table-top models were also made of the Dortmund-Ems area and these were studied by the hour in squadron 'classrooms'. So important was the mission that Sir Arthur Harris, now commanding 5 Group, personally sat in on a number of the rehearsals; but this was essentially a raid planned almost entirely by the men flying it. It was, in effect, an early version of the sort of drills the famous 617 'Dambusters' Squadron would use and improve upon three years later.

Satisfied that the rehearsals had gone well and that the show could go on, Flight Lieutenant R. A. B. 'Babe' Learoyd, who had been on the original Ems raid, made a solo recce over the area on the night of 11-12 August. He found that the defences had been strengthened by searchlights and light flak, and that there were signs of other emplacements being dug. So it was the sooner the better, and the moment Learoyd got back, the button was pressed by Harris for the all-important raid to take place that night, 12-13 August. The most difficult bit was selecting five of the ten crews in training. They were all good, and competition was as intense as if this had been a Possibles v. Probables trial at Twickenham . . . which was how the elite of Bomber Command looked at life, anyway, in 1940. Eventually pieces of paper were handed to the 'successful entrants', and it was found that the five crews would be led respectively by A/Squadron Leader James Pitcairn-Hill, Flight Lieutenants Learoyd, Matthews and Mulligan and Flying Officer Ross, making two from 49 Squadron and three from 83 Squadron. Among the 'rejects' was a young bomber pilot we have heard of before, and will hear of again, Guy Gibson.

Dortmund-Ems was an exceptionally brilliant attack. Ross, who went in very low, never pulled out of his dive and crashed in flames in the canal, with total loss. Each of the other four Hampdens was badly shot up. Mulligan was forced to climb again steeply and bale out with his crew. At least, all were taken prisoner. Matthews had to fly home on one engine. The other two planes, Pitcairn-Hill who had gone in first and Learoyd who had gone in last, had succeeded in getting their bombs over and under the target, and Matthews had struck very near.

It was altogether a major success. The aqueduct had been breached; the water was flowing out of the canal; it would be fourteen days before the damage would be repaired; and the movement of barges and other vessels from the Rhineland to the invasion ports had been measurably delayed at a vitally important time.

Flight Lieutenant 'Babe' Learoyd received the VC for his actions in this operation; A/Squadron Leader James Pitcairn-Hill, who was to die in another important raid a few days later, added a DSO to his DFC; and as soon as it was discovered that Flight Lieutenant Allen Mulligan was safe in a POW camp, he was given the DFC.

The precision of the Dortmund-Ems bombing made it an exceptional case. Bomber Command's night operations tended to be highly inaccurate, and the 1,450 tons of badly-aimed and faulty bombs dropped on Germany in July and August may have terrified the populations involved, but they did little damage to the factories and installations they were aimed at.

The knocking out of a tiny water-bearing bridge by a small force of skilled bombers inevitably became an immediate talking point with crews on both sides of the Channel. On the morning of 13 August, a few hours after the aqueduct-busters had returned to their bases in Lincolnshire, Luftwaffe crews were congregating to launch the widest-ranging daylight offensive on Britain since the war began. News of the Dortmund-Ems canal achievement, which filtered through to the unrelenting Germans as they were warming up their engines, must have had considerable effect on their resolve.

Over 300 bombers and 1,100 fighters of the Luftwaffe were committed to battle that day. And the next few days were to be make-or-break ones in the softening-up Adlerangriff blitz, prior to the Sea Lion invasion. Simply, the Eagle-Attack was designed to destroy the RAF in the same way as the Polish, Belgian and French air forces had been destroyed.

To succeed, the Luftwaffe needed a balance of cloud and sunshine, mixed their way. And, on 13 August, it seemed they had got it. Although the summer of 1940, like that of 1939, had been as heavenly as the war news had been hellish, overcast cloud had now suddenly descended on the Channel, while sun shone over England. It was exactly right. It must have seemed that the Fuehrer had a hot line to the fallen angels whose forte was the manipulation of the weather. The plan-of-the-day was to make heavy probing attacks to expose Britain's defences, from Southampton and Weymouth to Southend and the Thames Estuary, and also to attack airfields in many parts of the country. The conditions gave bomber crews the hope that they could approach their targets largely unseen. This hope was strengthened by the fact that the previous day heavy raids had been made on south and east coast radar stations, and it was believed enough had been knocked out to allow the bombers through. Also, with such widespread raids as were planned, it seemed unlikely that Fighter Command would be able to spread itself enough to cope. In this way, it was believed, vulnerable gaps would be found in Britain's coastal defences, to be exploited in the impending invasion.

All day the Luftwaffe droned over the Channel on a dozen all-important missions, each mounted by seventy to 150 aircraft; and all day Fighter Command managed to shift its interceptor forces in time to the right places, like giant moves on a draughts' board. They were substantially aided in this by the patched up radar stations, all of which were still functioning, with the sole exception of the Isle of Wight.

Quickly dealt with were Heinkels making for Eastchurch airfield and heavily escorted Stukas attacking RAF ground installations around the south coast. Both forces suffered heavy losses before noon. In the afternoon, there was heavy fighting in the skies over all parts of southern England, as raids were attempted on airfields, docks and factories. The city of Southampton was heavily damaged, as were several Coastal Command air stations. But, in less than twelve hours, forty-seven German aircraft were shot down for the loss of only thirteen by the RAF. It had been quite a day, and there was to be no sleep for radar staff or night-fighter crews when darkness spread its wings over England.

Goering had to keep his stiff-necked young fliers hard at it, around the clock. Both sides knew that the Battle was almost at its do-or-die climax, and its successful resolution had become a matter of pride and passion for the crews involved, apart altogether from the great issues of conquest or repulsion. Dowding's 'chicks' of Fighter Command were putting up performances that would put their names into the footnotes of history. Goering's 'eagles' may have had superiority in numbers of planes but the types of aircraft were mainly ill-designed for the purposes asked of them. And in the swaggering Reichsmarschall they had a leader flawed by misjudgements.

Anyway, on Goering's orders, the attacks on airfields, defence installations and factories were continued throughout the darkness of 13-14 August, and among the inescapable tragedies was the bombing by Heinkel 111s during the night shift of the Nuffield aircraft works at Castle Bromwich, with eleven direct hits, much damage and many civilian casualties. This must have been sheer luck, because the bomb-aiming of the Heinkels of 100 Group that took part was crude. Indeed in something like seventeen attacks on other aircraft factories that night and during the remainder of this period of the Battle of Britain, they only twice planted their bombs within five miles of the targets.

Fog and bad weather caused the cancellation of a vast programme of intended Luftwaffe attacks on 14 August, and on the night of 14-15 August. In the twenty-four hours, a meagre total of 500 sorties were flown at a cost of ten aircraft against eight lost by the RAF. But, unknown to the participants or to the spectators, 15 August was to be the peak daylight point of the Battle of Britain . . . the turning point . . . the day of days for Britain . . . the occasion when German planes would fall from the sunny sky over the farmlands of southern England like pheasants at a bumper shoot.

There were plenty of birds for Fighter Command to pot on 15 August. In an attempted all-out blow, Goering had sent over the full might of three Luftflotten, comprising 1,800 aircraft—nearly 1,300 of them fighters—in successive waves. While Luftflotten 2 and 3 were mounting a dozen major raids in the south, a force of fifty dive-bombers from Luftflotte 5 was approaching the Yorkshire coast. These were the very latest Junkers 88s, flying in from Norway and Denmark, and, because of their great speed, they had chosen arrogantly to scream like angry eagles across the North Sea totally unescorted, thinking to surprise the natives.

Thanks again to good British radar fixes, four squadrons of fighters from 12 Group were awaiting the Junkers over Scarborough and within ten minutes the fifty bombers were in serious trouble. More than half the force turned about and using full-boost made for cloud cover. A dozen dropped their bombs at random over Bridlington, accidentally blowing up an ammunition dump. Only ten got through to the target (which was the main bomber airfield at Driffield) where they did a certain amount of damage and destroyed a number of Whitleys on the ground. On the other side of the balance sheet, a quarter of the freshly-minted Junkers dive-bombers would never dive again, and many more were severely damaged.

When the total score for the daylight hours of 15 August was added up, Goering was to find that in one day he had lost an eighth of his bombers and a fifth of his long-range fighters—an unbearably serious development for the Luftwaffe. Plans had to be changed, and quickly.

The people of Britain, hundreds of thousands of whom had actually seen hated black-crossed Nazi bombers fall flaming from the sky, listened enraptured as the BBC told listeners—including many in occupied Europe with clandestine radios—that 182 enemy aircraft had positively been destroyed, together with another fifty-three probables. The figures were exaggerated for various reasons, some of them innocent, but not even Lord Haw-Haw could deny that the Luftwaffe's nose had been bloodied in the most dramatic fashion. Indeed things had been so bad for Goering on 15 August that it was to go into his diary as *schwarzer Donnerstag* (black Thursday) ... not the sort of thing so vain a man would write lightly.

Nor did Friday the sixteenth cheer him out of his state of shock. On this day he rounded up every available aircraft to make up a total of 1,720 sorties and suffered proportionately heavy casualties to those of the day before. The figures for the previous ten days were placed before the Reichsmarschall that evening and they showed that the Luftwaffe had lost a total of nearly 400 planes. He was thrown in a funk. General Holder had assured him that the RAF could be smashed in two weeks to the point that it could not put up any substantial opposition to the invasion forces, and he had told the Fuehrer much the same thing. Now he had to plead for time and for a switch of policy.

So shaken was Goering by the losses, insupportable even by an air force the size of Germany's, and particularly by the loss of trained crews, that he issued a personal urgent order that no aircraft should fly with more than one officer in the crew. He added, in one of the wierdest miscalculations of the war, that all attacks on British radar installations were to cease. Misinformed and too ill to weigh scientific evidence with any accuracy, he had underestimated the importance of British radar and the marvellous part it had played and was playing in parrying the Luftwaffe's offensive air strikes, whether these were mounted by day or by night.

It was to night bombing, with its smaller losses, that Goering was now forced to turn, like Bomber Command before him. Although the Battle of Britain would continue for some months, postponement of the Sea Lion invasion was inevitable, and Britain could breathe again. Hitler's six-league jackboot, so successful against lesser fry in Europe, had been lacerated by the needle concealed in Britain's crotch. The march of his day blitz had been blunted and halted for the first time. The great opportunity presented to him by Britain's critical weakness after Dunkirk had passed. The Fuehrer had led his shock troops up a blind alley for the first time, with an ambush at the end of it. Now, his only alternative plan lacked the sweet fruits of swift victory. The substitute night blitz which was soon to be ordered would take longer to mount and could never be rapidly effective, featuring, as it had to do, all the wrong types of aircraft for the job.

Until these night raid plans were ready, there had to be an overlap of tactics and Fighter Command would have to go on fighting full-stretch for some weeks. But the fact was that The Few had already won a battle as notable as Trafalgar. The Luftwaffe had failed to implement its orders 'to establish decisive superiority in the air and to wreak such havoc on the ground as would render the British helpless to resist invasion, or induce them to sue for peace'.

In brief, Hitler's forecast of victory over Britain by a 'snap checkmate' had ended in stalemate. The formulation now demanded of a new strategy had to be based on an extended war for which the German economy was unprepared and the Luftwaffe ill-designed.

The defensive battle which Britain had stonewalled its way through had not only been an immediate and dire necessity for the British but also a *sine qua non* of ultimate victory. No wonder a new spirit was abroad in Britain. No wonder laughter began to take the place of fear. Adlertag had come and gone. Instead of swooping to the kill, the eagle had fallen off its perch. And the British, with their inborn sense of the ridiculous, had begun to laugh at Hitler.

It was also autumn. Air activity had to lessen in winter, and there could then be no thought of a revised Sea Lion invasion plan until the spring or summer of 1941, by which time it should be possible to thump the mammal's sensitive nose still harder.

Air fighting would still be fierce, but on a much-extended timetable. And a partial disengagement in bad weather was inevitable—giving Britain time to think; time to work; time to grow; and time to begin reversing the bombing trend. The wave of German conquest which had swept so easily over Poland and western Europe had miraculously spent its initial force on the coasts of England.

The Adlerangriff had also painfully exposed the Luftwaffe's air limitations. On paper, it had been three times as strong and twice as modern as the RAF. But in fact its army-support concept had not fitted the cross-Channel blitz role. Its bombers had proved themselves too light and its fighters too short-winded for strategic employment of this sort. The Stukas had been a complete failure— almost as vulnerable against a first-class opponent over England as our Battle bombers had been in France. Goering had failed to develop his radar and ground control while blindly underestimating our efficiency in these departments. His reserves of crews were inadequate and his aircraft production lacked the vision of a Beaverbrook.

The art of war develops fastest when it is being practised. Used to quick victories, the Luftwaffe was confused by the failure of its long-established strategy. In the confusion and the bickering which followed, it learned no lessons and made no decisions for future strength through new aircraft types or refined technology. Thus, as the RAF survived and profited from its moment of greatest peril, the Luftwaffe passed its peak without knowing it and went into gradual decline. The German decision to switch to night bombing, with no true heavy bombers, in fact or in prospect, could be said to have laid the framework for the ultimate defeat of the Axis.

Churchill said it in the House of Commons on 20 August, 1940, with: 'Never in the field of human conflict was so much owed by so many to so few.'

The implied picture of a heavily-outnumbered Royal Air Force achieving a well-nigh miraculous victory by sheer gallantry and skill was appropriate to the emotions of the time. No one would wish to take away one word of that praise.

But it is important in recording the story of Britain's Bomber Command to recognise the true strengths and weaknesses of the enemy at the various milestones of the war, of which this was probably the all-important one. And these facts are quite clear, from hindsight evidence: (*a*) The disparity in numbers, when related to types of aircraft, was not nearly as great as was commonly supposed; (*b*) the German air officer corps was at this stage largely an aggregation of Spanish Civil War veterans, hastily-trained ex-ground soldiers and raw youngsters; (*c*) Adlergriffe's strategic aims had been foggy and shifting; (*d*) the Fuehrer had tended to panic in the face of set-backs; (*e*) the Luftwaffe had botched many of its raids because it could not adjust from the ingrained idea that its main role would always be the tactical support of large and mobile ground forces; (*f*) and its repulse was in large measure due to the logical consequences of its shortcomings in weapons and leadership.

In short, the Nazi flying forces defeated by The Few, in spite of their bravery, discipline and skill, were not the coldly efficient supermen German propaganda would have liked us to believe them to be.

Chapter Six

Meanwhile, back at the bomber stations the policy of attacking German aircraft factories plus aerodromes in occupied territories and barge concentrations on the coasts was continuing unabated. There was little capacity for wider policies, what with a total bomber force if anything rather smaller than it had been at the outbreak of war, and with the flow of replacement crews restricted to about fifty per week. In late August, however, a number of attacks had been made on synthetic oil installations, and the Scholven hydrogenation plant had been severely damaged.

In his 'never in the field of human conflict' speech on 20 August, Churchill had spoken of the tide of the war turning. But he was no more aware than anyone at that time that Hitler, who had withdrawn at the start of the Battle of Britain to his mountain retreat at Berghof, was already tentatively shifting his ground and setting his alternative sights on Russia. Understanding nothing of air tactics and, in Goering's words 'unable to think in the third dimension', he had already lost patience with the ebb and flow of air war, with its inconclusive daily statistics.

The Fuehrer's greatest flaw, which had not yet been realised, let alone analysed, in Britain, was again at work as our best ally. All his life, Hitler had been increasingly prone to grope for the easy solution—an appetite which post-war psychiatrists have ascribed to his petit-bourgeois instincts—but this flaw had been conveniently covered up for him in the satisfaction of the cheap victories of the first year of the war. He also had a womanish intuition which now told him, sooner than anyone, that Eagle was flying into failure and that, by his own command, Sea Lion could therefore not proceed. Should he be correct in this, a successful diversion would be necessary to bolster his neurotic pride. He would have to seek a quick success in Russia, after which Britain could be squeezed and starved into submission.

In thus ignoring the strategic imperatives, and forgetting the timeless lesson that the road to everywhere is the road to nowhere, the Fuehrer was already setting the seal of doom on his Third Reich at this moment in late August, 1940.

As he prepared his plans for the invasion of the Soviet Union and steadily moved the Wehrmacht's centre of gravity eastwards, Hitler kept from even his closest friends the fact that he had virtually accepted that Sea Lion would have to be postponed indefinitely. In an effort to maintain political and military pressure by keeping Britain in fear of impending invasion, he allowed last minute loading exercises and amphibious manoeuvres to continue as though the Channel-crossing awaited only suitable weather. And throughout the latter part of August, an average of almost 1,000 aircraft a day were hurled against British targets.

We did not know that he was bluffing, but neither were we in fear any more. Every day, the British Army and Navy were gaining strength. The RAF was tired, but in blunting, and repelling the Luftwaffe it had gained immense moral strength and purpose. The feeling was that all we had to do was to stay in business and we would win.

Initiative was returning to Bomber Command, and bomber crews were beginning to be able to show their power in more and more positive ways—especially in attacking the assembling invasion fleets. And, better still, the greatest of all German cities was to be offered suddenly and unexpectedly as a target for their pent-up feelings.

On the night of 24-25 August central and east London had its first taste of bombing since the days of the Zeppelins and Gothas of 1916-18. It was not a major raid and, indeed, there is some evidence that the capital was bombed by mistake.

Whether or not this is so, Churchill at once saw a righteous reason for switching to token attacks on Germany's heartlands and reacted immediately. Although the maximum bombing force available with the range to strike deep into Germany was scarcely one-tenth of what the Luftwaffe could send over England in reprisal; and although the distance from Bomber Command's airfields to the German capital was six times as far as that from the French coast to London, the Prime Minister proposed the immediate punitive bombing of Berlin.

The result was that on the night of 25 August, eighty-one British Wellington and Hampden medium bombers set out for the German capital from East Anglian bases. Although there were few night fighters on either side in those days, the 1,200-mile round trip was a taxing one for crews—particularly for navigators, who had to rely on dead reckoning and good luck to take them over the target areas, there still being no effective navigational aid available. There was dense cloud cover over eastern Germany and over the capital itself. Individual bombers were responsible, as was the custom, for finding their way there, and only twenty-nine aircraft succeeded in doing so. Those that did found Berlin well defended by two great rings, outer and inner, of searchlights and anti-aircraft guns, and during the three hours it took for all the planes to arrive and drop their bombs around the chosen industrial area, the flak fire remained intense. Thanks to the cloud cover, however, not one plane was shot down, although ten were damaged in varying degrees. In addition to their bomb loads—which were fairly light to allow for the extra fuel tanks carried—the British bombers dropped a few thousand leaflets suggesting that someone should do away with Hitler as a prelude to peace talks. Three water closets were also dropped by Hampdens of 61 Squadron.

It was not much of a raid, as far as damage was concerned, and no one was killed. But the Berliners were shocked as the first bombs in history dropped on their city. Goering had assured them many times that this could not happen. 'If it does you can call me by a Jewish name,' he had told the German people. Yet it was happening. Unsure of himself for once, Goebbels at first ordered that the raid should be played down. Then he had second thoughts and personally led a screaming match on 'the brutality of the British, who are the first thus to attack defenceless women and children'.

Other light night raids on Berlin quickly followed, and small numbers of Berliners were killed in residential areas, due chiefly to the rough and ready quality of the British bombsights. Goebbles continued to fume about 'cowardly English pirates' and Hitler vowed diabolical reprisals, which he defined in an irrational, emotional speech on 4 September as a firm intention 'to wipe London off the face of the earth'. His flaw was again showing for anyone with the discernment to read him correctly.

On 7 September it was obvious that something big was afoot when the normal daily targets for the Luftwaffe around the south coast and the home counties were left in peace. In the uneasy silence, the code word 'Cromwell' was issued, which meant 'invasion imminent' and in some places the Home Guard over-enthusiastically rang the church bells (the signal that the enemy had landed) as they sharpened their pike-staffs and loaded their shotguns, and were reported to be angry and disappointed when neither airborne nor seaborne troops appeared.

But when the German bombers finally crossed the coast in great force that evening and that night, they sailed in successive formations up the Thames, ignoring completely for the first time in many weeks the airfields of Kent and Essex, making straight for London town. They smashed their way past the capital's diluted defences (many guns and searchlights having been diverted to defend fighter and radar stations) and over a period of eight hours, they dropped 300 tons of high-explosive and 13,000 incendiary bombs over central and east London, scattering them widely around dockland, Woolwich, East Ham, Poplar, Bermondsey, Bethnal Green, Battersea, Waterloo Bridge, Westminster, Paddington and Dagenham.

The London Blitz had begun. And Londoners reacted with the kind of spirit of fortitude and humour that politicians relish and do not deserve. 'We'll survive,' was the cry, 'but let's give 'em double hell back!' Churchill was glad to do so: 'I undertook forthwith to see that their wishes were carried out,' he wrote later, 'and this promise was certainly kept.'

It was indeed kept, but only in the fullness of time. Every front-line crew in Bomber Command was at this time adding several sorties per week to its score. There was a limit to the further demands that could be made of them, with Hitler's invasion bluff all important. The Navy (heartened by the purchase from America of fifty elderly but sound destroyers) had a battleship-led fleet steaming in the Western Approaches. The Army had re-equipped and was poised to hold a line Gravesend to Portsmouth. The RAF was expected to deal unkindly with Germany's invasion fleet as it crossed the Channel.

Each day Spitfires and Hudsons of the RAF's Photographic Reconnaissance Unit had been flying along the full length of the enemy's coastline, from the West Fresian Islands to the Cherbourg peninsula, taking film of the assembling fleets of invasion craft, moving towards the Scheldt and the Straits of Dover. The numbers of craft were increasing frighteningly. By 6 September there were 205 barges at Ostend alone, with a similar number at Flushing and some hundreds between Dunkirk and Calais. With the fear of invasion predominant, these became top priority targets and the whole might of Bomber Command was thrown against them.

The boys went in with a will. They had a sense of being with Drake against the Armada or with Nelson against Napoleon's forces at Boulogne. These were urgent, immediate missions of vital importance, and the spirit was very different from that shown in the leaflet raids of the phoney war. The crowded targets of Flushing, Ostend, Dunkirk, Calais and Boulogne (which now held over 1,000 barges in harbour, plus another 600 up-river at Antwerp) became laconically known as 'the Blackpool Front' and every available aircraft had a go. On the night of 13 September alone, eighty barges were sunk at Ostend. Not too much care was taken to bomb accurately. The thing was to off-load your bombs around the waterfront, or on the assembled troops, and rush back for more. By mid-September, reconnaissance showed that nearly 200 barges had been wrecked—a magnificent effort by Bomber Command.

Meanwhile, Hitler's emotionally directed hate-blitz on London was continuing, to the point that between 7 September and 13

November, more than 12,000 night sorties would be flown, with London receiving over 13,000 tons of high-explosive and nearly one million incendiary bombs. In addition, this offensive was to claim 14,000 deaths in this period with another 25,000 injured.

When it was largely released from bombing barges, towards the end of September, Bomber Command again turned its attention to Berlin and to other German industrial targets. It had not the planes to match the Luftwaffe's blitz on London. But Commander-in-Chief Sir Charles Portal, knowing how inaccurate night bombing on both sides could be (with even wrong cities being attacked, let alone the wrong targets) was calling for de-briefing sessions offered little that was positive in any way in terms of detailed results.

A committee under Mr. Geoffrey Lloyd had been studying bombing plans, and among the evidence it had sifted was the fact that night bombing accuracy, even on practice ranges free from flak and other distractions, was seldom achieved with less error than 300 yards. It was also revealed that on live raids, only one-quarter of the bombs dropped were hitting the targets. Without flares or marker bombs, crews had to rely on moonlight or instinct or fires on the ground for the identification of their aiming points. It was fairly common for a bomber to drop its load on the first blaze it spotted in the approximate area of the target. Sometimes this worked, but as often as not they would be adding bombs to the troubles of colleagues shot down in flames shortly before. No cameras were carried, so that de-briefing sessions offered little that was positive in any way in terms of detailed results.

During September, 1940, Bomber Command lost some sixty-five of its 450 bombers in the course of 3,141 sorties in night raids, and another twenty-one were destroyed in landing accidents. It was as much as could be afforded at the rate of bomber production of the time. The British public, and 'sympathisers' overseas had in September contributed more than £5 million in cash towards the purchase of aircraft wherever they could be bought and the money was mainly spent in America, which was beginning to develop its role as our supporting arsenal. Alas, of the 2,633 aircraft she had exported to Britain since the beginning of the war, none were suitable as night bombers. In this respect, she was satisfying her own needs first, which was understandable, as Hitler had signed a formal Tripartite Pact on 27 September, bringing closer ties with Japan and increasing the threats to the US.

Britain had meanwhile turned up an almost embarrassing richness of leaders in the RAF. It is one of the ironies of the period that the all-conquering Reich—the storied land of military prestige and expertise—had reached one year into the war with an air arm headed by Goering, who was unable to put matters right and seemed unwilling to delegate his authority. On the other hand, the British, who had the tradition of muddling through and losing every battle but the last in true amateur fashion, now had an air force with a much more highly developed leadership. Probably the reason for this was that the fifteen years of air restrictions imposed on Germany by the Treaty of Versailles had left a gap during which leaders should have been maturing in the Luftwaffe, whereas it was in those very years to 1935 that Britain's senior fliers were becoming true professionals and natural leaders. Even now, at the end of September, 1940, Germany was still shortsightedly choosing to forego the creation of a long-range bomber force, whereas Britain's Bomber Command was counting the days till the first four-engined bomber would be available.

On 4 October, the Vice-Chief of Air Staff, Sir Richard Peirse became Air Officer-in-Chief, Bomber Command, in succession to Sir Charles Portal who moved up to the top job of Chief of Air Staff. Target selection for strategic air warfare was the responsibility of the intelligence staff (who provided the necessary information about location and protection) and the combined commands (who determined what would hurt the enemy most in terms of the war as a whole). In his new position of power, Portal now set about getting his way over 'carpet' bombing as opposed to selective bombing. Instead of oil plants and railway targets, he wanted to select, warn and bomb twenty or thirty German towns, and he felt he would have support in this as more and more German bombs fell on residential areas of London, which the newspapers were beginning to describe as 'terror bombing'.

An Air Staff directive was therefore drawn up and sent to Peirse containing draft bombing plans on totally new lines. There were to

7—TLC * *

be two main lines of attack in future. The first aim was to be the destruction of German morale and the second the knocking out of oil production. Selected towns were to be attacked every few nights by forces of between fifty and 100 bombers. Oil targets were to be included in these raids when moonlight and weather permitted identification of targets. Occasional assaults would also continue on railway yards and on naval targets. Peirse was told to adopt in future the German technique of opening a raid with fire bombs and thereafter working to spread the fires with explosives.

This was, in truth, the moment at which all pretence of adhering to the Roosevelt doctrine of 'no bombing of civilians' was abandoned. The fiction that bombers could attack 'military objectives' in towns with accuracy was set aside and Portal, in his honesty, substituted the much more sincere description, 'area bombing'.

Chapter Seven

War consists largely of acts that would be criminal if performed in time of peace. Accordingly, the whole notion of reducing crime in war was always rather preposterous. War crimes had been defined and re-defined over the years, and attempts were still being made in 1940 to control them by means of international committees and pronouncements from 'uncommitted' statesmen.

But what of the vast new horrors of the indiscriminate aerial bombing of cities towards which Britain and Germany were both now rushing? Could such criminal activity become acceptable under the doctrine of response to 'military necessity'?

Although experience of the barbaric futility of bombing was limited, the 'Rules of Warfare', as agreed by the Washington Conference on the Limitations of Armaments (1922), had in fact spelled out the dangers, in laying down that: 'Aerial bombardment for the purpose of terrorising the civilian population, of destroying or damaging private property, or of injuring non-combatants, is prohibited.'

At first this 'rule' and Roosevelt's commentaries on it had been heeded, more or less. But on both sides night bombing had become pretty much a game of blind man's bluff.

Consequently, as raid and counter-raid proceeded and it was recognised that high-level bombing by night on factories, railroads, docks, and the like, was less discriminating than had been anticipated, the inevitability of 'area' or 'terror' bombing had had to be accepted as an incidental and unfortunate concomitant of such operations.

And now all pretence that bombing could be morally defensible was about to be abandoned for the duration, and the more so because this was the eve of the destruction of Coventry and the blasting of Mannheim.

On the night of 14-15 November, 1940, a total of 437 enemy aircraft (forty more than the largest previous raid—on London on 15 October) took off in three great streams, directed at Coventry: their aim the futile one of breaking the will to resist of the English people. They were led by the first 'pathfinders' of the war—the experienced night-fliers of the leading Kampfgeschwader from 100 Wing, in their Heinkel 111s. A new target-finding device, known as X-Gerat, was being used for the first time (it having been realised in Germany by now that British Scientific Intelligence had learned to jam or bend the Knickebein radio navigation aid previously used in raids on London). The X-Gerat system was more sophisticated than Knickebein, and it worked very well. Briefly, it involved flying along a fine radio beam (which was centred on a coarse beam) until a succession of intersecting beams triggered a distance-to-target signal. Britain had nothing like it.

The Heinkel pathfinders dropped several tons of incendiaries on the centre of Coventry at 8.15 p.m. and for ten hours thereafter the main forces 'homed' on this inferno, and added to it a total of 495 tons of high-explosives, 900 incendiary cannisters, and 130 parachute mines. It was a callous and bloody raid. The whole heart of the city, including its fine cathedral, was razed to the ground; 380 civilians were killed and 800 seriously injured. It was of little account that Lord Haw-Haw explained smoothly that twelve aircraft factories and nine other industrial plants had been hit.

Righteously indignant, the British public demanded a city for a city, and the Government concurred. Within twenty-four hours the order had gone out to Bomber Command that in future they would simply aim at the centre of any town they were attacking.

The actual reprisal raid took a little time to organise, but, when it came, it was apparent that the preparation had been fairly thorough. Indeed, it had been obvious to Portal and Peirse for some time that, with only a very small bomber force, it was good tactics to make concentrated attacks on one target at a time. This was their chance to prove they were right. On the night of 16-17

December, the first of what was to be a series of such attacks was made on the city of Mannheim. This was to be the British answer to the Luftwaffe's rape of Coventry.

Alas, it was impossible to mount a mission on anything like the scale of the German one. To give over-active crews some rest, after a very hectic period, squadrons were standing-by in rotation and a total of only 134 aircraft could be mustered for Mannheim. Even so, this was more than one-third of the front-line strength of Bomber Command.

As with the Luftwaffe, twenty-four of the most experienced Wellington crews acted as pathfinders to begin the raid and light the target with incendiaries. Unlike their German opposite numbers, they had to rely on their navigators to get them there, but it was a fine moonlight night and all went quite well. The follow-up waves of Wellingtons, Whitleys and Hampdens had been ordered plainly 'to concentrate the maximum amount of damage on the heart of Mannheim', and 102 aircraft captains claimed at de-briefing to have done so. All swore to their intelligence interrogators that they had bombed the chosen target area and had left the centre of the city blazing fiercely. At once, Sir Richard Peirse issued a signal congratulating everyone.

The de-briefing on this occasion had been longer and more detailed than was usual, although the crews were obviously very tired after such a long and arduous raid. There were good reasons for this: (a) Mannheim was the 'dummy run' for what was to be a series of such city-centre raids; and (b) the first flight of Spitfire photo-reconnaissance planes had by then been working closely with Bomber Command for about a month, and they were due to survey the Mannheim damage later that day.

The subsequent analysis of pictures caused depression all round. Crews' 'eye-witness accounts' were hopelessly exaggerated and inaccurate. The validity of the theory of Bomber Command's capacity for area bombing was less strong in the light of detailed reconnaissance than might have been hoped. The photographs proved above all that the operation 'had failed in its primary object' (to quote the Official History) in that damage, far from being focused in the centre of the city, was widely dispersed, with the worst of the fires concentrated in the suburbs. This was doubly-galling because the Luftwaffe's bombing of London and Coventry had been so much more accurate.

So far, so bad. It was decided that subsequent 'concentrated raids' in the series—on Bremen, Wilhelmshaven, Kiel and other towns—would go ahead. But in the meantime more urgency was given to the new-fangled study, at all levels, of the excellent pictures the Spitfires were bringing back; and, to get nearer the truth in the matter, four days later a detailed photographic record was made of the twin oil plants at Gelsenkirchen which had been a primary target just before Mannheim. Again, claims made were almost completely demolished. According to the de-briefing records, crews of 152 aircraft said they dropped 140 tons of high-explosive bombs and several tons of incendiaries on the first plant, while 124 aircraft had dropped 122 tons of miscellaneous bombs on the second. The photographs, alas, showed no glowing picture of destruction. They revealed, in fact, that no major damage had been done to either plant.

At long last the need for better bombsights and more powerful bombs was recognised at a high level, and more money was pushed in these directions. It was all rather sad as a commentary on 'blind' flying by crews allied to 'blinkered' direction by technocrats.

Sadder still was the fact that to some extent the RAF was beginning to believe its own publicity. The press had been working hard for months telling the glorious tale of The Few, and, now that the main phase of the Battle of Britain was over, it had turned its attention to The Many—'the brave blue-eyed boys who are giving Germany what she deserves in answer to the raids on London and other British cities'. The Navy was doing little at this time worthy of propaganda, and the Army still less, so the papers were full of the exploits and the 'characters' of the RAF—all suitably glamourised.

One or two of the veteran fliers in Bomber Command *were* true characters and worthy of all that was said of them. They did not particularly care what people thought of them—which is the ultimate in professionalism. They were secure in the knowledge that they had mastered their jobs, and their chief aim was to use their talents to achieve survival through all the hard tasks that were being asked of them. The 'glory' was unimportant compared with the successful completion of a tour.

But these worthy types also included extroverts who had adopted handlebar moustaches and fishermen's sweaters as their uniforms of rebellion against the petty disciplines of the service. Alas, other miscellaneous immature crewmen sought to copy the mannerisms of these heroes, rather than their techniques, by playing to the adulation in which the public appeared to hold them, and trying to style themselves in the image their audiences expected. Extravagant dress and gestures, together with much line-shooting, became the way of life on pub crawls for many.

This trend was particularly hard on the raw youngsters who were joining operational squadrons in ever increasing numbers from Officer Cadet Training Units. Insecure and all too conscious of the fact that they had been stampeded through basic flying training in about six months, as against two years in peacetime, and greeted as 'sprogs' by everyone with a few sorties in, they tended to feel they had to seek operational experience before they were ready for it and too often failed to survive for long enough to tell the tale themselves.

They were green and bewildered, most of these young pilots and navigators of whom so much was expected. They were scared, too—scared as hell. Scarcely out of school, they had briefly taken up careers as solicitors' clerks, commercial artists, shop assistants, student-teachers, carpenters, stockbrokers, or what have you, before joining the RAF and becoming eligible, through intelligence and aptitude tests of a sort, for aircrew training.

Some of them had never been out of their towns or valleys and could not even drive a car or ride a motorcycle before they found themselves barking their shins on the cockpit trapdoors of whale shaped bombers, therein to squat insecurely on parachute packs in the dais-like pilots' seats, or to fumble with multi-coloured charts on their knees as they felt for their sextants and slide-rules.

It was an entirely new way of life in which everything was strange and complex . . . in which nothing related to, or could be judged by, previous experience. In a matter of weeks, at an age when adolescence was scarcely overcome, they had to make the acquaintance of, and master, incredibly complex monsters, the sinews and nerves of which were miles of wire, the brains of which were a multiplication of instruments tuned to such unknown elements as radio waves, inertia, magnetic force and atmospheric pressure, and the muscles of which were a series of levers or controls of baffling multiplicity.

The young pilots had to learn in double-quick time to steer these aircraft along the grass and take them safely into the unknown deep of the night, while their navigator-colleagues sweated their way through their many necessary calculations, like detectives sifting and weighing evidence but obliged always to come up with the right answers.

No young men in history had ever had to take in and spew out as much complex information in such a short time. Training methods were still primitive and haphazard. There were not indeed many instructors in the world who knew what it was all about themselves. Actual experience in the air had to be the main teacher. It is perhaps an indication of how elementary and sparse was the total knowledge of aviation and of the elements at the end of 1940 when it is recalled that at that time the Atlantic, for instance, had never once been flown in winter and the whole subject of navigation had only been stabbed at here and there on the safer routes and in reasonable weather conditions. The air was the upper world of the future, but in 1940 fliers were only able to peer dimly through its slightly-open door.

So it was that the part-blind led the blind man and, as the reaper kept hacking away quietly at the semi-professionals in the squadrons, inevitably the fledgling, fresh-as-paint officers, NCOs and ORs from the flying schools stepped all too soon into the breach of fear.

The slaughter of the innocents, sacrificed perhaps to satisfy ill-digested and inconclusive plans, was getting under way. And in the fairly heavy raids on Germany in December, 1940, almost as many British bombers were lost through the inexperience of crews, allied to hazards of navigation, weather, fuel miscalculations and crash landings, as were brought down by flak or by the small number of night fighters then in service.

There was so much that could go wrong for aspirants, however keen and intelligent, on their first few missions. Briefing tended to be curt and sketchy in those days. Nervous but eager, a young skipper would lead his crew aboard the monster they had been allocated, which was not always the one in which they had made their station familiarisation flights. Adjusting and securing their

Sutton harness and parachute packs, they would go into the engine-starting drill and would give the thumbs up to the ground crew as the engines burst lumpily and smokily to life. So far, so good.

A few minutes of warm-up, while the oil temperatures rose and the oil pressures dropped to normal, with the rev-counter needles swinging idly, and the cockpit checks would proceed according to procedures learned parrot-fashion in school. Chocks away, an inch or two of extra throttle, and the big bomber would be jerking its squealing way down-wind around the perimeter track, with hot blue smoke wreathing around it in the night air. A touch on the brakes at the start of take-off would bring the wayward crate into line ... and from that moment on, any one of a hundred things could go wrong before touch-down on return from the raid.

It would be easy, for instance, for an inexperienced pilot to be initially panicked into charging across the grass for take-off before he was quite ready for it, because an impatient controller, with other planes surging at the bit, was giving him continuous green light on his Aldis lamp. In such a way did many a plane end up enmeshed in the perimeter fence.

Or a nervous skipper might ham-handle his throttles at this stage, with the result that the plane would skid around the airfield in an alarming and humiliatingly uncontrollable semi-circle to the danger of all ... or the brakes might gum up as the bomber was accelerating to leave the runway, with fatal results ... or maybe an engine would hiccough frighteningly on take-off, whereupon the pilot might pull the mixture lever back hastily and another young team would finish, before it had begun, coffined in an untidy blazing metal box in an adjoining field. Too often in take-off the only route taken was the direct one towards the station mortuary slabs.

Once aloft, a new set of possible troubles would quickly line up. Each and every medium bomber in that period of the war had erratic characteristics of its own, when airborne as well as on take-off. The Wellingtons, for instance, all behaved curiously in rough air, some much more so than others. In particular, the control column would wander waywardly backwards and forwards on its own, as the elevator cables moved to match the flexings of the light but strong webbed, Geodetic fuselage. In that it had been allowed for in the design, this was normal. Indeed it had already become an in-joke with crews that no one had ever been able to record the true measurements for the Wellington's span or length because they were never twice the same. But this yawing of the 'joystick' could be so extreme in turbulence in older marks that young pilots encountering it for the first time could become excessively anxious about its effect on their flying skills and were therefore all the more accident-prone.

Similarly, the characteristic nose-down attitude in flight of the ponderous, slab-sided 'Barn Door' Whitley and its reluctance to do what it was told to do, were disturbing on early acquaintance, as, indeed, was the excessive swing to port which made the Mark IV such a handful on take-off. The 'old lady's' wings and fuselage gave the impression that they were going in different directions and the perennial difficulties of synchronising the twin Merlin engines could be scarifying equally for navigator and pilot in attempting to steer a true course.

In turn, the Handley Page Hampden, or 'Flying Tadpole', although an easy to control and 'forgiving' plane, had the major disadvantage that its extremely narrow fuselage (three feet wide at the broadest point) had a claustrophobic effect on new crews and tended to produce fatigue on a long flight. Also, should the pilot be wounded, it was nearly impossible to remove him from his cramped cockpit so that another crew member could take over the controls and this led to a number of disasters that might otherwise have been avoided.

The relationships between pilots and their navigators (who served the double function of co-pilot in five-man Wellingtons and Whitleys, but were solely navigators in four-man Hampdens) were vital to the success of a sortie. Bereft of any effective navigational aid, and having to rely on dead reckoning, good luck and improvisation, they had to work hard and sympathetically together on every flight if they were simply to get to the target and back, whether the enemy had a go at them or not.

The first lesson of the air then was for the navigator to read off the rectified air speed (which corrects speed indicated for instrument and position errors). True air speed is then discovered by correcting for altitude and temperature differences. When actual windspeed—a real difficulty—was applied, the ground speed of the aircraft could be ascertained. Absolute accuracy in such calculations was essential if the correct course was to be followed. Whereas a 'clock' could measure air speed accurately at a constant latitude and temperature, the inevitable variations in these factors, caused by varying flying conditions, would produce errors which, in those days, no instrument could overcome. Constant vigilance was therefore necessary.

Frequent checks of the fuel meters on the main panel was another part of the navigator's drill. Having noted the rate of petrol consumption he would have to calculate the true hourly rate so that he could say how much fuel remained in the tanks at any given moment. This could vary from pilot to pilot. The altimeter reading (never 100 per cent accurate) would also have to be adjusted for barometric pressure and temperature, to give the approximate height of the plane—and this drill, too, would have to be repeated several times on a trip, with the navigator singing out the readings to the pilot.

Meanwhile, periodically the pilot would be checking his gyro compass against his magnetic one, adjusting the scale of the former to correct the reading. As the gyro was steady, and did not swing from side to side as did the magnetic compass, it was much easier to steer by it.

But always the navigator had the serious responsibility of keeping constant track of progress—noting any change of speed or direction and any factor of temperature, altitude or engine revolutions that might affect the course that had been set, while keeping an eye on the western sky, in case a star fix should be called for—watching Orion and the bulbous moon swinging downwards at fifteen degrees per hour.

So the flight over occupied territory would proceed, usually at heights that could not be reached by flak or searchlights, with the pilot anxiously peering at rivulets of oil lashed into dancing patterns on an engine cowling by the slipstream, while the navigator beside or behind and beneath him—in his role as human lodestone—was checking the scores of entries in his flight log, keeping his accounts of the plane's track over the earth, the cloud layers, the wind, the drift, and the possibility of ice. . . .

Ice was often a killer that winter. Primitive de-icers were making their appearance on the wings of the new marks but not all bombers had them and when they did they could not always be depended upon to do their job. Sometimes weather charts would show belts of snow and ice to be avoided en route, but as often as not such dangerous hazards would be encountered without warning, or at heights where they should not have been.

Suddenly a young crew could fly into a sinister cloud layer. Within minutes, in the absence of the pulsation of de-icing boots, the speed of the plane would begin to slow and, if they knew their stuff, the pilot or navigator would shine an Aldis lamp (a sort of portable car headlamp with a handle and a trigger switch) out of the side windows to confirm that creeping ice was indeed seizing hold of the leading edges of the wings.

It was always necessary, in such circumstances, to act with great speed. Within a few minutes three or four inches of angry, ragged corrugations of frozen water could build up on the wings. Not only would this add considerable weight to the plane; it would also change the leading air foil from the smooth curve the designer had intended to an irregular blunt shape which would throw eddies into the slipstream, destroying the air pressure lift which kept the wings of a plane level in flight. At once the nose would begin to dip and, although the pilot, if he knew what he was about and was watching his artificial horizon, could pull back on his stick and keep the nose up for a time, this would also reduce airspeed and, if left alone, the ice would soon win by stopping the plane dead in a stall from which there could be no recovery.

In the few minutes before this could happen, the pilot would have the choice of attempting to climb the plane out of the ice layer (with an ever-heavier gross weight to force upwards) or to dive down in the hope that the temperature nearer the earth would be above freezing and that he could get out of it that way. Either choice could be the wrong one . . . and many were the consequent victims claimed by such of nature's 'shrouds of doom'.

Having successfully overcome such a difficulty by luck or good judgement, the navigator would then be faced with the fact that it had been impossible during the crisis to keep track of the fluctuating airspeeds, heights, temperatures and compass-readings. The plane might now be as much as 100 miles off course. If the stars were visible, another position could be calculated by sextant, but this could take twenty minutes or more. If there were no stars, a rough and ready course, either to home or to nowhere, would have to be risked.

This was one aspect of weather difficulties which could lead to the plane crashing out of fuel in some area so far off course that no one would ever know what had happened to it or why. Other crews setting off in moonlight might find themselves in comparable crises because the meteorological forecasts were 'so full of monkeys'. It is generally agreed nowadays that, although many things have to be taken into account in weather forecasting, such as cloud behaviour, temperature, pressure and humidity, the single and most important factor is air mass—the boundaries, seams and nature that characterise each one and, most of all, the fronts that mark the end of one air mass and the beginning of another.

But frontal-analysis, as this science is now known, was apparently difficult to achieve in the early part of the war. Anyway, time and time again bombers set off eastwards into the night sky, their crews happy in the assurance that it would be a moonlit, cloudless night, only to find a row of thunderstorms over the target, or an unexpected line of squall preceded by rolling clouds on the route home.

Flying around storms or through cold fronts on the way to the target could use up precious fuel, and, if there was an additional period at the end of it, as there often was, during which the pilot would fly around in circles looking for the actual target, it was never too difficult to reach that other major killer, the macabre Point of No Return.

A perfect navigator would always prevent this happening, but as there were no perfect navigators, any more than there were perfect people, it could and it did. Navigation is a pursuit of truth, and meticulous log-keeping gives it its strength. Whatever the emergency, the navigator should have all the facts to hand as the basis for instant decisions. In addition to his log, he should keep a graph showing, on the horizontal co-ordinate, the number of miles flown, and similarly noting, on the vertical co-ordinate, the amount of fuel consumed. On the same graph, a slanting black line or curve should show the planned fuel consumption related to miles, and he should add to this a red line detailing the *actual* fuel consumption in flight. Without overcomplicating a difficult picture, it should also be added that provision ought to be made on the graph for irregularities, such as the failure of one engine or the need for the plane to turn back before reaching its target. Perhaps most important of all would be a star on the graph indicating the point beyond which there would not be enough fuel to turn back. As there were no petrol filling stations in the heavens, and as there were no hard shoulders on which a plane could park until help reached it, this was inevitably known as the point of no return.

If he kept this record (or How-goes-it graph, in the jargon of the RAF) carefully and diligently, any navigator should have been able to tell the pilot at all stages of the flight whether they could go on any longer, on the basis of hard facts, not guesses. If his red line of actual performance turned out to be much worse than the black lines of pre-flight intent, he might have to warn his skipper before they ever reached the target area that they had gone as far as the petrol situation would allow.

Anyone who deems it too crazy for words to think of planes being sent on bombing missions, in late 1940, in which the fuel position could easily become critical must certainly have a point; but the fact is that there were as many back-room boys who could not do their arithmetic in those days as there were navigators who had difficulty with spherical trigonometry; and one simple tale should serve to hammer home the fact.

At this period, ill-defended Malta was being hammered by Italian bombers and by the Luftwaffe's long-range Fliegerkorps X, and was putting up the sort of brave, blind defence that was to make her the George Cross island. Fighters were desperately needed for this defence. So, it was decided at the Air Ministry to fly in some aircraft via the aircraft carrier *Argus* which was cruising in the Mediterranean. A squadron of Hurricanes was assembled on the ship and, on 17 November, 1940, two Skuas led twelve Hurricanes on what should have been a straightforward flight to Malta. But only one Skua and four Hurricanes arrived, and three of these made miraculous landings with less than five gallons each in their tanks. The other eight Hurricanes and one Skua had been lost at sea, without seeing a shot fired in anger, having run out of fuel.

Someone in the back room had made an incredible miscalculation. Because of Italian fleet movements, the planes had been flown off the *Argus* about 460 miles west of Malta. As they were being led by Naval planes, the Hurricane pilots did not know how far they were expected to fly. And the back-room boy, having got his figures wrong, had failed to tell them to take extra fuel tanks.

This could happen at the end of 1940, and so it was that British bombers over Europe were sent on missions with only just more than enough petrol to get there and back. Too many of the planners had never had the scarifying experience of flying for long distances in a bomber. A hundred gallons surplus must have seemed a lot to them. But it could represent maybe an hour's flying (or very much less in the teeth of an unforecast head wind) and could be used up unwittingly or unpurposefully in any one of a dozen ways. With such narrow margins, it was all too easy for pilots to go bankrupt without realising it.

So it was that sometimes planes were lost unnecessarily on their way back from Berlin and other cities, through using up too much precious fuel. Before or after they had dropped their first bombs they were liable to find themselves stuck up in the merciless sky with not enough fuel to take them the last few miles over the North Sea or Channel. So they would crash-land in enemy territory, or they would attempt to pancake in the sea, or they would simply fall to earth in England trying desperately to reach their base.

The crews, and particularly the young ones who had only theory, rather than experience, to help them in an emergency, could scarcely be blamed for these 'point of no return' disasters. The big bets were placed when the basic decisions were made before the bombers ever left the ground. All too often the margins of fuel, weighed against bombload and range, were too slim, even for canny, crafty professionals of long experience . . . and the meteorological forecasting had a lot to answer for, too.

Sometimes, when all had gone fairly well on a sortie, there would be terrible tragedies on the way home. The pilot, the navigator, the gunners and the bombardier would all have carried out their instructions to the letter. Exhausted they would be flying along, looking forward to their bacon and eggs, their fabric damaged perhaps and the plane full of cordite fumes, but otherwise intact.

Then, contrary to the forecast, they would run into hellish weather. This could bring a sequence of hazards.

Maybe, to get above the icy clouds, they would fly higher into the thin air than the flight plan ordered. Oxygen bottles were still in short supply, but when they were carried, quite often they went wrong. The insidious effects of oxygen-lack were insufficiently known then, and it was only after some crews who had experienced it managed to get home and tell the tale that the carrying of oxygen tubes and masks became obligatory. Indeed, so serious was the danger that mobile decompression chambers were to be taken around bomber stations in 1941 to demonstrate the strange effects of anoxia.

Starved of oxygen for even a short time, crews would become incompetent and idiotic. The initial effect would be somewhat similar to pouring alcohol into an extrovert character. Everything would seem euphoric, and crazy actions, including the adoption of outrageous flying attitudes, would follow, with everyone falling about giggling as the plane was mishandled. One pilot reported that he felt he knew better than his instruments. He ended flying upside down, his Sutton harness biting into his shoulders, while his feet floated away from the rudder pedals, and while the air of the cockpit became animated with dust, shell cases and spam rolls. His fellow crewmen found it hilarious and only because he banged his head did he come-to sufficiently to get the plane the right way up and down to a safer, if cloud-filled altitude.

This pilot problem was bad enough, but the effect of anoxia on navigators was invariably disastrous. In losing cohesion, they could not jot down even simple words, let alone concentrate on their charts. One or two logs survive from 1940 with formless scrawls on them. Their writers got home purely by luck. Many did not.

Even when oxygen supply was not a problem, flying above bad weather always was. There was a curious, if ephemeral, feeling of security in being on course high in the heavens, alone against the limitless range of all existence. It was difficult, under such circumstances, to adjust to the fact that getting to base would almost certainly involve plunging down through banks of rain, cloud or fog of uncertain depth. If the radio was working, and the plane was in range, there might be information available about the minimum

9. *Every bomber had a camera by this period of the war and target pictures were obligatory. This was taken during a raid in the winter of 1943-4. The aircraft was apparently flying through searchlight glare at the time.*

10. *Although the massive allied air armadas have crippled the Luftwaffe by April, 1945, allied bombers continue to meet sporadic enemy opposition. This dramatic picture shows an 8th Air Force Fortress plunging earthward after an ME 109 had shot away one of its wings. This incident took place after an attack on an airfield near Oranienburg, during which a total of 305 enemy aircraft were destroyed in a single day's operation on Tuesday, 10 April, 1945.*

11. *Lancaster in flames.*

height of the cloud base. If not, there was the ever-present danger of diving down and down through swirling, amorphous grey vapour, or ten-tenths cloud, and finding at a dangerously low height that the plane was too close to the earth or sea for safety, with no let-up in the nil visibility. Or, similarly, on nearing home it might be discovered that fog, high winds or accidents had suddenly closed down the home base and the alternatives.

In such circumstances, a young crew could panic and fly off into death in the unknown Atlantic, in trying desperately to find a compass reading which would lead them to a visible coastline or other landmark from which they could map-read their way to some safe field. Or they could circle above the clouds, looking for a gap, until they ran out of fuel and crashed. Even after finding a haven, *and* a welcoming flashing green light, they might be under such strain that the landing would be fluffed and another mass grave would have to be dug, bearing the simple words on cold stone: 'Crew of four. . . .'

In brief, much, too much, has been written about brave bomber crews setting out for Germany to fly relentlessly through blinding searchlights and searing flak . . . to place their bombs in the heart of a raging inferno before streaking home, all guns blazing at enemy night fighters . . . and to land ultimately on one engine with the navigator leaning over a dead pilot to bring the rest of the crew to safety. . . .

Such things did happen once in a while. There was, for instance, a famous picture in the press just before Christmas, 1940, which showed a Wellington landing from a raid with all the fabric missing from the fuselage aft of its wings. And, at about the same time, a Hampden of 83 Squadron staggered home under extraordinary circumstances, after receiving a direct hit. Its fuel tanks on both wings had been holed; fire had enveloped the navigator's and rear gunner's cockpits, melting the aluminium floor, and causing the latter to bale out; the plane's wireless-operator/gunner, Sergeant John Hannah, had then forced his way aft and had somehow, despite severe burns, extinguished the inferno roaring through the bomb-bays; not content with this he had crawled forward again and, finding that the navigator had also baled out, forgot his anguish in helping the pilot to land the crippled bomber. His subsequent VC was undoubtedly one of the best-deserved of the war.

But *every* crewman who boarded a night bomber (and did so again and again and again) faced nightmares of danger and fear which were so unnaturally extreme that they still haunt many of those who have survived to this day.

Chapter Eight

The first three months of 1941 brought weather of a severity comparable to that experienced in the winter of 1939-40, and all the Cabinet's best-laid plans for a bombing blitz on Germany had to be severely curtailed as a result. The principal one to suffer was a new Oil Plan. An extraordinary piece of information had been placed before the War Cabinet at Christmas, 1940, which suggested that earlier bombing attacks on plant had already reduced German production of synthetic oil by 15 per cent.

This remarkable intelligence report, which was to be shown after the war to have been almost totally false, was accepted as fact, although it was based on the dropping of a total of only 540 tons of bombs (less than 7 per cent of Bomber Command's total effort in the period concerned), and it formed the basis for yet another incredible switch of policy, formulated in an Air Staff order to the AOC-in-C, on 15 January, 1941. This declared that 'the sole primary aim of your bomber offensive, until further orders, should be the destruction of the synthetic oil plants'.

The new plan called for the despatch of 3,400 sorties against seventeen installations, on the high-grade fuel from which the turning of a variety of German wheels depended. An added attraction was that nine of these plants were believed (again wrongly) to account for more than 80 per cent of total production. And it was estimated that these plants could be totally destroyed within four months. It was in fact a ridiculous plan, and typical of the paper-work altars on which so many bomber crews were being sacrificed in the early years of the war. But at the time it was being punted as 'a heavy and possible fatal blow to Germany', and even 'a quick death clinch'.

The fact was that Bomber Command lacked the bombs, the navigational aids, the planes and the expertise to hit such targets with any accuracy at night. If nothing else, the reconnaissance pictures obtained at Gelsenkirchen should have rammed these facts home and exposed the Air Staff for the blind idiots they were. Peirse and Portal were both in favour of the plan; but documents recently made available under the thirty-year rule have indicated that Churchill had grave doubts.

When it came to the crunch, however, the gods that protect civil servants and air chiefs came swiftly to the aid of the planners and prevented their crass miscalculations being found out. Throughout January, February and March, 1941, ice, snow and fog restricted the oil offensive to the point that only 221 sorties could be flown, against the 3,400 ordered, a state of affairs which the official historian of Bomber Command records trenchantly in the words '... it was in effect the Admiralty which had got the Air Ministry out of the mess [it was in] for if Bomber Command had, at this stage, been left free to carry out the oil plan, it would have done a great deal more damage to its prestige than to its targets'.

The explanation of the Admiralty's role in this is that before the end of March, a new major crisis of defence and survival had arisen and had inevitably provoked another instant change of bombing plan. Sir Richard Peirse was now told by the Air Staff, under direction from Mr. Churchill himself, that for the next four months he was to give priority to attacks on German U-boats and other aggressive surface-craft associated with what was becoming known as the Battle of the Atlantic.

Germany had decided to starve us out of the war and was seeking, with every weapon she could muster, including a fairly large force of Focke-Wulf Condors, to cut our sea lifelines —particularly those in the Atlantic. As this was a purely defensive exercise, which could not harm the Axis except in a negative way, it was bound to dilute the positive effects of the strategic bombing effort once more. The use of medium bombers against naval craft should also have been looked at harder from the point of view that, if Bomber Command could not find and hit factories and oil installations, let alone the centres of cities, with any accuracy, it was unlikely that it could pin-point ships and submarines to a degree that would be helpful in curbing the new Atlantic menace. But to some extent a compromise was reached, with experience, in that a significant part of Bomber Command's efforts came to be directed against German naval towns and harbours, rather than against U-boats or other craft in open waters.

The first, and main targets for a time, were the battle-cruisers *Scharnhorst* and *Gneisenau* in Brest harbour. These were subjected to attacks every few days, starting with a 100-bomber raid on 30-31 March, and were kept out of action by damage. The two ships, after a brief and successful career in the Atlantic had become holed-up temporarily on the Biscay coast for victualling and maintenance while the *Bismarck* and *Prinz Eugen* took over, or tried to.

The only really serious damage was, in fact, done to the *Gneisenau* by a Beaufort aircraft of Bomber Command's poor relation, Coastal Command. In a 'suicide' attack at low level in daylight, a Beaufort of 22 Squadron planted a torpedo amidships on the cruiser, but never came out of its dive. Flying Officer Kenneth Campbell, the pilot, was posthumously awarded the Victoria Cross.

Meanwhile, despite the atrocious weather, the Luftwaffe had been continuing its blitz on Britain throughout the winter months on a scale far surpassing anything that Bomber Command had been able to achieve on Germany. The second phase of the German terror attacks had lasted from the bombing of Coventry in November, 1940, to the end of February, 1941, and had featured thirty-one major raids (some of them by 300-400 aircraft). Eight of these raids were on London, and the others were on cities as far apart as Glasgow, Cardiff, Liverpool (and Merseyside) Southampton, Manchester, Birmingham, Sheffield and Swansea, often featuring two or three raids in as many nights. The weather had inevitably taken a hand with the

Luftwaffe also, reducing the number of sorties from 6,000 in November to 1,200 in February, but even this latter figure made Bomber Command's 221 sorties in the first quarter of the year look pretty puny by comparison.

Nor had Germany's night raid losses been heavy. Only seventy-five of their aircraft had been destroyed in the course of more than 12,000 sorties. The only encouraging note was that British night fighters were beginning to come into play, in the early months of 1941, and had claimed twenty-five of the seventy-five losses; indeed, night fighters would take an increasingly-important 'bite' from attacking waves and from lone fighter-supported raiders in the remainder of 1941 and thenceforward, because the brilliant Beaufighter had now been brought into service. This splendid night-flying plane, with its top speed of 330 mph, not only had an unprecedentedly-powerful fire-power of four 20-mm cannon and six machine guns, it also carried an Al Mark IV radar which enabled it to 'see' in the dark. It could be directed to its target by a ground controller, who could see both the enemy bomber and the intercepting Beaufighter on the screens of his GCI (ground control of interception) radar sets.

Technology had been given more money, and another forth-coming result was that some guns were also radar-directed, and these were being supplemented by rocket batteries, similarly controlled. Even more importantly, Dr R. V. Jones, who had discovered and dealt with the German Knickebein target-finding device, had now come up with an answer to its more-sophisticated successor, X-Gerat. Radio-jammers he had devised, known as 'Bromides', had been issued to defence units through-out the south of England early in 1941 and had caused confusion in Luftwaffe raids on a number of occasions. And when Germany came up with a more-advanced version, Y-Gerat, another scientist, Dr. Robert Cockburn, of the telecommuni-cations Research Establishment, quickly had an answer ready in a jamming-device named Domino, which led in turn to many hundreds of bombs being dropped away from the target areas.

Both sides had also gone strongly into the bluff and counter-bluff business of 'dummy' targets. Some of the exaggerated claims made by Bomber Command crews were undoubtedly caused by the fact that the Germans had rounded up large numbers of craftsmen from the theatre and advertising exhibition worlds and had set them to work building dummy cities in open country near the main Bomber Command targets of that period. As soon as a raid on a particular city was seen to be imminent, fierce fires would be lit in the middle of the illuminated cardboard/plywood dummy city, and often a heavy weight of bombs would be mistakenly dropped into this false inferno, while the German defences fired anything but dummy flak at the bombers.

In time, our navigators came to recognise these decoys, partly because some were constructed with somewhat extreme thoroughness, laid out in straight lines and neat squares, and partly because the fires lit were too furious to be true. The trick then came to be to navigate to near the dummy (which could usually be seen for miles) and then, knowing that the decoy was X miles from the real thing, turn off to the city proper.

Another bluff much practised by British bomber skippers in the experimental days of early 1941 was to carry copies of Luftwaffe emergency cartridges, the originals of which were issued for use only when a German aircraft was in distress. They had been duplicated by some enthusiastic boffin in London and were issued very unofficially to crews. The drill was that when an RAF bomber had blundered over a strongly-defended area on its way to the target, or on its way back, and was being heavily attacked, the crew would switch on the plane's navigation lights and would fire one of these emergency cartridges; dramatically and providentially, as soon as one of these red sparkling lights appeared, flak would cease. This ploy continued to be a success for months, presumably because the Reichswehr were not too hot at plane identification, and had been told off by their Luftwaffe colleagues for shooting up friendly aircraft (a mistake not uncommon among British anti-aircraft units also).

Decoy 'targets' were meanwhile taking a different form in Britain and, instead of stage 'props', the English versions were constructed by army units with military skill and cunning. A secret unit, under the command of Colonel John Turner, a retired Director of Works and Buildings, made bogus airfields their speciality and by the winter of 1940-1 there were more than ninety of these in open country around the general areas of Bomber and Fighter Command bases in the south. Not only did they feature mock buildings of a type now standard to the RAF; they also had the authentic flare-path and other lights, and even included wood-and-canvas, full-scale imitation aircraft. With Doctors Jones and Cockburn bending the Luftwaffe's beams and Colonel Turner luring them to phoney targets, quite a quantity of bombs were being misdirected harmlessly week after week after week by the spring of 1941.

Col. Turner also worked on a dummy city idea, and did it better than the Germans. He timed his decoy fires, which were codenamed 'Starfish', to start slowly just as the German path-finders appeared, and to build up steadily thereafter. His first dummy town collected sixty-six bombs intended for Bristol, and subsequently a Starfish site near Hayling Island was hit harmlessly by 170 bombs, 32 landmines and 5,000 incendiaries.

Other secret 'undercover' devices were less successful, including one called 'Mutton' which involved dropping quarter-mile lengths of piano wire, each with a parachute on one end and a bomb on the other. It was a crazy idea, which was played around with for some time at the Royal Aircraft Establishment, but it never really worked. In any event, many German bombers now had cutting devices fitted to the leading edges of their wings, mainly as a measure of safety against balloon cables. This idea had first been thought up in Britain, and had been introduced to 5 Group by its commander, 'Bomber' Harris, some months earlier. They were made to order by a little firm he called in—Rose's of Gainsborough.

So it went on, with invention being met with counter-invention and the scientists on both sides trying somehow to steal a march on the enemy, while cloaking their ideas in secrecy and disguise. Word had got around that the Luftwaffe had important research and development establishments located in the depths of the Black Forest in the mountains of south-west Germany. So a plan was set afoot to destroy large areas of the forest by fire. The weapon devised for this was known as 'Razzle'. Each Razzle consisted of a celluloid folder, about six inches square, containing a piece of phosphorus embedded in damp cotton-wool. The idea was simply that when the cotton wool dried out, the phosphorous would smoulder, the celluloid would burst into flames and, hopefully, where they fell the trees would be set alight. Some tens of thousands of these Razzles were dropped over the mountainous parts of the Black Forest over a period of about a year, usually by planes, with normal bomb load also carried, on their way to other targets. Some fairly good fires were started on several occasions, but in the end the scheme was gradually shelved as being unlikely to bring any dramatic results.

On an important new front, too, an organisation had by now been set up to ferry American-built aircraft across the Atlantic, but Hudson planes for Coastal Command were the main priority at this stage. In turn, Canadian Pacific Railway had established an Air Ferries Department and soon Canadian-built bombers of British-design, together with crews trained in Canada, some of them British, would be making the then-arduous flight to Northern Ireland via Gander, Newfoundland. Top Imperial Airways' pilots assisted in pioneering the route.

The state airline had also daringly opened up a service between London and Stockholm on 2 March, 1941, to ferry small but urgently needed Swedish-made articles, such as special types of ball-bearings, springs and electrical equipment. Very important passengers were also carried, and a total of 1,200 such trips would be made between 1941 and 1945, with the inevitable loss of a score of aircraft. But the 'neutral' Swedes were supplying ball-bearings in large quantities to Germany as well as to us, and were swapping secrets in both directions.

The 'Lease and Lend' Bill, signed by President Roosevelt on 11 March, was undoubtedly one of the most important milestones of the early war, enabling, as it did, the United States to sell, transfer, lease or lend any defence article, providing the receiving country's defence was deemed to be vital to the defence of the United States. Britain was obviously the main initial beneficiary. No bombers were involved in the early stages, but within weeks much-needed ammunition was flowing to hard-pressed English airfields and to their AA defence units.

Meanwhile, elsewhere in the world Britain was moving into a period of struggle when everything was turning sour. We had captured Tobruk, but Rommel had been sent to North Africa to take it back. We had landed an expeditionary force in Greece but would shortly have to evacuate it. Bombing successes were necessary to boost morale at home, but what with bad weather and a policy based on winning the Battle of the Atlantic, the 'persuasion industry' at the Ministry of Information in Bloomsbury was having a thin time in this direction.

In truth, something very dramatic *had* happened in Bomber Command, but it was too early to trumpet about it ... in case of a characteristic backfire. Surreptitiously, selected crews had been undergoing training in the first of the eagerly-expected four-engined bombers to come off the production lines. There had been snags, gremlins, bugs and serious prototype crashes. But, secretly, a few of the 'heavies' had been flown, together with battle-tried 'mediums', in raids on coastal targets in February and March, care being taken that none of them should go any distance inland, in case they crashed and the Luftwaffe got a look at them.

The British decision, in the late 'thirties, to proceed with the design and manufacture of four-engined bombers had been one of the most enlightened of the period and to some extent it counterbalanced the many wrong judgements that were made within the same Air Ministry at the same time. Germany may, indeed, have lost the war because she failed to make a similar decision. This is not to say that bombers alone could ever have won wars, but if the Luftwaffe had had true heavy bombers when we were on our knees in 1940, the invasion of Britain might have been enabled to proceed, with results that can only be guessed at.

It was on the now-forthcoming heavy bombers that the whole of Britain's air strategy was to be based. That they had taken so long to reach squadrons was regrettable, but the original designs had had to be modified in the light of battle experiences.

The Short Stirling, which had made its first flight in May, 1939, was the first of the breed, and the only British bomber to be used in World War II which had been designed from scratch to take four engines. But it was a disappointment from the start. On the day it was due to make its maiden flight from Short Brothers aerodrome at Rochester, Kent, its undercarriage collapsed, which was prophetic, really, besides being the means of delaying the flight test programme at a critical time. Indeed, the huge plane, built to specifications drawn up by the Air Ministry in 1936, would never become a real success owing to its extreme weight and, consequently, its low ceiling, although about 2,350 would be produced by 1944.

The Stirling's shortcomings were due, in fact, to the shortsighted limitations of the original specification, which had characteristically insisted (presumably for reasons of economy or lethargy) that the wing-span should be less than the 100-foot door width of the standard RAF hangar and that the fuselage cross-section size should be dictated by the size of standard RAF packing cases. The designers were therefore forced to create a wing of low-aspect ratio and high induced drag, with an inevitable reduction of its operational ceiling.

Wing-loading weight, in relation to lifting surface was an aspect of aircraft efficiency to which more attention should have been paid. Experience should have shown that a light aeroplane with big wings, like the one in which the Wright brothers had pioneered heavier than air flying, had tended to be slow-flying but was safe as a butterfly, while a heavy one, with small wings, could be designed to fly fast and straight, and to land 'hot' like a duck.

To some extent the Stirling fell into neither category, but had faults of both.

The one plus factor that the small wing gave the bomber was useful manoeuvrability, but its design was to mean, alas, that it would be very vulnerable to fighter and flak attack, especially in daylight, at the modest heights at which it was forced to fly. Indeed, in flights to Italy, later in 1941, it would have to fly through the Alps, rather than over them, because of its lack of power—a serious shortcoming that would lead to unnecessary loss of life.

The Stirling's defensive armament was fairly good. Nose and tail turrets were standard. Ventral turrets were also a feature of the first few Stirlings produced, but these reduced speeds at critical moments and oddly-shaped dorsal turrets had to be substituted.

There was much evidence of Short's flying boat design experience, particularly in the fact that the fuselage construction featured rectangular sections with rounded corners. The wings, which also showed relationships to Sunderland and Empire flying boats, had their leading edges armoured and were provided with balloon cable-cutters.

The flat-sided fuselage, allied to small wings, gave the plane a distinctive appearance which was to make it easier to recognise by German AA and fighter crews and therefore more liable to be shot at, and its slow speeds (a maximum of 245 mph at sea level, and a cruising speed of about 200 mph at 15,000 feet) did not make it less vulnerable. But its manoeuvrability, for so large a plane, was something to be wondered at. The Stirling could literally be stood vertically on its tail and could be stalled in this position, whereupon it would drop its nose and return to level flight after the briefest of dives.

Because its wings were mid-mounted, the Stirling's undercarriage had to be stepped unusually high goemetrically to give an appropriate ground-to-plane angle. This resulted in a dangerous side-swinging effect in take-off, in answer to which its pilots had to be very sensitive in using their throttles. Improvisations to the plane, in the light of battle experience by other bombers, had led to armour-plating, plus additional armament, on a scale that had increased the design gross weight from 52,000 pounds to 70,000, and this fact had made laden take-offs still more hazardous—especially from the muddy grass fields that were features of Bomber Command's continuingly primitive operations in 1941. There were, therefore, even more take-off crashes of Stirling bombers, when they came into service, than there had ever been with Wellingtons, Hampdens and Whitleys.

New methods of training, pioneered by No. 7 Squadron of 3 Group, the first squadron to have four-engined bombers (in place of their ancient Wellingtons) had had to be carefully devised, particularly in view of the fact that the Stirlings featured a seven-man crew of pilot, co-pilot, navigator/bombardier, radio operator, engineer/gunner, and two other gunners. Many teething troubles were ironed out by this squadron, and drills were laid down for crews in what was much more a team operation on the flight deck than had been the case with the medium bombers.

One of the many design features which 7 Squadron quickly faulted, but which was maybe understandable in a plane which had been dreamed up five years earlier and which had been committed to production before anyone had had any experience of operational conditions and requirements, was in the matter of bomb-load. As has been mentioned before, the Air Staff's view, was that only rarely would bombs of more than 500 pounds be required. So the Stirling had been deliberately planned to carry up to two-dozen 500-pounders. Although ways were subsequently found of fitting in anything up to seven bombs of 2,000 pounds weight, as an alternative, the mode of construction of the 42-foot bomb-bay—which had two girders running down the middle, dividing it into three reduced-size sections—made the plane useless for carrying the much larger bombs that would be coming forward in due course.

The 500-pounder, and its 250-pound stable-mate, had been the 'sacred cows' of the armaments' staff in the 'twenties and 'thirties. Nor had the war, with its corrective evidence, made much difference to their hidebound attitudes. Aircraft designer, Barnes Wallis, for instance, had more or less dropped everything, on 3 September, 1939, to concentrate on air weapons, as being the most fruitful field for making a major contribution to winning the war. Knowing that all planes then in production had been designed for small bombs (the more so as the Wellington was his own design) and conscious of the fact that not only did big bombs need big bombers with special bomb-bays, but also that size was not the only criterion of explosive devastation, he had drawn up full plans for a huge 'Victory' bomber and for a range of bombs designed to do specific jobs therefrom. He was also working on the idea of pressurised cabins for bombers which would enable them to fly at 35-40,000 feet, and bombsights which would enable them to drop their loads fairly accurately from such heights, if they could see. And he had even suggested, and had drawn up, a list of priority targets which could have disastrous snowballing effects, if knocked out, on the German economy.

But Wallis had such difficulties, in the first eighteen months or so of the war, in getting anyone to listen to him, let alone help him to get production going, that it was only when he duplicated and posted his ideas to seventy or more leading citizens, and got the Special Branch on his shoulders as a result, that some heed was paid to his ideas. Fortunately, although a natural eccentric, Wallis was a fighter, and he kept plugging away for nearly four years until he eventually got his way . . . with the incredible Dambusters squadron the main result.

But, at this period in the war, there was little imagination or skill being applied either to bombs or to their accurate strategic delivery. Indeed, despite the fact that the first 4,000-pounder 'blockbusters' began to reach bomber squadrons in March, 1941, and the first was to be dropped by a Wellington in an attack on Emden on 1 April, armaments generally were still dragging far behind aircraft development. In the first eighteen months of the war, the main weights in use by Bomber Command had been the inevitable 250-pounder, (of which some 70,000 had been dropped) and the equally-undramatic 500-pounders (of which 55,000 had been dropped). This was a depressing record. Not only were the small British bombs defective and inefficient, as has been related over the period concerned; when they did go off they did very little harm, thanks to the idiotic proportion of explosive to casing (which was now only about 27 per cent, compared to the German's corresponding ratio of 50 per cent) and the amatol explosive itself was still relatively ineffective.

Anyway, when the first three of the initial batch of fifteen Stirlings to be delivered took off from Oakington, Cambridge, on the war's first four-engined bomber sorties, on the night of 10-11 February, 1941, their bomb-load was restricted to 500-pounders—a mere sixteen to a plane; it was like using tanks to carry peashooters.

These they dropped on storage depots at Rotterdam and then the giant bombers flew home safely. The only mishap was that one plane had an engine failure. This was not serious, as one of the virtues of the Stirling was that it could maintain height at any weight with one engine out (although it could not do so with two engines cut at any weight over 50,000 pounds).

Partly because of teething troubles encountered by 7 Squadron, production was built up very slowly. In addition to the fifteen planes sent to Oakington for preparatory work, only twenty-one Stirlings would be supplied to squadrons in the first quarter of 1941.

Meanwhile the marks of the other two four-engined types were also being developed rapidly. These were the Lancaster and the Halifax, both of which had stemmed from two-engined bombers. It has been reported that the way the Lancaster came about was that, in 1938, Air Chief Marshal Sir Wilfred Freeman, Air Member for Development and Production, was visiting the Avro company with his deputy, Air Vice Marshal Sir Arthur Tedder—both good men and true—to see how the Manchester twin-engined bomber project was coming along. They were disappointed at what they saw and heard; it was full of bugs, and a prototype had crashed on a test flight. But in the office of Roy Dobson, the chief designer at Avros, they were asked if it was correct that there looked like being a surplus of the much-favoured Rolls-Royce Merlin X engines coming forward. On being told that that was so, Dobson produced a desk model of the triple-tailed Manchester III, to which he added extra wing sections with two extra engines. The two staff experts were impressed and authorised him to go ahead with the idea. Through this shrewd and intelligent afterthought was born perhaps the greatest of World War II bombers, the Lancaster—which was just as well for Avros as well as for Britain, because the Manchester, with its equally unsatisfactory Rolls-Royce Vulture engines, was mainly a failure as a bomber, although it was to be used for the first time, in a raid on Brest on the night of 24-25 February, 1941, and intermittently thereafter.

The Lancaster Mark I prototype had first flown with great success on 9 January, 1941, and production was being rushed forward so that deliveries to squadrons could be effected later in the year, whenceforward its bomb-carrying feats would be legion, as will be recounted later in the story.

The Handley Page Halifax, the third of the makes of four-engined bombers that were to give the Third Reich, in honour of Churchill's promise, 'the shattering strokes of retributive justice', was faster off the assembly lines than the 'Lanc'. Having been produced as a much-enlarged version of the firm's unsatisfactory Vulture-powered HP 56 medium twin-engined bomber (disappointing in the same way as the Manchester) the Halifax also featured four of the advanced Rolls-Royce Merlin X power units. The prototype had first flown a few days after the outbreak of war and first deliveries had been made to No. 35 Squadron at the end of 1940.

'From Hell, Hull and Halifax, good Lord deliver us,' Lord Halifax had quoted from an old Yorkshire prayer at the christening ceremony for the first Cricklewood-built Halifax. When it is considered no fewer than four out of ten of all the heavy bombers built in Britain in World War II were Halifaxes, it is probable that Germany should have harkened to the last two parts of the prayer.

A new method of split-assembly, which Handley Page had introduced to the Halifax production lines, meant that the bomber could be divided into sections for transportation and repair, and also meant a speeding-up in the recovery and rebuilding of 'bent' aircraft. Four separate assembly lines had been established, at subsidiary plants, in addition to the two main Handley Page factories at Cricklewood and Radlett, as a group production effort of a completely novel sort. These factors and others of an equally imaginative kind led to speedy deliveries and to production records for the Halifax. And they obviously had some bearing on the very large proportion of Halifaxes employed by Bomber Command in the middle period of the war.

Raw materials were in very short supply all round, with U-boats claiming all too many cargoes in the Atlantic. In effect, Britain was short of everything and the aircraft firms with the most go-ahead executives tended to corner rather more than their share of scarce metals when priorities for the materials for the tools of war were being settled. (Severe shortages of metals had indeed been one of the main objections to Barnes Wallis's plans, for a giant bomber and

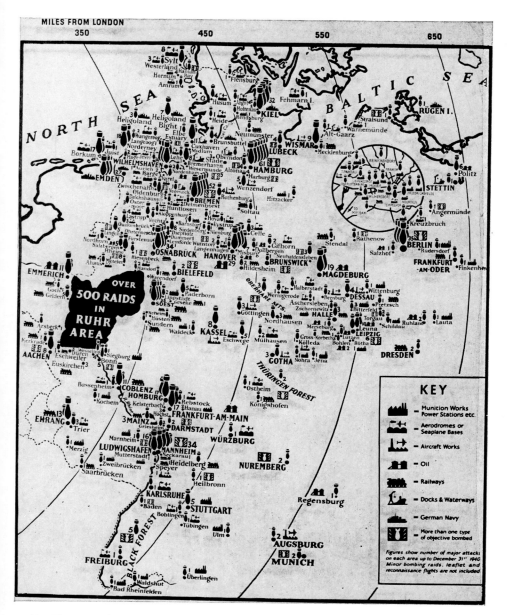

12. *This map shows raids on Germany up to 31 December, 1940. It was impressive as propaganda, but the bombs were small, and the effects on the Reich were negligible, relative to the sacrifices made by Bomber Command. Nevertheless, after Dunkirk it was the only means we had of striking at the German homelands.*

| La forza del destino... | Die Macht des Schicksals... | La forza del destino... | Die Macht des Schicksals... |

RUDOLF HESS
Nominato Luogotenente del Führer
il 27 Aprile 1933.
Secondo successore designato
di Hitler.
**Attualmente prigioniero di
guerra in Inghilterra.**

RUDOLF HESS
Stellvertreter des Führers.
Ernannt am 27ten April 1933.
An zweiter Stelle in der
Nachfolge Hitlers ausersehen
**Jetzt Kriegsgefangener in
England.**

Maresciallo del Reich
HERMANN GOERING
Primo Ministro di Prussia
Comandante in Capo della Luftwaffe
Commissario del piano quadriennale
ecc. ecc. ecc.
Primo successore designato di
Hitler.
Futuro
?????

Reichsmarschall
HERRMANN GOERING
Ministerpräsident von Preussen
Oberbefehlshaber der Luftwaffe;
Beauftragter des Führers für den
Vierjahresplan.
usw. usw. usw.
Zur Nachfolge Hitlers bestimmt.
Zukunft
?????

13. *Leaflet raids on Italy and Germany were an astonishing feature of night bombing in the early part of the war and were continued spasmodically to the end. The German side of a two-language leaflet reproduced here is typical of those dropped in the middle period of the war.*

14. *De-briefing scene, complete with sandwiches, tea and twin-like Intelligence Officers, after one of the first raids on Berlin in August, 1940. The official caption of the time describes how 'the crews of the machines left the Berliners a startled as well as a frightened people'.*

bumper bombs, by Beaverbrook and others. In wartime, even more than in peace, having a sponsor who 'knows his way around the shortages' was every bit as important as having a stupendous idea.)

Anyway, six Halifaxes, chosen from the first twelve machines produced, and flown by the re-formed 35 Squadron, at Linton-on-Ouse, had made their operational debut successfully and without incident in a raid against Le Havre on the night of 10-11 March, 1941. These were to be known as Mark I Series I Halifaxes. And two nights later these same planes became the first four-engined aircraft to drop bombs on Germany, with an attack on Hamburg. Subsequent marks followed fairly quickly, with higher gross weights and with increased fuel tankage. Before the assembly lines for the transport version of the Halifax would be closed down in November, 1946, more than 6,000 would be built, and this versatile plane would have continued in service with Bomber Command until the last day of the war.

The Mark I Series I Halifax had a wing-span of 99 feet, a length of 70 feet and a height of 21 feet. Its maximum take-off weight was 55,000 pounds and its maximum speed was 265 mph at 17,500 feet. With an operation ceiling of 22,800 feet, its range (with a bomb load of 5,800 pounds) was 1,860 miles. It featured a nose turret of two Brownings, a mid-upper and a tail turret with four. Some versions also had two Brownings in beam positions and the numbers of crew could therefore vary upwards to a maximum of seven. An astonishing total of 13,000 pounds of bombs could be carried at a pinch. Later versions would be powered by Bristol Hercules engines, with aircraft span and length increased.

The original important decisions by design teams in the mid-'thirties to use four engines in 'the bombers of the future', although it misfired in some ways, was undoubtedly right and was certainly farsighted. You may ask, why four engines for a planned heavy bomber: why not five, six or three? The answer, worked out in 1935, was that four was the right number relative to required range and speed. It was also reckoned to be correct for safety and economy. The facts had been statistically recorded that a single-motored plane had a 500-1 chance of making a longish flight without engine failure, while a twin-engined one had a 25-million-to-one chance against failure of both power-units. But the longer the flight, the worse the

9—TLC * *

odds, for the very good reasons that (*a*) the two engines could never be wholly independent; and (*b*) the further you fly on one engine, with the other one doing nothing, the greater the strain on any weaknesses it may possess.

Planes with three engines were discarded for the obvious reason that the third was unlikely to keep the aircraft aloft on a long flight if two failed or were knocked out. And, by analogy, four engines were considered ideal because they could really do the job and survive in the event of two engines failing or being hit. The odds against three or more engines failing, in turn, were so great that there would be no real benefits in building an aircraft with five or six. It was also calculated that, setting aside the hazards of flak and fighter shells, one engine in a plane was liable to fail about once in 6,000 hours of flying and, when that happened on a four-engined plane on a long flight, the remaining three engines could carry on without any serious difference in performance, except in the minds and hearts of the crews. All three types devised—the Stirling, Halifax and Lancaster—could also struggle home on two engines.

Studies had also been carried out into the so-called 'engineering curse' which was said to limit the natural range of any size of aircraft to about 750 miles. It was reckoned that it took about two-thirds of the total lift to hold a plane up in the air. Of the remaining third, at least half would have to be fuel, leaving about one-sixth for bomb-load. Long flights meant more fuel and fewer bombs. No matter how the early designers played around with new ideas they were invariably driven back to these original sins of the engineer's curse. Nor did bigger planes, such as the new, heavy bombers, make any great difference to this 'law of nature', except that they needed more and bigger engines, fatter fuel tanks and longer runways. Also, fuel consumption rose proportionately with power and speed. Lightness of aircraft was no real help either. because, after a certain point, it reduced strength.

The answer to greater range with higher bomb-load turned out to be streamlining. This was not fully understood in the late 'thirties or even in the early months of the war (although in the previous twenty years it had led to the cowling of the engine, the elimination of struts, and the retraction of landing gear) but fairly dramatic improvements were effected, as the war proceeded, by the aerodynamic smoothing of various protrusions and humps, allowing the planes to slide ahead faster through the sticky air, so that each gallon of petrol drove it just a little further, increasing the range or the bomb-load, albeit ever so slightly at first. These were the main ways in which the Halifax, Stirling and Lancaster became more effective over the years. They could never be described as 'poems of engineering', but from the start they were unique in world aviation, and they were also as timely as they were welcome. Alas, there were too few of them in 1941 and electronics had not reached a stage at which they could be used operationally.

Maybe one of the reasons was that many of the Air Staff and a majority of the politicians had reached an age when men normally retire from the hustle of life and were incapable of grasping the technological needs and challenges of these vessels scaling ever-new paths in the virgin sky.

Chapter Nine

It was inevitable, as 1941 dragged on, that all eyes were on Bomber Command far more often than was desirable. Since the fall of France, Britain had stood alone against desperate odds. Throughout the Western Hemisphere millions were watching us and seeing Britain's hope as their own. The Wehrmacht still lined the entire Atlantic coast of Europe and dominated the Continent. The UK's main task was to defend the homelands and stay alive to fight another day by improving supplies, organisation, mobilisation and training. Things were going badly in the Middle East. It would be years before the initiative could pass to us in Europe. Only through Bomber Command could the British public and our friends on the fence or in occupied territories be allowed to savour retributive justice. But Bomber Command also needed time to gather strength. With only a few hundred aircraft spread over many tasks, and with squadrons being diverted to the Mediterranean or 'loaned' (never, in fact, to return) to Coastal Command, it was too much to hope, whatever the Master Bombing Plan might be at the time, that much spice could be supplied therefrom to a public whose appetite for successes in return for long hours of productivity was strong and unsatisfied.

Inevitably, the civilian population of the British Isles was going through a crisis of its own. Churchill was by no means the hero in 1941 he was to become. There were rumbles of rebellion and criticism of the leadership from all sides of the political fence. The British had hastily cohered when threatened and were preserving a somewhat-shaky façade of unity, even in the negative period of 1941. The decadence of the 'thirties was still visible beneath the hopefully democratic surface, and society was still permeated with privilege and exploitation. The black market was flourishing and 'jobs for the boys' continued to be something of a national scandal.

These things inevitably had their effects on the boys of Bomber Command. They knew the spotlight was on them. They knew there could be no let-up for them until the war was won. They were being asked to stretch their efforts to the limits of endurance. They *had* to believe in what they were doing, because the chances were they would have to give their lives for their beliefs. They resented the lusting for German blood, as much as they resented the corruption and cynicism, by the public and the politicians, for the very good reason that they were in the front line and should have been consulted about what was possible and what was not.

The skippers (and some of their crew members) were mainly quite exceptional young men at this stage in the war. Volunteers to a man, they had been chosen for their education, their powers of leadership and their enthusiasm for flying. Some were immature and others had become cynical, but in the main they were clear-eyed, cool-headed, fast-reacting young men of the sort that would have made sports stars, racing drivers and mountain climbers in peacetime. Later, in the years of rapid expansion of Bomber Command, the quality would inevitably be diluted, but in 1941 they were mainly the cream of the cream. Three things were letting them down, and they felt it deeply. Two have already been mentioned—public urgings for them to do more destruction (which at its worst was like the screeching of the crones outside the Bastille) and the lack of understanding consistency of the air and political leadership. The third was that the standards of support were not up to the quality of aircrew. There had been fourteen RAF men on the ground for every one in the air, and in the case of ground crews and administrative staff—both categories important in many ways to the success of a mission—selection seemed not to work well, in that many were 'lazy buggers' lacking in urgency, in skills and in sensitivity to the crews' needs or problems.

That, despite all these irritations and weaknesses, the young men who flew and crewed the bombers faced the fears that were their daily cross, and gave of their best from the depths of their guts, is more than Britain deserved or should have been able to hope for in the valley of despondency that was reached in the middle of 1941.

The fruition of Hitler's extraordinary decision to attack Russia had a cheering effect in June. Although the Soviet Union was an ally of uncertain strength, at least we were no longer standing alone. The second phase of the Luftwaffe's blitz was also weakened from the moment of the invasion of Russia on 22 June, as more and more planes were demanded on the eastern front. Thenceforward raids on Britain would be much reduced, with 'skip-bombing' of ports, airfields and ships at sea Goering's main policy for a time, as a supplement to the German navy's increasing attempts to strangle us by blockade. German leaflets stating that Britain would starve by the end of the year because she was steadily losing the Battle of the Atlantic were dropped in East Anglian villages on the night of 11-12 June.

These switches of tensions did not relieve Bomber Command of any of its headaches. Indeed, Churchill deemed it vitally important (having said in a broadcast on 22 June that 'any man or State who fights against Nazi-ism will have our aid') that Russian gratitude should be stimulated by even greater bombing efforts being seen to be done on our part. To achieve this, yet another bombing plan was needed. So, peremptorily on 9 July, the four-month period of assistance to the Admiralty in the Battle of the Atlantic having been completed, a new directive was hustled to the AOC-in-C of Bomber Command. Signed by the Deputy Chief of Air Staff, but thought out at a higher level, it said simply: 'I am directed to inform you that a comprehensive review of the enemy's present political, economic, and military situation discloses that the weakest points in his armour lie in the morale of the civilian population and in his inland transportation system.'

There was some real sense in this. It had been finally digested that oil plants were too small to be hit with any accuracy, even by moonlight, and that towns and railway systems (particularly those in the Ruhr area) offered much more suitable targets, with the possibility of comparable disruption being caused. Sometimes the targets would coincide; sometimes not.

The Air Ministry directive was quickly followed by an even stronger one from the Chiefs of Staff, with the authority of the War Cabinet. In it, they expressed their desire that the root sources of the German war machine, plus 'the economy which feeds it, the morale which sustains it, the supplies which nourish it and the hopes of victory which inspire it' should be attacked at once with vigour. These were probably the 'winged words' of Churchill himself, but it plainly meant that 'area bombing' was now fully authorised, whatever the consequences. As with many of the Prime Minister's utterances, this order (whether actually worded by the great man or not) showed more optimism than realism, although to be fair it is on record that he questioned some of the detailed forecasts put before him by his air advisers. At that moment in time, Bomber Command had a front-line strength of fewer than 400 planes. Even with crews shuttling almost daily across the North Sea, risking their planes and their lives through fatigue as well as in running the gauntlet of ever-increasing flak, the number of targets that could be bombed, even minimally, was ludicrously small. The total tonnage dropped by Bomber Command in June had been little more than 4,000 tons.

But Churchill was on the spot and had to talk big, whether we could act big or not, because Stalin had got in direct contact with him for the first time early in July and was already demanding 'a second front'.

There was a slight overlap in the bombing plans in the remainder of July, with attacks on enemy ports and shipping continuing. Brest, Lorient, Rotterdam, La Pallice and Cherbourg were the main targets, and, in the course of the sixty-third attack by Bomber or Coastal Command on the apparently invulnerable battle-cruisers, *Scharnhorst* and *Gneisenau,* in dry dock in La Pallice and Brest, a squadron of brand new Halifaxes succeeded in hitting the *Scharnhorst* five times. Typically, two of the armour-piercing 500-pound bombs dropped penetrated the deck of the cruiser but failed to explode, and the other three effected only superficial damage. But the story was played up in the press for all it was worth and the crews were delighted at achieving such accuracy.

Railway marshalling-yards around the Ruhr were to be the principal transport targets under the new plan, with the object of cutting off the remainder of Germany and occupied Europe from the most productive source of supply, and direct attacks were to be made on the centres of Hamburg, Frankfurt, Berlin, Bremen, Hanover, Stuttgart, Mannheim and other important towns. In these ways it was hoped that fighter and flak defences would have to be stretched to the maximum instead of being mainly concentrated in the Ruhr.

In addition, with Stalin demanding (as bombs fell nightly on Moscow) that still more should and could be done to draw German fighter planes away from the Russian front, a temporary resumption of day bombing on a modest scale was authorised. Targets were chosen, mainly in France, which were within the combat range of British support-fighters, and four-engined Stirlings, with their powerful defensive armaments, joined the traditionally day-bombing Blenheims in a series of raids which became known as 'Circus' attacks. Because the Spitfires mainly concerned could only fly short distances if they were to hold anything in reserve for dog-fights with Messerschmitts (the principal object of the exercise) the targets chosen were comparatively unimportant ones in occupied territory, and the Luftwaffe only took the bait if the tactical conditions favoured them.

Blenheims, now very much the poor relations in Bomber Command, were not restricted to occupied territory entirely, and towards the end of July, 1941, Winston Churchill toured 2 Group Blenheim bomber stations, and made a personal appeal to crews to strive even harder to draw Luftwaffe fighters westwards in daylight missions. 'I am relying on you to help Russia in this way,' he told them, 'and so to help us all in the long run.'

The Blenheim was still no match for enemy fighters, but experienced crews had learnt over the past year or so to use cloud cover to dive in and out on a target before they could be intercepted. Sylt and Bremen were chosen as additional daylight targets for 105 and 107 Squadrons, stationed at Harwell (and among the young pilots involved in the Sylt mission was cricketer Bill Edrich, then a novice Pilot Officer).

The main raid on Bremen was mounted within a few days of the Prime Minister's visit and was led by an extraordinary Australian, 27 year-old Wing Commander Hughie Edwards, a peacetime flier who had won the DFC a few days earlier for an almost suicidally low attack on a destroyer off the Dutch coast. The raid on Bremen involved an unprecedented flight, for a wave of Blenheims, of 150 miles across German territory.

Edwards led fifteen selected crews from the two squadrons in what was to be one of the most daring raids of the war. They crossed the North Sea at a few hundred feet, believing that cloud would give them a measure of safety over the target. Alas, the sky was clear and blue all the way, and as they dashed for the town, from east of Bremerhaven, the light bombers ran into a positive jungle of barrage balloons defending Germany's second largest port. The Blenheims were flying too low to avoid the cables, so they ploughed on through, depending on the cable-cutters on their wings to do their stuff. Somehow the formation reached the dock area where flak and machine gun fire came up at them like a firework display at Westminster on Guy Fawkes day.

Edwards and his intrepid companions were now flying just above the rooftops and several planes had to bank steeply to avoid pylons, chimneys and ships' rigging. Repeatedly hit by shrapnel or bullets, they nevertheless succeeded in dropping their 1,000-pounders in the heart of the dockland area, before swinging away towards safety. Two aircraft suffered direct hits at this point, and crashed among the port warehouses. Another two were forced inland and never seen again. In the remaining planes there was much damage and many personal injuries, and about half of the elderly Blenheims had to be written off when they somehow got back to base.

Edwards was rightly awarded the VC for this astonishing raid (which had had such a traumatic effect on the German command that Goebbels himself went on the air to explain it away) and his two crewmen got the DFC and DFM respectively. Later, Edwards was to lead a squadron of Lancasters on Eindhoven, for which he would be awarded the DSO, making him the first man to win 'the big three' (VC, DSO, DFC) gongs in World War II—a feat only to be equalled by Guy Gibson and Leonard Cheshire.

Meanwhile, as night raids proceeded on German cities, and while Churchill was meeting Roosevelt in Placentia Bay, Newfoundland, to draft joint war and peace aims in the Atlantic Charter, the War Cabinet's scientific adviser, Lord Cherwell, thought it time to set up a committee to examine flash photographs taken by night bombers during 100 separate raids in June and July, involving twenty-eight different targets.

The de-briefing records, which were also examined, showed that, of 6,105 bombing sorties involved, crews on 4,085 claimed to have pressed home their attacks, and Cherwell wanted a detailed check on this. Photo-analysis, covering 600 pictures in all, resulted in the depressing conclusion that fewer than one aircraft in three had dropped its load within five miles of the designated target. In some cases, any two sticks of bombs in the one raid might be as much as ten miles apart, in opposite directions from the target. And in some particular Ruhr raids, only one-tenth of the bomber crews who claimed to have reached the target were found to have got within five miles of it. All the other bombs had dropped 'very largely in open country'.

The only small consolations were that the results achieved in raids on nearby French ports were much better than those in the Ruhr; and full moonlight was shown to improve accuracy considerably.

The War Cabinet met at once to consider the report and demanded proposals for action from the Chief of Air Staff, who admitted at last that Bomber Command would have to live through the rest of the year with a smaller degree of effort while, in addition to building in numerical strength, somehow or other tactical methods would have to be revised by the introduction of improved navigational and bombing aids. The spring of 1942 thenceforward began to be talked about as the springboard period for the destructive bombing of Germany.

Bombing for most of the rest of 1941 therefore became more a public relations exercise than a major programme. Single sorties, at the discretion of the skippers, spread over a night period came into vogue again, instead of attempts at mass raids, and as many targets over the whole spectrum as possible were attacked for reasons of morale at home and surprise abroad. This is not to say things were easier for crews. When they were not bombing they were familiarising themselves with new aircraft and techniques. And altogether they were still so thin on the ground there was little time for fun or even relaxation.

Some had 'temporarily' joined Coastal Command—seventeen squadrons in all having been transferred since April—for the continuing battle for the Atlantic, and, from this source came one of the most astonishing and improbable tales of war to brighten the front pages of British newspapers on 28 August, 1941. Apparently Squadron Leader J. H. Thompson was patrolling the convoy lanes in his Coastal Command Hudson, flying through low clouds above stormy seas off the Hebrides, when his second pilot yelled out that there was a U-boat to starboard. Turning sharply, Thompson saw that the German submarine was diving, so he made a straight swoop at it, and dropped a stick of bombs across its wake. The U-boat surfaced again at once, whereupon Thompson attacked it again, this time with his machine guns. Instead of the return fire he expected, when he saw the crew leaping from the hatch, the Hudson pilot, on his third run was faced by about forty German sailors waving white flags in the form of handkerchiefs and shirts. The incredulous Thompson wirelessed the news to the nearest surface craft and circled his captive submarine until help arrived. He was credited with the only capture of an under-water craft by an aircraft in history. The U-boat was taken in tow by a destroyer and was subsequently used by the Royal Navy.

In September, 1941, after two years of war, it was revealed that a total of 35,000 tons of bombs had been dropped by Bomber Command in twenty-four months for a loss of 1,300 bombers. It was a puny tonnage (which would be equalled in a single week later in the war) and a bitter loss of aircraft manned by brave crews. This proportion of planes destroyed to bombs dropped certainly could not be sustained, particularly as the new heavy bombers were reaching squadrons at a rate equivalent to only one bomber per week. Talk of expansion was all very well; but the front line crews could see all too little sign of it. They still had to slog away mainly in obsolete and obsolescent aircraft; their life expectancy was still calculable in weeks.

On 10 November, Prime Minister Winston Churchill, in a speech at the Mansion House, said: 'Now we have an Air Force which is at least equal in size and numbers, not to speak of quality, to the German Air power.' It was a curious definition of the statistics. Talking in all theatres of war (for, in addition to the Middle East, we now had fighter squadrons in Russia) and all commands, we had several thousand aircraft, certainly. But poor Bomber Command was at the nadir of its fortunes, having no more planes than a year before, and being still unable to muster any more than one-third of the total German bomber force.

Maybe Churchill was seeking to put new heart into the RAF, for a terrible meteorological misjudgement a few days before had led to an unparalleled tragedy, which had lowered morale at a time when it was none too high, anyway.

Nearly every available bomber in England had been mustered for prestige raids on Berlin, Cologne, Mannheim and the Ruhr on the night of 7-8 November. Out of 390 planes that set out in fairly good conditions, thirty-seven bombers failed to return. They had run into appalling weather over the Continent, contrary to the met. forecasts they had been given, and although no exact details were assembled or released, it is thought that most of the almost one-in-ten planes which failed to return had been led to disaster by thunderous anvils of cloud in which they hopelessly lost their way to crash in occupied territory.

It was too much. During the remainder of 1941 (while the Americans came into the war and dominated the headlines, giving Stalin two 'hot' lines to scream down) and the first few weeks of 1942, Bomber Command's main efforts were again concentrated on attacks on the German battle-cruisers lying in Brest, with negligible results. It was with something like relief that, on 12 February, 1942, crews learned that the *Scharnhorst* and *Gneisenau* (the cause of so much frustration in that, for a year, they had exposed the inaccur· acy of British bombing) had made their escape up the Channel . . . although it has to be said that they were prevented from doing any more damage to our Atlantic shipping.

It was the end of a sad chapter. With the spring would come a new AOC-in-C, who really understood bombing problems from hard experience; with him would arrive the Lancaster and—even more importantly—life-saving navigational radar aids.

Chapter Ten

The arrival of Air Marshal Arthur T. Harris at Bomber Command HQ in a wood near High Wycombe, Buckinghamshire, on 22 February, 1942, was as explosive an event as it was important. He had been recalled from Washington, where he was head of the RAF Delegation, to take over at short notice as AOC-in-C from Sir Richard Peirse, who had taken his departure on 8 January, having been posted to India, apparently as a scapegoat for the general failure of bombing policy.

Harris was very much the right man at the right time. Once again, Britain's penchant for muddling through and somehow contriving to pull a leader out of the hat when it was almost too late was being demonstrated dramatically. As Chamberlain begat Churchill, so Peirse begat Harris, and in each case the will to go on fighting was reinforced just in time by the injection of iron at the top. In all the war, we never got anywhere near the cold executive efficiency of the German autocrats, but by God we were blessed in every major emergency with men of spirit and of courage, however flawed they might be in other ways.

Harris's arrival at the top of the Bomber Command heap was as timely, and in the same sort of way, as Montgomery's would be a few months later for the Eighth Army at Alamein. In both cases the men in the front line had fought bravely for years with ancient equipment (including 1918 armoured cars in the one case and bombs of similar vintage in the other) until they were weary almost to the point of disgust.

In the case of the bomber crews, their dedication had been made use of to test ideas they had found to be beyond the capabilities of their aircraft. They had reached the point where better reasons would have to be given for continuing sacrifices. They wanted positive, unequivocal leadership. And they wanted planes.

Just as Montgomery would dig in at Alamein until he got equipment worthy of his Desert Rats, so Harris was the realist urgently required by Bomber Command in February, 1942. A flier himself, who had led his first flight against Germany's Graf Zeppelins in 1916 and had flown on bombing missions in this war, Bert Harris was a rough, tough firebrand of a leader who knew what he wanted and why. From the moment he arrived at High Wycombe, and crushed all opposition to his single-minded ideas with characteristic unsmiling glares over his half-moon spectacles, few doubted that a new era had begun for Bomber Command. Indeed it had, and Harris would be one of the most fearless, ferocious and controversial figures on the Allied stage for the rest of the war.

To his utter astonishment, the new AOC found on the day he arrived at High Wycombe that his Command was down to less than half its establishment, and all he had to do his bidding was a mixed parcel of 68 heavy, 257 medium and 55 light bombers—a total of 380 serviceable aircraft with crews. He spent hours that first day drumming up more planes from every conceivable source, and checking on what new crews were coming forward. Numerical strength was important to Harris. He learned that only about 200 new aircraft per month were being delivered, and he wanted to know why. Nobody escaped the sharpness of his tongue that week, from the Prime Minister down.

Later, Eisenhower, who would develop a great respect and affection for Britain's bomber chief, was to describe Harris as 'the individual who originally wanted to win the war with bombing alone, and who was supposed to have derided the mobilisation of armies and navies'. That was certainly his attitude in February, 1942. He demanded more and better planes; bigger and more powerful bombs; and if the other services had to go without as a consequence, that was their worry. He had no fancy ideas about bombing. 'Let's finish the war by beating the hell out of the Hun', was Harris's brisk attitude. 'Maybe one day we'll be able to bomb scientifically every time. But until we reach that stage, let's mainly send over fleets of bombers to flatten Schicklgruber's houses and demoralise his workers.'

Support for this view came at once from Lord Cherwell. In a minute, addressed to Churchill in March, 1942, the Cabinet's scientific adviser offered an analysis of German attacks on Birmingham, Hull, Liverpool and other towns which suggested that every ton of bombs dropped had made from 100 to 200 people homeless. He reckoned also that the average operational life of an RAF Bomber Command crew was fourteen sorties, and that in the course of these it could drop nearly 40 tons of bombs, putting 4,000-8,000 Nazi families out of their homes. His experts had worked out that 22 million Germans were concentrated in fifty-eight towns—all within reach of our bombers. Starting at once and building up to mid-1943, when there could be 10,000 heavy bombers in service, mass raids on these targets could lead, he figured, to one-third of the entire German population being rendered homeless, with high absenteeism in the factories an equally important bonus.

There was a simplicity about this vision which appealed instantly to Air Marshal Harris, who had the same approach to war in the air as Trenchard and Douhet before him. He had inherited a force which, in two-and-a-half years, had frittered away its strength in a series of misconceived plans which had done little to hurt Germany or awaken the British fighting spirit. To hell with pin-point bombing. It could come later. For the moment, it was time that the Nazi masses were shown that they were all responsible for the war. 'Let's break their spirit,' said Harris, a forceful figure of few words; and he set about seeing how to get the scheme going as speedily, economically and wholeheartedly as possible. There would be no further opportunities for the time being at least for post-mortems on why the level of sophistication in bombing techniques was scarcely enough to ensure that bombs landed within five miles of their targets, even when the bombers found the right towns. A town was a town when scruples were swallowed and true 'carpet' bombing was the policy.

Paradoxically, the first major raid initiated by Harris was a precision one. There was in his pending tray an intelligence report that the Renault works at Billancourt, near Paris, was but lightly defended. The moon was due to be full on the night of 3-4 March, so he prepared to send a mixed force of 200 bombers, led by the most experienced crews in the Command, on a series of low-level sorties that night, if the weather was favourable. In fact, conditions turned out to be perfect; the first bombs dropped from a few hundred feet by the leading planes miraculously landed plum in the middle of the huge factory; and subsequent damage caused by the rest of the force cut Renault production sharply for several months. Alas, this was a 'one off', as they say. Not for a long time would the circumstances be just right for such a dramatically successful raid. By the end of the month, indeed, Bomber Command was again committed fully to area bombing.

Although there was an overlap of the old technique of bomber skippers going off on their own within a specified night period and doing their best in their individual ways, Harris was soon to change this, intent as he was on using large fleets of heavy bombers, led by skilled navigators and using the very latest equipment available, to stun the Hun in the course of well-organised mass raids. Second pilots and navigators were sent on intensive courses with this aim in view; bomb capacities and marker flares were examined towards more effective lighting and firing of target areas; it was all go-go-go.

In March, new four-engined Stirlings and Halifaxes, which indeed offered new conceptions and permutations of bomb-loads, were beginning to come forward in reasonable numbers and the Lancaster was at last ready for squadron service. But, best of all, 'Gee', the first of a series of navigational aids specifically designed to help bombers to their targets, had just come to hand. Harris saw to it that examples of Gee—which was still in very short supply—were fitted and tested in a small number of selected planes without delay.

Gee had emerged from a Cherwell-inspired investigation into navigational aids, as to the flying of bombers over long distances. It was better than the German Knickebein and Gerat devices. Gee's master transmitter, in effect, laid an invisible radio grid over the nearer areas of the Continent, so that a navigator in a plane fitted with a Gee receiver could plot his position at any time to an accuracy which varied from zero near home to within six miles at a range of 400 miles from the transmitter. Unlike Knickebein, which gave an accurate fix only where its beams intersected, Gee could be used at any point along the route within the limits of its beam length.

As it happened, the first raid in which Gee was used was not an ideal one to demonstrate its usefulness. Harris had long been convinced that, weight for weight, incendiary bombs were far more effective than high-explosive types in built-up areas, and now he had a chance to prove it. In a sense, he was following rather than leading in this, in that the Germans had already shown in London and elsewhere what fire raids could do; but at least he had firm views on what was what and was seeing to it that the appropriate squadrons were given suitable supplies of incendiary bombs and knew how to use them to the best effect.

The city chosen for Harris's demonstration was appropriately the mediaeval Hanseatic port of Lubeck (population 153,000) on the Baltic, north-east of Hamburg, with its fire-prone timbered houses. It was beyond the Gee range, but half-a-dozen of the 230 mixed bombers (including a few four-engined types) which set off on the night of 28 March had Gee receivers and Gee-trained crews. This was considered worthwhile on the basis that Gee would at least set them on a spot-on course for a good part of the outward journey and so would reduce their dependence on luck and dead reckoning in finding the target.

Again the night was moonlit and the planes in the van, with Gee on board, were able to reach the coastline at the right point without a time-wasting search. They then 'struck a match for the others', in the new slang of the crews, by illuminating the target with flares, from fairly low altitudes, and they also got a good fire going with their incendiaries. This meant that the following waves of bombers (inexperienced crews for the most part) without benefit of Gee, were able to see the blaze from fifty miles away and add to the flames over a period of ninety minutes by dropping 144 tons of incendiaries and 160 tons of high-explosive. Thirteen bombers were lost, five of them through navigational errors; but Harris had made his point that any of Germany's many old towns (with their narrow streets and wooden buildings) could be laid waste by bombers carrying a high proportion of fire bombs.

The results were spectacular as never before, and supported Harris's other theories on flares, navigational aids and the useful

10—TLC * *

communication of skills from experienced leaders to novices during actual raids.

In de-briefing, 190 of the crews claimed to have dropped their bombs into the fire and, for once, few of their logged reports were off the mark. Harris had incidentally increased the number of cameras carried by this fleet of bombers, and the immediately-printed results of these flash pictures confirmed that a great deal of damage had been done. Photo-reconnaissance (carried out now by a Wing of Mosquitoes) moved in a few days later and showed that nearly half the city, covering some 200 acres, had been flattened. Analysis showed that at least 2,000 houses had been destroyed, largely by fire. In addition, cement and canning factories, an electrical generating station, some warehouses and the railway station had been destroyed or damaged, together with the Reichsbank, the Gothic market hall and the twelfth-century cathedral.

It was an astonishing boost for morale—service and public. The war had been going badly. Hitler was more than ever on top of the world, what with drive-through successes in southern Russia; with his U-boats destroying 700,000 tons of British-American shipping a month; and with his minions systematically looting Europe with Germanic thoroughness. The Mediterranean was becoming an Axis lake, with Germany and Italy holding most of the northern shore from Spain to Turkey, and the southern shore from Tunisia to within sixty miles of the Nile. The Germans were about to link up, too, with the triumphant, all-conquering Japanese in the Indian Ocean. It was an incredibly depressing picture for the Allies. America was not yet ready to play a major part, although the US Bomber Command (the first American air headquarters in Europe in World War II) was being established in Britain. The main eventual aim of the Allies in Europe—to invade the Continent—was already being planned, but could not be undertaken for many months. Until Allied strength was sufficient truly to turn the tide, only the RAF's Bomber Command could take the war to the Axis in Europe.

It was a tremendous responsibility, but Harris's carefully-conceived carpet-bombing plan certainly seemed to be about to pay important dividends. The raid on Lubeck was a major success in terms of prestige and propaganda. It also presaged the taking to the German people of some of the horrors they had previously been inflicting on others. And, for almost the first time in the war, a Bomber Command attack on a German town had not only caused concern in the area of the raid but had raised something of a panic in Berlin itself, where Goebbels had been shocked into breaking off from crowing about the millions of Russians who were starving to death to threaten querulously further reprisals on Britain. Hitler was equally upset and quickly authorised the initiation of a sharp series of raids in April on similar British cities—'any listed in Baedeker'—beginning with Canterbury, Exeter, Norwich and York. To do this, some ninety Luftwaffe bombers had to be withdrawn from Sicily. Inevitably the terrorangriffe series soon petered out (though extensive damage was done to the cities involved) after some 2,000 tons of bombs had been dropped, for the simple reason that the bombers involved were more urgently required on the Russian front and in the Middle East.

Alas, the Lubeck raid had once again been something of an exception—an experiment rather than a stepping-stone in the main plan. Lubeck was not a town of great industrial importance, as would be the cities of the Ruhr on which Bomber Command's sights were mainly fixed. Also, as a port it had been fairly easy to find at night. The inland industrial targets to the west of Lubeck were soon to prove to be much more difficult to pinpoint, and would be found to be much more heavily defended by searchlights and flak batteries.

Night fighters of the Luftwaffe, operating in 'boxes' in the sky, were also becoming a major worry to the RAF's bombers, and were often necessitating switches from moonlit to murky nights, as offering possibly the lesser of two dangers. About three planes in every hundred were now having to ward off German fighters on night raids—almost a threefold increase on the year before—and almost as many RAF bombers were being brought down by the Luftwaffe as by light and heavy flak. Searchlights had also multiplied considerably and were brighter than ever, often blinding British crews at the all-important bomb-release moment of their missions. And German radar, greatly improved in the past few months, was being used more and more to direct fighters, flak and rockets to concentrations of bombers.

Four-engined Avro Lancasters were now being delivered at a rate of about three a week and high hopes were held for them, based on their speed, height, sophistication and variable, capacious bomb-bays. Powered by Rolls-Royce Merlin engines, and outstanding from the start in terms of production design, these great new planes could astonishingly carry a bomb weight of 14,000 pounds for more than 1,600 miles, at 210 mph, although originally designed to carry only 4,000 pounds.

The Lancaster I then in use had a gross weight of 60,000 pounds. It could fly at a top speed of 287 mph at 11,500 feet, and had a service ceiling of 24,500 feet.

The ill-starred Manchester bomber, from which the Lancaster had evolved, although disappointing and destined to have a brief life of a year in service (with only seven bomber squadrons using them) had made its operational debut in a night attack on Brest on 24-25 February, and a number of Manchesters had been lost through big-end bearings failing in the complex Vulture engines. The Lancaster, by contrast, the first of which were built around Manchester airframes, had been found in prototype tests to be almost uniquely uncomplicated and reliable in structure and power units. The Lancaster looked like being (as indeed it was to be) the best heavy bomber any nation would have in the war.

The first two Lancaster squadrons, Nos. 44 and 97, at Waddington and Woodhall Spa, Lincolnshire, had become operational on 2 March. They were both 'Empire' squadrons, the first nicknamed 'Rhodesia' and the second 'Straits Settlement'.

A growing number of crews and squadrons from all parts of the British Empire were now assembling in Bomber Command, as the Empire Training Scheme got thoroughly established.

Two Lancasters from 44 Squadron were first into action in mine-laying sorties in the Heligoland Bight on 3 March, and the same two planes dropped bombs on Essen on the night of 10-11 March. But news of the great new bomber was to be kept from the public for another week.

Daylight raids, with their even greater hazards for crews, had not entirely been abandoned, and on 17 April, a 'special' long-distance precision raid was authorised on the MAN diesel-engine factory at Augsburg, Bavaria, about thirty miles north-west of Munich. It was to be the occasion for the unveiling to Britain and Germany of the mighty Lancaster and it was also to be a test of the abilities of the new planes to fly by day in self-defending formations. Carefully selected and briefed, twelve crews from 44 and 97 Squadrons, led by Rhodesian Squadron Leader J. D. Nettleton, set off from the tulip fields of Lincolnshire on their momentous mission in perfect spring weather.

The Maschinenfabrik Augsburg-Nuremburg (MAN for short) factory was turning out engines for U-boats, and it was a target which Harris and Churchill had agreed could only be attacked in daylight if sufficient accuracy and damage were to be achieved.

Unescorted because of the distance from base, the twelve Lancasters swooped on the target from a few hundred feet, having evaded the radar screen, hoping for surprise. Over the target, they were so low that the murderously heavy flak was having to be fired with open sights at point-blank range, hitting the planes and the factory buildings indiscriminately. The bombing from 100 feet or less was so accurate that the diesel-engine assembly shops were severely damaged by a score of direct hits. Inevitably seven of the twelve Lancasters were shot down, but it was conceded that no other aircraft in the world could have done better on a 'suicide' raid of this sort, and Sqdn. Ldr. Nettleton was awarded the Victoria Cross—the first of ten Lancaster skippers to be given the top award for valour in the war.

Churchill personally congratulated the squadrons and told Harris privately that it was a magnificent effort in which the results justified the sacrifices. Nevertheless, it had been a chastening and frightening experiment, and Bomber Command would not attempt a repetition of the Augsburg type of daylight raid until the very different conditions of 1945.

Unlike the reliable-from-the-start Lancasters, the year-old Stirlings and Halifaxes were still suffering from the sort of teething troubles normal to new types of aircraft. For example, from a batch of seventy such 'heavies' brought into service in the early months of 1942, more than sixty were temporarily unserviceable from one cause or another. These difficulties indeed were causing much loss in lives and time at a vital stage in the air war.

The Stirling was still badly handicapped by its weight and

was limited in the bomb-load it could carry as well as in the heights at which it could fly. Its heavy armaments had accounted for quite a number of Messerschmitt 109 and 110 fighters, but German pilots had discovered that a burst of fire in the direction of the fuselage roundels of a Stirling could put the tail turret out of action, so that various modifications were now having to be made to the plane. Much to the relief of the crews of 3 Group, Harris had simultaneously decided to switch all Stirlings to night operations.

The most remarkable feature of the Stirling was that (like the Wellington) it could absorb an astonishing amount of damage and still stagger home. In the course of a collision with a night fighter at this period, for example, a Stirling of 75 Squadron had four feet cut from its starboard wing, a huge hole torn in its fuselage and part of its rudder wrenched off; it nevertheless flew on, dropped its bombs and reached its base safely five hours afterwards.

Lightly-loaded, Stirlings (although hard put to it to reach 12,000 feet) were sent over the Alps week after week to bomb Genoa, Turin and other industrial towns in North Italy. On one such raid, a Stirling managed to fly for four hours on two engines before making an emergency landing in the North African desert. Although they were inferior to the Halifax or the Lancaster in terms of speed and altitude capability, the Stirlings were regarded with some affection by their crews because of their astonishing resilience.

The under-engined Handley Page Halifax I was also undergoing changes at this period. It, too, had been switched to night-sorties-only, and attempts had been made to improve its rather disappointing defensive armament. The recently-tested prototype Halifax II, with a Boulton-Paul turret similar to that featured on the Lockheed Hudson, was even heavier than the Mark I, and this factor, allied to drag from the new dorsal turret, seriously affected the ability of the Merlin engines to keep the plane aloft. When fully loaded, it developed an alarming tendency to spin uncontrollably, with subsequent losses of valuable planes and crews. Streamlining led to an improved version, the Halifax B Mark II Series 1A, with slightly more powerful Rolls-Royce Merlin XXII and XXIV engines. And, at the same time, the bomb-bay doors were modified to permit the carrying of larger bombs. The length of the plane was also increased by 18 inches, and the combined changes resulted in a welcome overall improvement in performance of about 10 per cent.

In March, 1942, a Halifax Mark II was the first British bomber to carry experimentally a secret new radar bombing aid, known as H2S, with a strange ventral radome shape, which would become a major British success later in the year.

An all-British bomb sight had been invented by this time by a Farnborough scientist, Richards by name. It was an intricate and delicate mechanism, involving gyro-scopes, which he had christened SABS (for stabilising automatic bomb sight). But Harris, when it was offered to him, would have none of it, for the time being at any rate. Always caring about his crews, he deemed it too complicated for them to have to deal with in the midst of their many other tensions during a raid. One of the SABS's drawbacks was that a bomber using it would have to approach the target on a straight and level course for at least 10 miles. It was put on one side for possible future use. In fact the bomb sight was an airborne computer.

Although shipping losses were foremost in the minds of the War Cabinet, and although 44 per cent of Bomber Command's effort was having to be devoted to minelaying and to attacking European ports that were linked with the war at sea, Harris was now deeply engrossed in plans for his next big night raid. He accepted, as part of an unhappy inheritance, that each day he would have to allocate some of his precious bombing force to such duties as the covering of convoys in mid-Atlantic and the hunting for U-boats. But he also bombarded the Cabinet with memos urging that shore-based aircraft could do more to win the Battle of the Atlantic if they could concentrate on bombing Germany with ever-larger fleets of planes.

Rostock was to be Harris's next target—an important seaport and manufacturing city on the Warnow river, eight miles from the Baltic coast; another old town with much timber in its city-centre buildings—and a means of helping to prove to his superiors that he could do much to win the war through area bombing alone.

Rostock was attacked on four nights running, from 23 April, by Gee-led forces which ranged from fifty to 130 bombers, comprising a total of 468 aircraft over the period. In all, 440 tons of HE bombs and 310 tons of incendiaries were dropped, repeating the Lubeck pattern. Again, remarkable successes were recorded in recce pictures. The important Heinkel and Arado aircraft factories were seriously damaged; seven-tenths of the city was destroyed, mainly by fire (including 1,800 houses and the three main churches); and 100,000 people, from a population of 123,000, had to be evacuated.

When the Rostock results were analysed, Churchill was so pleased that Harris was able immediately to promote his 'secret weapon'—a plan he had nursed for years as the ultimate answer to his critics. This was to send 1,000 bombers on a defence-saturating raid against a large German city. Churchill considered and approved the plan at once—warning only that the probable loss of 100 precious planes would have to be faced.

Harris did not have anything like 1,000 bombers to hand to proceed with his scheme, but he was a master of improvisation. Although deliveries from factories were increasing rapidly, the intake of squadrons was well below the promised programme. Indeed Harris at that date could scarcely boast an average of 417 aircraft and crews available each night for operations (representing only one-tenth of the Armada of 4,000 heavy bombers that had been planned to be in service in mid-1942). But, by hauling in some squadrons from the Middle East and rounding up a miscellaneous collection of planes, including Ansons and Blenheims from Coastal Command, plus 367 miscellaneous planes from training and conversion units, he somehow saw to it that he could muster a total of 1,046 aircraft for the job.

The crews listed for the operation were equally random, including some who had not even completed their OTU training, together with a few hundred 'greybeards' who had thought they would never fly in anger again. Appropriately, Harris named the proposed raid Operation Millennium.

This translation of theory into practice before the real strength of his forces had been worked up was an astonishing risk and seemed to some a foolhardy act of bravery by a persistent and single-minded commander. But the C in C himself had no doubts about the rightness of his decision. He wanted to stage a dramatic preview of what could be done by a growing Bomber Command armada in the year ahead.

On the basis of excellent weather forecasts, Harris (now Sir Arthur) ordered a Command Broadcast at ten minutes after mid-day on 30 May, 1942, and gave the simple instruction 'Operation Plan Cologne' to the CO's at fifty-two airfields throughout the country. Late that evening the magical total of over 1,000 aircraft took off and headed for Germany. They were mostly twin-engined planes, but they included 338 of the latest Stirlings, Manchesters, Halifaxes and Lancasters, some with the camouflage paint scarcely dry on their huge fuselages.

Total war was taken to the citizens of Cologne that night in the course of the greatest air operation in the history of warfare. The university city had been chosen partly because of its importance to Germany's war effort. As one of the leading industrial cities of the Reich (population 770,000) it had a vast concentration and range of factories and plants, featuring the production of manufactured machinery, electrical goods, chemicals, textiles, foodstuffs, paper, iron goods, vehicles, lumber, rubber goods and Cologne toilet water. It was also an important river port.

Again aided by Gee, crews of 898 aircraft claimed to have reached the target and to have dropped 1,455 tons of bombs, including the staggering total of 970 tons of incendiaries. Crews also reported gleefully that they had been able to see the fires of Cologne from 150 miles' distance on the way home; and subsequent reports from the 'underground' there indicated that the blaze could be observed clearly from towns on the Dutch coast.

Thanks partly to diversionary sweeps, by fifty RAF intruder fighters, aimed at creating diversion and confusion over Belgium, France, Holland and Germany, many Luftwaffe night-fighters were pinned down and most Bomber Command casualties resulted from the blindingly heavy flak over the city, and from collisions or navigational errors. Nevertheless, forty-three valuable bombers failed to return and 116 crash-landed or got home damaged. The total-loss ratio was 3.6 per cent, and the 'insupportable loss rate' for Bomber Command at the time was 5 per cent.

It was something of a triumphant occasion. At dawn the next morning, the first photo-reconnaissance plane took pictures of

Cologne from 23,000 feet and reported a pall of smoke, rising to 15,000 feet, in the shape of a giant cumulo-nimbus mushroom. Subsequent analysis indicated that buildings over an area of 600 acres had been destroyed—a figure which almost equalled the total of destruction caused in all previous bombing raids on Germany during the war.

The hell Germans had been inflicting for years on others was being meted out in return, with interest. Churchill, who was intent on pursuing every course that would inflict injury on the Nazis, immediately congratulated all concerned on one of the great victories of the war. And Sir Arthur Harris was to write in his memoirs: 'The dominating offensive weapon of the war was at last being used.' It certainly was not his fault that (as post-war examination of German records was to show) the dominating weapon had offered only temporary successes. As to the Official History of the Air War points out: 'Within two weeks the life of the city was functioning almost normally.'

With the full support and co-operation of the Prime Minister and the Chief of Air Staff, Sir Charles Portal, 'Bomber' Harris had not only done his homework for the main raid with care and flair; he now showed that he also possessed imaginative foresight by launching post-raid sorties on Cologne of a completely new sort.

An excellent pilot himself, Harris had been tremendously impressed by the performance and capabilities of a legendary new light bomber that had begun to reach squadrons a few weeks before. This was the Mosquito, a plane which had been so different in all respects from any other aircraft being built anywhere in the world at the time of its birth that it had come within an ace of being stillborn.

Whereas the Wellington, the Halifax and the Lancaster had precariously come into being as private enterprise improvisations stemming from botched Air Ministry specifications, the Mosquito had not even had the slim advantage of being based on such requirements. Geoffrey de Havilland, fed up with Government interference, and without any public money whatsoever, had chosen to conceive, in the late 'thirties, a light day-bomber based on his successful Melbourne Air Race Comet. Named initially the DH98, it was to be a powerfully-engined plane that could fly at speeds that would enable it to evade the German fighters then in production. It was also to be light and streamlined, as no aircraft had ever been, by being made by a revolutionary process his experts had evolved in the de Havilland wood-working shops.

When the designer presented plans and a model of the exciting plane to the Air Ministry, at the end of 1938, they more or less laughed in his face, telling him smugly that 'they knew' from experience that no bomber could ever evade any fighter. As far as they were concerned, the DH98 was a non-starter.

But there was in the Air Council a remarkable man, who has been praised earlier in this book for his unstuffy outlook, Air Marshal Sir Wilfred Freeman, then Air Member for Development and Production. He had seen the Mosquito's possibilities from the start (having been roped in on the studies unofficially) and he now chose to do battle for a year against the stone walls of indifference and ignorance at the Ministry, while de Havilland, a man of equally unshakeable conviction, went ahead with his plane on a private enterprise basis. And in December, 1939, Freeman managed to get an order placed (more or less on his own authority) for fifty Mosquitoes. Inevitably, the Air Ministry watered down the project by stipulating that the planes should be built for photo-reconnaissance instead of as bombers. Additionally, for several months even this limited programme was in jeopardy. Supplies of engines and components were denied de Havilland's, on the grounds that they were needed for other, better-established types, and the Mosquito found itself, at the time of Dunkirk, at the very bottom of the aircraft priority list.

Freeman and de Havilland fought on, believing that blood was thicker than red ink, and by July, 1940, their persistence had the result of persuading the Air Ministry to promote the Mosquito to the long-range fighter role. During 1941, the two tired champions at long last got their way when larger orders were placed for an unarmed bomber version of the plane—destined in the future to be the greatest vehicle of precision bombing of the war. And it was to this great new plane that Harris now turned for a dramatic post-script to the first-ever thousand bomber raid.

The intrinsic beauties of the Mosquito were that two powerful Rolls-Royce Merlin engines had been incorporated in the smallest and lightest possible airframe, combining clean aerodynamic lines with a tremendous power-to-weight ratio, and giving it a performance no other aircraft anywhere would equal before 1944. Like all beautiful aircraft, its flying characteristics were impeccable. It was also the most versatile plane of the war and in demand by all Commands for all purposes.

Geoffrey de Havilland had personally demonstrated to Air Marshal Harris the Mosquito IV bomber's incredible potentialities; he had executed upward rolls with one airscrew feathered and had taken it to near-enough 400 mph in level flight—an unprecedented speed for any sort of warplane.

Mark I versions of the Mosquito had been delivered to the RAF in late 1941, and these had been made much use of by Harris in securing pictorial confirmation of the devastation caused in his first mass-bomber raids. Flying at about 23,000 feet, the recce-Mosquitoes had eluded everything the Luftwaffe had been able to send up against them and had been able to mount as many as ten photo-sorties a day when required.

The Mark IV Series II bomber variant—the first to be delivered—had improved performance on the Mark I recce-plane, the Mark II fighter and the Mark III trainer. Featuring Merlin XXI, XXIII and XXV engines, with lengthened nacelles, they were designed to carry four 500-pound bombs, with shortened vanes, and were capable of adaptation to take a single 4,000-pound bomb.

The first four unarmed, 385 mph Mosquito bombers had only just been delivered to the first squadron—No. 105 at Bourn, Cambridge—when Harris decided to throw them into the breach in May, 1942; and from then on the Mosquito was to become one of the C-in-C's favourite weapons.

On the first bombing outing occasion on the morning after the giant Millennium raid, the four Mosquitoes swept in from the sea like lightning, harassed the Cologne authorities in their attempts to clear up the stricken city, terrified the populace still further, outpaced the interceptor fighters, and skimmed home to report to the bomber chief-of-chiefs.

'Old Harris didn't half rub his hands in glee when we told them how we had the Hun scuttling into the holes the big boys had made the night before,' one of the observer-navigators reported on their return to Bourn from reporting direct to the wood at High Wycombe where the AOC held court.

It was a fantastic beginning for de Havilland's bouncing baby and for the AOC-in-C's prescience. The gleam in Harris's eye from that day forth got brighter. He was lucky enough to have taken over at Bomber Command at a time when technological research and aircraft design were offering new opportunities for aggression. Equally, the RAF was fortunate in having found a leader who had a sure instinct for making the best use of his new material. But, on the day after Millennium, not even 'Bomber' Harris could have known that as well as largely taking over the role of daylight bomber—outpacing fighters and confusing flak batteries in a technique of dive-attacks and low-level passes—Mosquitoes under his direction would also perform the greatest feats of low-level target-marking as 'pathfinders to the pathfinders' in the incredible 617 Squadron's precision raids of the last couple of years of the war . . . or that, because of their almost-limitless versatility, Mosquitoes would eventually be built in forty different versions—all of them successful.

In any event, the AOC had again turned his mind to his main plan of carpet-bombing German cities. And only two nights after Cologne, on 1-2 June, the vast Bomber Command armada of 1,000 bombers was in the air again—or almost. Because of losses and damage in the earlier raid only 956 aircraft (including 340 from training units) could be assembled.

On this occasion the very-heavily defended inland Ruhr city of Essen (population 660,000) was the target, and the results were a great disappointment after the dramatic successes of the past few weeks.

Germany's defences were prepared this time, with a line of mobile flak assembled all the way along the route to the target, and the bombers had a rough time throughout the 150-mile journey from the Dutch coast to the inland city, and back. The intention was to include the vast Krupps armaments works at Essen in the bombing. In fact, cloud and industrial smog over the Ruhr sent the leading planes astray and, in the subsequent confusion, marker flares and incendiaries fell over a wide area, including the numerous communes and small towns adjacent to the town. Over 700 crews claimed to have bombed the city, but photo-recce by Mosquitoes showed little damage to Essen, whereas bombs had apparently dropped over a very wide area of the Ruhr. The Official Historian was to sum up in due course in the stunning words: 'The Germans were not even aware that a great raid on Essen had been attempted.'

Harris immediately demanded that there should be a speed up in testing and manufacture of a radar-based invention, known as Oboe, which had been devised at Farnborough to enable planes to drop bombs accurately through clouds, but it would be many months before any of these would reach squadrons. And meanwhile, weather was to remain the greatest enemy of bomber crews.

The number of aircraft that failed to return from Essen was thirty-one, but about 150 were also damaged and Bomber Command was forced to lick its wounds for several weeks. Not a few of the thirty-one were lost tragically through mid-air collisions over the target, and this was obviously going to be a major future worry in mass-raids.

Indeed, bombing of important inland targets in the Ruhr, even with the help of Gee, was proving a very different matter from in-and-away attacks on more lightly-defended minor cities and coastal towns of the Lubeck and Rostok categories. Apart from overland troubles en route, there was the problem of height in approaching the cones of fire and searchlights that ringed the industrial areas of the Ruhr. Particular targets were easier to pin-point at below 10,000 feet but this ensured a torrential flak bombardment. If, on the other hand, the bombers were sent in at comparatively flak-free heights of 15,000 feet and more, they would probably have night-fighters to contend with, especially as at that height (often with layers of cloud beneath them) they would have to swan around for some time if they were to identify the chosen city, in the midst of the solid industrial squalor beneath.

Gee was a navigational aid of only reasonable accuracy, which might take the leading planes to within a few miles of their destination. The target still had to be seen to be hit. This invariably gave the Luftwaffe's radar-directed fighters time to get into position for interception, and it gave radar-laid anti-aircraft guns a chance to fix on the bombers' path. It could also cause a sort of 'motorway madness' of the air, in which the British bombers—many in the hands of inexperienced crews—bereft of navigation lights, and therefore invisible to one another, would speed inexorably into hellish collisions in cloud or smog, to fall flaming to earth.

So it was that crew training, navigational drills, and marine-inspired traffic disciplines in the clouds had to be tightened immeasurably after the promising but daunting night raids of the early summer of 1942.

Variable winds over Europe, of random direction and velocity, were also the cause for increasing anxiety. Better and better navigators were the answer to this and to so many problems of weather and collision crashes. A good navigator was one who could think out the winds when they troubled his plane, and feel them almost, as a bird senses them through the barbules of its feathers. He had to know the wind like a brother. Skilled navigators, by careful reading of the conditions, could even contrive to get a boost from a favourable tail-wind, on the way home, that would get his crew back to base quicker and safer from a long, gruelling sortie than if he had chosen the shortest geographical distance across the earth's curved surface. Maps of air pressures, offering clues to pressure-pattern flying were in their infancy in 1942, but amazingly some navigators seemed able thus to feel the wind and adjust to it, bucking westerly head-winds and making use of both high and low pressure areas by veering right or left to find tail-winds.

Gliding had been a favourite hobby of fliers in the RAF for several decades and, in the summer of 1942, the idea was hit on of encouraging would-be navigators, as well as pilots, to take up the sport on the basis that there is no better way to learn the intimate secrets of wind and weather than by flying a sail-plane. Every movement in controlling a glider depends on the wind or an

orographic effect, and to soar like a bird it is necessary to make
intelligent but not foolhardy use of the thermal air marked by rising
cumulus clouds. Also, the weather's moods have to be watched if a
safe landing is to be ensured. Thus, in albatross-like flights, by day
and by night, did many a Bomber Command navigator learn a bit
more about the vital science that had been so neglected in the first
three years of the war.

Goering was of a like mind at this time over sail-plane training,
and glider experience was a must for most Luftwaffe pilots, observers and navigators, with weather-study the main purpose of the
exercises. In fact all the early training by the Luftwaffe was in
gliders. It was at this time that an incredible gliding tragedy had
sent four German fliers to their deaths.

Hitler had personally ordered an investigation into the effects of
thunderstorms on aircraft behaviour. Like the obedient Nazis they
were, five leading pilots took off in gliders from a field in the Rhon
mountains and flew straight into the centre of an enormous explosive thunderstorm. They were immediately swept mightily
upwards through swirling rain, with lightning cracking and flashing
around them, as their wings strained and split and the fear of God
rent their aching breasts. Within a few seconds all five made the
decision to bale out. It was a terrible mistake. As soon as their
parachutes opened in the turbulent air, violent updraughts swept
them at about 200 mph, like weird umbrella-powered moon rockets,
through the rain, snow and hail of the mushroom's stem into
freezing 30-below-zero thin-air levels of the storm's dark anvil top,
at 30,000 feet or more. There they were blown up and down at
Thor's will for hour after hour. Before long they resembled frozen
statues, their blood apparently congealed and their ears pounding
from the still-tumultuous thunder.

These incredible details of the terrors built into the heart of a
thunderstorm would not be available were it not for the miraculous
fact that one flier floated gently to earth when the storm subsided.
He was thawed out in hospital, but he had lost most of his fingers
and toes and his face was horribly disfigured by frostbite. His
Fuehrer in due course saw him personally and told him he was a
hero of the Fatherland. His words in reply, alas, have not been

15. *This official photograph, issued when four-engined bombers first came into service in 1941, shows the gear carried by a rear-gunner. It comprised:* (1) *Helmet;* (2) *Oxygen mask/microphone;* (3) *Oxygen tube;* (4) *Inter-com lead;* (5) *Dog-clips for chest-type parachute;* (6) *Mae West life-jacket;* (7) *Tapes for Mae West;* (8) *Quick-release for harness;* (9) *Parachute-harness webbing;* (10) *Lambswool lining to leather flying-jacket.*

16. *The faces are grim as crews are briefed for a raid in the difficult days of May, 1942. The station commander (the Group Captain in the centre) has joined the Wingco and the Intelligence Officer to emphasise the importance of the raid.*

recorded. His four companions were never found and may still be riding the skies for Germany—victims of their leader's Wagnerian whim.

Thunderstorms, both thermal and 'mechanical', were all-too-common for British and German fliers alike in that moody summer of 1942. The tremendous electric powers of nature, which had only begun to be examined in the limited pragmatic understandings of industry, and in limited radar probes by weather men, could be as frightening as close bursts of flak to young crews flying along the still largely-unknown paths of the sky over Europe. Although it was known that an aeroplane should be one of the safest places to be if lightning struck, extreme turbulence could be almost unbearable in a slow and clumsy bomber. Many a crew gave prayerful thanks to the aircraft workers who had built such strength into their planes as for a few interminable minutes they bumped, bounced and skewed through cumulo-nimbus storm clouds, expecting the wing spars to give way at any moment.

It was learned, through grim experience, that flight through the blackest part of the storm was safest, from the point of view of lightning or thunderbolts, but threatened wild vertical winds; that high-flying in such conditions attracted lightning and wing-icing; and that flying under a storm would usually mean encountering violent up and down-draughts plus heavy rain and hail.

It was always a difficult choice, with 20,000 feet generally the altitude of greatest danger; and the unpredictability of such storms—with the meteorological experts still pretty much in the dark over their causes and effects—led to some of the most scarey nights of the year for Bomber Command crews, as they bumped through nature's battleground of hot-and-cold up-and-down-draughts of alarming force. Three cases were recorded in 1942 of four-engined bombers being flipped upside down in such conditions. They returned home to tell the tale. An unknown number were lost from this cause or because they tried to fly over or under the explosive tempers of the wayward thunder god.

Hail in itself can do a great deal of damage to an aircraft. Even in innocently flying on the fringes of bad storms, some bombers, in those days of 1942, sustained large amounts of damage from almost

11—TLC * *

invisible barrages of heavy hail. Dents as big as ping-pong balls were caused to the wings and fuselages of a number of planes before this particular hazard was realised and coped with. Again it has to be mentioned that, even at this middle stage of the war, flying was a baby science and something new about it was being recorded in flight logs almost every day.

Chapter Eleven

The big build-up in the strength of Bomber Command, which Churchill was now describing as 'our immensely powerful weapon', was proceeding apace in the summer of 1942, but to Harris, its dedicated AOC-in-C, the facts of strength were illusory and frustrating. As fast as they could be trained, crews were being siphoned off to the Middle East (over one thousand crews having been claimed by Lord Tedder for his Desert Air Force in the first three months of 1942 alone), the Far East and elsewhere. Production of planes was running at nothing like the rate promised, but the figures would have been more impressive had it not been for the fact that considerable numbers were being diverted by the Defence Committee to commanders at new bases in at least twenty countries. The war which, two years before, had involved only Britain, Germany and Italy was now truly global.

World-wide, the RAF's total of front-line planes in mid-1942 was nearly 5,000, but Harris was still stuck with an employable raiding strength little greater numerically than the Command had boasted at the outbreak of war. Older types of bomber, having had their day, were being phased out or diverted to other uses. The introduction of four-engined aircraft was tending to slow down production in terms of numbers. The Halifaxes, Stirlings and Lancasters were costing more in money, time and materials, with consequent headaches for manufacturers. New assembly lines were slow to evolve. Bugs were still being ironed out. Ground crews were having to be sent on intensive courses to get 'genned up' on the new types; and failures leading to crashes during test-flying of production aircraft were disturbingly frequent.

Although arguments on the basis of counting heads and planes were not the whole story, with many vital factors including the courage of his crews not reducible to statistics at any time, the AOC was still bearing the largest responsibilities of any service chief in this period, and had the War Cabinet on his back for much of the time. Bomber Command was still sharply in focus in the international spotlight and was expected to perform wonders in raising morale at home; reducing morale in Germany; and siphoning off Luftwaffe air strength from the Russian front.

As the Cabinet counted heads and asked for bigger and better raids, equally to help the Russians and to impress the Americans, the AOC had to argue effective strength in terms of leadership, training, serviceability of planes; reserves of crews and aircraft; relative locations of units to targets . . . and a host of other factors. The prolonged demands on experienced crews, too, had reacted against the fitness and freshness of those who had survived. The headaches at High Wycombe seemed endless. . . .

Despite his problems, Harris had nevertheless already performed some minor miracles. By June, 1942, Germany had been made to suffer about as much bomb damage as England; the Luftwaffe was being compelled to deploy much of its army-co-operation air strength to defend the Reich's industry, to the point that, whereas 50 per cent of its aircraft had been on the Russian front in 1941, the figure was now 30 per cent and reducing; and the thousand-bomber raids he had scrambled together had cheered up the British people no end.

Another fascinating side of the blitz tactics of the new Bomber Command AOC-in-C was that Hitler was in such a rage over the carpet-raids that he had not only temporarily caused valuable aircraft to be withdrawn from mine-laying and other anti-shipping operations to add to his army-support fighters . . . he had also issued a number of new priorities for future reprisals on England, including the giving of an immediate go-ahead for the FZG 76 pilotless aircraft and for the A-4 long-range rocket. Harris's 'harriers' were hurting the Fuehrer's pride, whatever they were doing to his industries.

But the problem remained; how could Bomber Command go on carrying and waving interminable crosses on behalf of the free world when its strength, in aircraft and crews, could only justify raids by some 200-300 bombers on ten nights per month, drawing on a manpower strength that was down to less than half its establishment?

The temporary answer once more was to hit the leadlines hard by following the rule that if you had only a limited bomber force it was good tactics to hold off for a week or two and use the bludgeon again. This was what Harris chose to do in a fifth major saturation attack.

So it was that, on the night of 25-26 June, the second and last raid until 1944 by more than 1,000 bombers took place. The magic figure was achieved by borrowing aircraft from Army Co-operation Squadrons, by calling on Coastal Command for 100 planes and by involving 200 aircraft and crews from training units. The bombers involved ranged from the elderly to the latest of the four-engined types.

It was to be an unhappy night for Bomber Command, as well as for Bremen, the chosen city, but in the late afternoon the omens seemed good. Weather planes had been sent over Germany to double-check the meteorological forecasts. Almost perfect conditions were the prediction, with clear, moonlit skies. The news was flashed to the sixty airfields involved and the 'green for Bremen' signal was received with mixed feelings by 5,000 aircrew standing-by, who again included many veterans from OTU's and HCU's.

June, 1942, was a disquieting time for the commanding officers around the bomber wings. In the early years of the war there had always been a handful of experienced crews in every squadron to give it backbone and to inspire a necessary camaraderie of a unique sort. The fledgling crews then had peers to look up to and learn from—skippers who were recognised as outstanding leaders, together with their 'old soldier' crews, who might lord it a bit in the messes and nab the best benches to lounge on at briefing, but who were always an inspiration to have around.

But, increasingly over the years, the few had nearly all been plucked from the midst of the many. They had been downed, burned, blown to bits, drowned or, at best, taken prisoner. Their ends had been statistically inevitable. They had bought what time they could. They had wiped slates clean in boozers for their departed comrades and had drunk up, knowing that the same last rite would be accorded them in due course. They had collected their gongs and moved up rapidly in rank until the day came for them to write the letters of condolence to their friends' next of kin. By then the ghosts were more real and the night shivers came to them more often. More and more, life consisted of sleeping, flying, drinking and sweating. Whatever you did, you were done for in the end. No one, except the very luckiest of bastards, could buck or baulk the creeping cold truth that eighteen sorties would likely be one too many and a tour two too many. Luck became the only lady that mattered.

Sometimes the final call would come in company, as when practically a whole squadron would be wiped out in a mass raid. Sometimes it would come alone on an individual sortie. In either case it was seldom a quiet tap on the shoulder; usually it was violent and only occasionally was it swift. There are statistics for 1940, 1941 and early 1942, which indicate that Bomber Command casualties totalled a few thousand souls. The facts and figures mean nothing. Who can list, classify, or clothe with flesh and blood the gutsy professionalism on the one hand and the innocent amateurism on the other that should have characterised the bleak entries on the list?

The whittling down was most noticeable in a reduction of laughter. Hesitancy and inexperience were the begetters of a new grim seriousness. So few in number were the 'aces', the line-shooters (in the nicest sense) and the expounders of bombing techniques around the squadron ante-rooms that intelligence officers were now duty bound to see to it that every novitiate should read the squadron profit and loss accounts—the operations' record books—to gain therefrom some sense of what had been . . . some feel of the traditions that could and should be followed.

'It reminded me of a quote from "All Quiet on the Western Front," ' a survivor who was a rookie in 1942 recalls grimly. 'You would read page upon page of death and disaster, stated in brutally blunt language, and you'd think "So this is glory?" And you'd remember the German in the film who was told by his schoolmaster that to be foremost in battle was an honour not to be despised, to which he replied with a simple catalogue listing his experience . . . "out of my class of twenty, nine are dead, three wounded, four missing, and one in the madhouse . . ." '

To think this way, however, was rare. Fortunately for them, most OTU freshmen believed what they were doing to be worth-while, not to say noble. Their rewards, as with the soldiery of World War I, were hand-made shoes, perhaps; or manly mous-taches and neckerchiefs . . . and the adulation of girl friends and families. Maybe the squadron had been all but knocked out thrice over. Maybe it had been reduced temporarily to a single section. Maybe the old faces, the old jokes and the carefully-conceived techniques were gone for ever. They would replace them with their own variations . . .

Alas and alack, the truth was that theirs was to be a different sort of life. The so-called 'glamour' days of pioneer flying were all but over. In the future, it would be largely a matter of bus-driving-in-convoy for the many. Their resultant life style, too, would inevitably be diminished. The days of individuality were giving place to the days of the poor bloody infantry of the air.

Nobody was more disturbed than 'Bomber' Harris by the general whittling away of experienced crews. Most of all, he was appalled to see how few of the 'true blues'—the peacetime profes-sionals and reservists—remained on his strength. Of the men who had been under his command in 1939 and 1940 (in 5 Group and elsewhere), scarcely any were still listed as alive and fit in June, 1942. And who could wonder at this when a graph would show a crew's operational progress—*any* crew's operational progress—with a 90 per cent chance that the thin blue line would end in a red dot long before thirty missions had been completed.

The lengthening list of crews who had failed to return from operations, plus the inevitable losses through injury and death through planes crashing on landing or lost on non-operational test flights, had been too high for too long, relative to the numbers of men flying. Total continuing losses of 5 per cent or more were not only more than Bomber Command could bear; they offered such slender odds of survival that morale had to suffer; and there was the very real danger of Bomber Command reaching the point that nearly every crew involved in a raid would be making its first sortie.

As he thought about these things, and prepared to send his entire force on its fifth giant raid of the series, Sir Arthur Harris was formulating a theory which would answer at least some of these problems later in the year.

Meanwhile, back at the bomber stations, between the last weather check in the late afternoon of 25 June, 1942, and the final cockpit checks by 1,027 crews in the late evening of the same day, things were happening to the skies over Europe that would have led to a last-minute postponement of the raid had anyone at Bomber Command been aware of them. Missions on this scale could be and often were called off at the last moment. It had happened on the second of Harris's five great raids. Hamburg had been chosen as the target on 29 May. Crews had been briefed, bombs loaded on aircraft and everyone had been standing around in nearly 100 crew rooms ready for the off when bad weather over the target had reprieved Hamburg. Bombs had had to be unloaded and then, the next day, all the lengthy procedures had to be gone through again for the new target—Cologne.

This time, alas, there was no last-minute cancellation. The 1,000-plus crews smoked the last of their interminable crew-room cigarettes, boarded the vans that took them to their aircraft, and scrambled into their appointed places, feeling sick in their stomachs and showing irritability they did not mean.

At last the doors of the aircraft clanged shut, the inter-coms were pronounced OK and the thousands of engines sprang into life. From a dozen English counties, assorted fat planes rose shakily heavenwards to rendezvous at their east coast 'Clapham Junctions' of the sky, to be shunted and built up into migratory forces flying east with their deadly loads.

Clouds can be many things to many people, but in the summer of 1942, before radar beams were being used in bombers to pierce them, they could destroy, in a few minutes, the hoped-for results of thousands of hours of careful preparation. As the giant armada droned, roared and wheeled around the Ruhr towards Bremen, on that pleasant moonlit June night, the weather was as predicted. As usual, they were blinded by the fantastic glare and dazzle of the 'searchlight belt', comprising about 2,000 in number, with its attendant flak, which the Reichswehr had laid down from the Dutch coast to Paris, and which could not be avoided. Then, suddenly, they were in heavy cloud—a scudding greyness, rising from a base of a few hundred feet to God only knew what height. Almost at once there were crashes. Two Stirlings bumped wings and spun to earth; a valuable Lancaster lost its tail to an unknown 'friend' and screamed earthwards like a pigeon dipped in plaster, with only two of the seven crew able to scramble out and float to an uncertain reception at the hands of a frightened and angry Ruhr population.

The vast armada ploughed onwards, the young skippers gripping their sticks with nervous fingers, as they made the change-over to blind flying . . . uncertain of what to do for the best, and somewhat mistrustful of their instruments in the swirling shrouds . . . while the navigators sweated as they checked and re-checked the readings they jotted in their logs . . . and gunners peered all around into the murk, glimpsing shapes that might be friend or foe, their thumbs hovering over the buttons of their weapons. Over a wide area of cloudscape, R-T crackled and spat, as the part-sighted tried to aid the blind with such comforting words as 'There's a bogey* up your arse. It might be one of ours. Can't tell in this bloody clag.' In fact, there were no German fighters up that night and friend squirted bullets at friend a dozen times, in the un-nerving bumping world of never-ending sponge-like vapour. All that was needed to complete the nightmare, a survivor recalls, was for some celestial loud-speaker to roar out Ride of the Valkyries.

It was a night when St. Christopher was pulling no strings. Factors had to be weighed on factors—some fixed, some variable. Alertness was all. Contingencies had to be piled on contingencies; decision on decisions. Fear had to be licked by disciplines—by weighing the known facts and figures and making the best use of them.

The high, wide, woolly and gusty ocean of cumulus through which the bombers were forced to fly that night produced every emotion, from rational and cool, to do-or-die madness and stark

* An unidentified aircraft.

fear, in the hearts and minds of the many inexperienced pilots and navigators caught in the jungle of the clouds' deadly embrace for the first time.

Some lost the confidence and concentration so necessary to flying on instruments. They found themselves looking wildly around at the black ever-changing shrouds which were clawing at their windscreens instead of at the dials of the standard blind-flying panel, while they listened-out nervously for some *saving* message on their headphones, trying the while to ignore the roar of the engines, amplified by the clouds.

In the moments when the terror held them, errors could easily be made which would lead not only to no hope of reaching the target but sometimes to the more awful fate of no hope of getting home—to the ultimate disaster of remaining in the belching evil vapour, lost and terrified, until the last drops of petrol spluttered through the engines, with the 'abandon-aircraft' signs flashing and new dangers opening with the para-chutes. As Confucius has it, 'a man who has made a mistake and is not in a fit state to correct it has made two mistakes already'. Over the Ruhr on that June night, the philosopher was proved right in the experience of at least a dozen crews.

The most successfully navigated planes were the ones driven and steered by those who kept their heads down and did not think beyond watching the six-instrument 'blind' panel. They kept track by the compass of how they were heading; they watched the airspeed indicator to chart their speed; they kept time by their watches; they checked the drift meter and the artificial horizon; the altimeter told their height and the ther-mometer their temperature ... and that was about the spread of it.

Inevitably, many crews were only half-hearted in their at-tempts to find the actual target. They dropped their bombs at the first glimmer of light beneath, and, as the high-explosives went 'crump crump, crump' behind the tailplane and blew the incendiary flames into wide-spread fires, they would turn for home, causing other following bomb-aimers to add to the wrong blazes. Inevitably, as a result, the country houses of the Ruhr's industrialists suffered more than their factories that particular night.

Meanwhile new problems were facing the raid 'leaders.' By this time, German scientists had found ways of interfering with or bending the beams of the Gee radar device the leading aircraft were carrying. They, too, became confused and scattered as the narrow beam (hard enough to follow at any time) split and deviated.

Bombs were dropped more or less indiscriminately over a 100-mile area of the Ruhr, and less than a fifth of the total of more than 2,000 tons fell in the general confines of Bremen. The only consolation, that would be drawn from reconnaissance photographs over the next few days, would be that a few planes were seen to have succeeded in hitting the Focke-Wulf factory in the heart of the city. But post-war German records were to show that production of aircraft at the factory was but little affected.

It was more obvious than ever that the menace of cloud over a target had to be tackled systematically and thoroughly by the scientists—preferably before any other raids on this scale should be attempted. There was a certain amount of political capital and morale-boosting prestige still to be reaped from the very fact of this giant raid and the ones that had preceded it, but facts were facts and behind the scenes it was impossible to believe that the Bremen raid had been a success, when it was measured in results achieved against effort put out.

By dawn on 26 June, it was grimly clear that, in all, fifty of the thousand raiders had failed to return from Bremen because of collisions, flak, navigational errors and other equally horrific causes. Another seventy had been severely damaged in the air or in landing.

Coming home from such a mission was usually as frightening as going out. It was necessary to cross the coast at certain defined points to avoid being fired at by British ack-ack. The height of the cloud base, through which it would be necessary to descend at some moment, could never be estimated accurately, even when radio signals were received from experts, passing on other crews' experiences, or reports from coastal areas. If, as on this occasion, the cloud zone was below 1,000 feet, the let-downs of planes had to be made with the greatest of care, whether over sea or land. In the latter case, it had to be embarked upon over flat country. Even hills a few hundred feet high were a major worry. The drill was that if the plane was still in cloud when the altimeter (only roughly accurate) read 500 feet, it was best to climb and try again later.

Such repeated descents could be incredibly un-nerving, to the point that a few minutes of heartbeats, with the engine throttled back, seemed like a lifetime of hard work; and, conversely, a glimpse of 'geography' below would be greeted with a shout of joy on the inter-com.

Emergency homing (steering on a given course) was much in use that night by planes in trouble for one reason or another, but, with so many planes aloft at one time, the radio waves were as jammed as the air lanes, and there were inevitably unhappy queues over the principal bomber stations, leading also to the last-minute fear of being picked off on landing by a German night fighter, or even, mistakenly, being shot at while circling by a Beaufighter.

Having reached their bases, and somehow floated their aircraft to a reasonable landing, there was the news to be faced of friends lost or missing. Bacon and eggs, with a strong cup of 'char', was the standard meal at the end of a raid, but there were many green crews (green in sickness as well as in experience) who could not face food, or bed, that morning, and who dreaded the questions of the intelligence officers.

Guilt was a curiously common factor, as they stood around disconsolately, wondering if they were lacking in guts and thinking about friends who had faced the worst and who had not come back. A few who were safely home had not even tried to get through to the target, but had swanned around until it was time to come home, and had dropped their bombs harmlessly in the sea. Would it always be thus, they wondered, or did courage come gradually?

Many of the 'timid' ones would be found out subsequently in training, and 'put away' in a sort of 'glasshouse' reserved for the punishment of those who were 'lacking in moral fibre'. It would be a harsh judgement in most cases. But total war was harsh and becoming ever more unfeeling.

Meanwhile, at Bomber Command HQ, the total cost was being written in the various account books, with the inevitable conclusion being reached that the Bremen raid had been all too expensive in crews and planes. Conferences were called; records of production were examined anew; and, most of all, secret sessions were convened on speeding up the introduction of navigational and bombing aids. The mood was grim but the intention was clear. The whole concept of Bomber Command would have to be re-thought, Harris still insisted: 'We are the only people who can win the war. And we *are* winning it.' But, in July, 1942, he took a clean sheet of paper and started re-planning his Command from scratch.

Chapter Twelve

Hitler was expecting us to invade Norway in the summer of 1942, or at least to seize a base in the north of that country to protect our sea-routes to Russia, and, although such was not the War Cabinet's intention, it was important that the Fuehrer should be kept guessing. Bomber Command was therefore called upon from time to time—in addition to its other tasks—to make difficult sorties into the mountainous areas of Norway's irregular 1,500-mile coastline.

Among the priority aiming points in this prickly zone was the German battleship *Tirpitz* (larger than the *Bismarck* and posing a serious threat to the Murmansk convoys) which was temporarily anchored in Aasen Fjord, near Trondheim. This was a particularly difficult target, as the fjord lay between steep cliffs ranging up to 2,000 feet, and was well defended by ship-borne as well as land-based anti-aircraft units. But Churchill regarded the *Tirpitz* as 'of extreme importance' and four squadrons of Halifaxes were sent in by moonlight to do their damnedest. They flew over the coast at 8,000 feet and could see the long fjord clearly in the moonlight some ten miles ahead. The drill was to make low-level passes at less than 1,000 feet, which was somewhat suicidal in the circumstances but offered the only hope of knocking out a capital ship.

Smudge-pots of smoke had been lit to obscure the target and heavy flak (some of it almost horizontal, from adjoining mountain-tops) caused the four-engined bombers to buck and weave as they flew low towards the battleship to drop their mines. Over the target heavy concentrations of light flak from the ships downed a number of Halifaxes, and most of the twenty-two planes that had reached the target were damaged to a greater or lesser degree.

But in the ultimate climb-out from the surrounding walls of cliff an unprecedented hazard was encountered by the survivors. The moon was bright, the water shone a phosphorescent blue and mountains flashed past on each side like pale moody giants. As the Halifaxes climbed screaming to expected safety at the end of the lengthy fjord, and their altimeters showed them in the clear at well over 2,000 feet, the leading crews saw to their horror in the moon's glow that they were heading straight for a massive unscheduled mountain wall, looming straight upwards beyond the end of the fjord. Two of the leading three planes took violent evasive action and went into inverted dives into the grim waters beneath. The other planes climbed on, apparently hopelessly, and, to their heart-stopping astonishment, flew straight through the mountain until they were flying in clear skies. It had been an optical illusion.

They had run in fact into a masquerading cloud, hovering above the mountainous wall and so like the snow-capped cliff as to be terrifyingly solid in the pale night light. It was a hellish phenomenon to encounter blind in such a narrow path of flight, and it had led to the loss of at least two planes that might otherwise have got home. In all, half the force of Halifaxes was lost on this unhappy raid, and among the eleven which staggered home to make emergency landings on the nearest Shetland airfield, or wherever they could find an early haven, one landed with 160 holes in the fuselage and its dinghy blasted out of its stowage in the wing. When the assorted survivors got back to their bases, two messages awaited them. One was a signal from Churchill which called the raid 'a feat unsurpassed in the annals of British arms' and the other was a report from a Mosquito photo-recce plane that the *Tirpitz* was apparently undamaged.

In addition to the disastrous loss of some of these Halifaxes, due to too fast avoiding action, this new plane was suffering a series of unexplained crashes through sudden, unexpected inverted dives, resulting from rudder stalling. A lengthy investigation was put in hand and it eventually indicated that in certain flying attitudes the plane's triangular fin would stall without warning, with the result that turbulent air passing through the gap between the fin and the rudder would lock the rudder hard over and cause the fatal dive. New rectangular fins were devised to rectify this alarming, not to say deadly, fault, but it would be some months before full modifications could be effected, and meanwhile the Halifax crews had to continue flying their planes with more than usual care and with their fingers crossed.

Although no further 1,000-bomber raids were possible for a couple of years after the end of June, 1942, partly through the need to leave training units in peace to get on with the vital job of turning out sufficient crews for the big bombers that were beginning to supplant the twin-engined medium jobs, Harris's front-line strength was still being stretched almost beyond endurance, with crews clocking up an average of eighty hours on 'ops' per month, when fifty hours was considered as much as the average nervous system could take.

Churchill had promised to 'pulverise' Europe from the air, and Harris was his whipping boy when things were going badly elsewhere. Bomber HQ at High Wycombe was too close to the PM's week-end retreat at Chequers for comfort. As a result, the AOC-in-C had to wear even more hats in this period than the PM himself. The proclaimed war-winning Air Ministry plan he had taken on—the elimination of the Reich's fifty largest cities—had had to be set aside in the face of unfulfilled deliveries of planes and crews, and of never-ending miscellaneous demands from the soundproof bunker deep beneath Downing Street. These included raids on U-boat bases; mine-laying expeditions into German coastal sea-lanes, locks and river-mouths; attacks on Italian factories to ease pressures in the Middle East; the sacrificial Norwegian raids; aid for Coastal Command in convoy escort and hunting of raiders; sweeps over France and Holland, taking in transport concentrations and other 'targets of opportunity' . . . the diverse demands seemed endless, and the strain would have to be even greater had not the Cologne debacle led to a more cautious approach to weather conditions.

Until new weather aids, based on miniaturised radar and

17, 18. These before-and-after pictures show the Eder Dam, which was breached by the Lancasters of 617 Squadron, led by Guy Gibson, on 16-17 May, 1943, in perhaps the greatest raid of the war. The special mines used had been designed by Barnes Wallis and had to be dropped from a height of not more than 60 feet. The reservoirs at Mohne and Eder were emptied and the Sorpe dam suffered considerable damage. Eight of the aircraft and fifty-four aircrew men were lost in the brave and dangerous raid.

19. *Wing Commander Guy Gibson (centre) shares a joke with other surviving Dambusters after the Buckingham Palace investiture in which he received the Victoria Cross. On the right is the legendary Micky Martin.*

20. *It is November, 1943, and the Berlin series of raids is under way. There had been heavy losses, but the young crew of R for Robert are back safely with their Stirling bomber.*

radio devices, could be perfected and produced in quantity, more and more reliance was being put on reports from Mosquitoes of Bomber Command's newly-established Meteorological Flight. But the 'Mossies' had to vary their procedures, or the Reichswehr would have been alerted earlier to each night's target, so accuracy of met prediction for a Continental area could only be partial, with the incidence of weather-induced accidents to bombers still alarmingly high.

Atmospheric pressures, with their effects on wind, temperature, cloud and weather generally were much better understood by crews themselves. It was now an established part of flying drill that, when passing through any weather front over Europe, the planes' drift was always to the left; when flying from a high barometric area towards a low one, the altimeter would show a greater height than the true one; and in a climb the wind could be expected to increase and veer clockwise with height— simple facts of navigation when viewed now, but not widely propagated in the earlier years of the war.

Supporting small-scale forecasts, now known as micro-climatology, covering local bomber station areas (and vital to the knowledge of what conditions might be like for planes returning from a long night mission) were even more likely to go wrong. To be fair, weather predicting is the most difficult of sciences even now, as one who checks back on long-range forecasting will know. Even the most conscientious of met men around the bomber stations, constantly checking the combined and changing factors of temperature, pressure, humidity and motion over irregular masses of land and sea, were driven to admit that native country yokels were right as often as they were.

So it was that, partly in self-defence, pilots, co-pilots and navigators with a nose for weather were gathering local lore so that they could anticipate changes in conditions without having to rely entirely on met reports from their 'experts', who tended to be affectionately known as 'guessers'.

Most of the Bomber Command airfields were in the cold dry east of Britain rather than the warm damp west. But it was the extreme local variations to this charted division of climate that came to be looked at more thoughtfully—the area phenomena that could produce thunderstorms over one airfield while its neighbour was in sunshine; that could invoke buffeting squalls at one end of Lincolnshire and breathless calm at the other; that could bring in local fogs at one side of a bay and severe frosts at the other.

Local lore was eagerly gleaned from natives in each bomber area and a surprising amount of it—especially those parts that were based on pure observation—was found to be accurate and helpful. 'A halo round the moon' was an important example that checked out. The strong winds (and rain) it forecast invariably came to pass for the sound reason that the ring was caused by refraction of light through ice-crystal clouds, the forerunners of a warm front with its attendant hard-blowing depression. Similarly, 'mackerel sky and mares' tails make tall ships carry low sails' was a good way of remembering that broken alto-cumulus clouds (resembling a fish's scales) would probably be the fore-runner of fronts bringing wind and rain. Swallows were seen to dip low before rain for the good reason that they were catching bugs unable to fly high because of abnormal humidity in the air . . . which also held good for swarming bees. Red sky (at night or morning) were confirmed as reliable for forecasts of good or bad conditions respectively, and 'clear moon, frost soon' was also soberly approved.

Many of the local sayings were based on an understanding of atmospheric pressures—as with the way changes of pressure can cause creaking bones or aching corns, and can make a drain smell strongly before a storm. And a curious extension of this lore, that might have saved lives had it been taken seriously, was published privately at this time as a semi-scientific thesis on the psychological effects of low-pressure conditions on airmen. The writer was a university-frustrated clerk at the Air Ministry. He propounded the theory, based on his own research, that the most disastrous bomber raids over three years of war had taken place on nights when there had been a sharp drop in barometric pressure. In his private paper he married this fact to general information he had compiled which indicated that in conditions of falling pressure generally, more road accidents

occurred; there were more crimes, suicide attempts, fluffed examina-
tions, and lovers' tiffs; more dogs went mad; more luggage
was left around; more babies were born; and more people got
drunk more easily. He considered from this that crews, with the
many demands on their time while flying, found it less easy to
concentrate and remember drills when the barometer was low.

His incredible report was shelved, to gather dust until the
'seventies, which seems a pity in retrospect. In a footnote on
the part temperature and humidity play in people's lives, he
claimed to have dug out the allied fact that the Bank of
England had a rule earlier in the century that important ledgers
and files were locked away during pea-soup fogs because in
such conditions there was always a dramatic increase in errors
made by the clerks and executives.

Whatever the truth of this last point, fog had continued to
prevent flying on many days and nights for the first three years
of the war—radiation fogs inland on summer nights and advection fogs sweeping in from the sea at all times of the year,
often late on humid afternoons—either type tending sometimes
to hang around for days.

These were bad enough in preventing flying, but when they
swept over much of east and central England unexpectedly,
aided by the belching smoke of its innumerable factory chimneys, while aircraft were away on a raid, they could be, and
often had been, absolutely disastrous. The Bank of England
could well have been right about fog, which seemed to provoke
the sort of madness among bomber crews. Again and again in
cryptic flight logs from the bomber missions of the early 'forties
it is hysterically mentioned. 'Bloody, bloody fog. Drives you
mad, mad', was typical. The black mists appeared to penetrate
the brains of fliers and cause a sort of panic reaction in the
calmest of them. Its vapours threw out judgement of distances,
safety margins, and geometric angles. It caused extreme irritability, recklessness and allied dangers. It was a killer on a major
scale, the more so when it was faced by crews exhausted from
a long mission. Fortunately, by the middle of 1942, help was at
last at hand in this respect for the much-tried crews of Bomber
Command.

Earlier in the year Churchill (ever the enthusiastic dabbler) had instructed the Petroleum Warfare Department to investigate methods of dispersing fog at airfields to enable aircraft to take-off and land in limited visibility. The highly-successful result of this investigation was FIDO (the Fog Investigation Dispersal Operation) in which petrol burners were installed at intervals along the edges of runways and lit to clear the immediate area of fog, while providing additional light for landing. The first FIDO beneficiaries were emergency bomber landing strips of vast proportion at Carnaby (Yorks), Manston (Kent) and Woodbridge (Suffolk). These airfields were chosen because the latest approach-and-landing aids had also been installed there, including GCA (Ground Control Approach). Twelve other bomber stations were to install FIDO before D-day, and altogether 2,524 landings and 182 take-offs were to be achieved in conditions of dense fog during the war, thanks to yet another 'Churchill baby'.

An equally valuable life-saving device simultaneously then in successful operation was an emergency radio system for helping lost and disabled bombers to find their way home. This was known by the code name 'Darkee' and was transmitted on a frequency of 4,220 kilocycles. The radio operator of a plane in trouble could call up Darkee control and, when his signal was received, he would be asked to circle while Darkee tracked him. He would then be given a course to fly on, a barometric setting, and details of the highest obstruction on the route. On arrival above the chosen field, the plane would be talked down. Darkee, in conjunction with FIDO, saved many a bomber in distress and both were a great comfort to many crews under strain. But, generally speaking, radio communication was less satisfactory than it should have been at this stage of the war. Apart altogether from the increased sophistication of German jamming of radio waves, there were all-too-frequent break-downs of equipment, static was often heavy, and laborious emergency messages had to be sent in morse under certain conditions of height or distance.

Meanwhile, as the bombers did their best as ubiquitous raiders, on the home front all was gloom. No white flags were being raised, but white feathers were being handed out to any young man who looked as if he should be in uniform. Perspex rings allegedly made from the windscreens of crashed German planes were all the rage to brighten the greyness of civilian life deprived of luxuries and fenced in by restrictions which had begun to seem endless and pointless. The long and continuing sequence of failures in war had created a sour staleness and an increasing demand for positive action in the shape of a second front.

Set-backs in the sand of the Middle East and grim news from the snows of Stalingrad were bad enough. The degree to which Britain's overseas commands and her Russian allies could be supplied depended directly on the amount of shipping available and here the picture was almost unrelievedly depressing. Sinkings of Allied or neutral merchant shipping at the hands of U-boats alone had run at an average of half-a-million tons a month in the first seven months of 1942 (a total which would have been even higher had not Bomber Command kept U-boats and warships in Norwegian waters, for fear of invasion there). A high proportion of the unbearable total of sinkings up to July, 1942, had taken place on the Atlantic seaboard, owing to the incredible failure of the Americans to introduce a convoy system in this period, or even take the most elementary defensive and offensive sea-air precautions in the area.

One way and another, Churchill's prestige and powers seemed in serious decline. There were rumours that he was ill and that he was to be ousted in favour of Beaverbrook or Sir Samuel Hoare, or was at least about to shed some of his responsibilities. Immediately after the shock of the fall of Tobruk at the end of June, 1942, a motion was placed on the Order Paper in Parliament, which stated: 'That this House, while paying tribute to the heroism and endurance of the Armed Forces of the Crown, has no confidence in the central direction of the war.' The attack was beaten off, but ugly rumours remained that Churchill was 'not the man he had been.' Additionally, left-wing Labour MPs were putting it about that the Prime Minister was deliberately delaying the invasion of Europe so that Germany and Russia would destroy each other and leave most of Europe clear for the big business-style democracy, controlled by America and Britain. Beaverbrook, despite his alleged pre-war demands for compromise, was believed now to be the principal proponement of a speedy invasion of the Continent, and there was undoubtedly some truth in his words that 'the Coalition Government's stock of goodwill . . . was nearing exhaustion'. There had to be victories soon, and Churchill knew it better than most.

Russia's attitude was adding to Winston's restless but frustrated urge to get something positive going. Stalin was still unwilling to accept the difficulties Britain faced in mounting amphibious operations. He continued to scream for a sacrificial landing on the Channel coast, as the only means of drawing off some part of the vast German forces that were moving into Russia. The Americans, too, were urging an early invasion of the Continent, so that they could get on with the war in the Pacific. But, in fact, any such adventure could not be contemplated at least until 1943.

The American bomber force in Britain was building up very slowly and was not yet flying in anger. Roosevelt had undertaken to establish an Army Air Force in the UK of 3,500 operational planes by the spring of 1943 (including seventeen groups of heavy bombers and ten groups of light bombers), but so far there was little sign that such an ambitious target could be achieved. In fact, this particular promise was making things even harder for the RAF. The Americans could no longer afford to allocate to Britain the ordered planes—one-third of our total estimated supply for 1942—agreed the year before, and on which we had been counting; and this at a time when the ever-more-urgent plan for a cross-Channel invasion was aggravating the war-material priority situation and causing the Air Ministry to have to fight ever harder against the Admiralty and the Army to keep the bomber programme going even reasonably well.

After many anxious consultations with his Chiefs of Staff, Churchill had come to the conclusion that the best practical method of attack available to him in 1942—in addition to Bomber Command's efforts in Europe—would be an invasion of North Africa, to be code-named Operation Torch, and he managed to persuade Roosevelt that this had to be the next move, against the claims of US General Marshall who wanted a second front in Europe before anything else. So it was that, in late July, Roosevelt nominated General Dwight D. Eisenhower (already established with a planning HQ in London) to take charge of Torch as a joint British-American enterprise.

That this was the right decision could scarcely be denied when, early in August, a large-scale exploratory raid was made on the French port of Dieppe by 5,000 Canadian troops and 1,000 British Commandos, resulting in casualties of about 60 per cent of the numbers engaged. We simply were not ready to cross the Channel with any hope of success. More than sixty squadrons from Bomber and other commands had supported this abortive raid and whereas the RAF had lost over 100 valuable aircraft, the Luftwaffe's losses totalled around fifty. The Bomber Command AOC-in-C then had again to use his direct-access-to-Churchill advantage to persuade the PM to allocate the production priorities he now needed even more desperately.

Meanwhile, in the midst of these unforeseen losses, and the torture of all his quart-in-a-pint-pot problems in July and August of 1942, Harris had somehow also found the time to think deeply about his urgently nagging idea for conserving and suitably employing the rapidly diminishing number of his veteran crews, as part of his general re-thinking and re-planning of Bomber Command.

Harris was inordinately fond of his 'old lags' as he called them, but it had always disturbed him that they tended to throw themselves into more 'ops'. If and when they finished a tour, they would try every trick to avoid the compulsory six months' rest period (usually spent coaching crews in advanced training units) and to get back into action. It was almost a sickness, this fevered impulse to go on and on. Sometimes there were reasons that were even deeper than keenness to get on with the job and finish the war. With the Poles it was a bitter, enduring hatred of the Germans. With some British boys it was perhaps the urge to get revenge for families killed in the Blitz. It could even be a semi-neurotic death-wish. Whatever it was, these were lives that had to be fulfilled while being conserved. They had to be allowed to take part in missions but in expert (and at the same time safer) roles.

Massed in with inexperienced crews in raids they were too often shot down or collided with or picked off by fighters unnecessarily in the general melee, as if they were 'just another crew'. They had specialised experience and the feeling had been growing in Harris that they should be given specialist jobs.

After early doubts, Harris had come round to persuading himself that by siphoning off his old lags in a specialist squadron (and later a group) he was doing them a favour and helping bombing accuracy at the same time. They could become 'shepherds' to the inexperienced, the more so as efficient new navigational and bomb-aiming devices would shortly become available. This would give the veterans job-satisfaction and could at the same time give them a stronger chance of survival. At one time he had thought that such a move might have the opposite effect and cause the slaughter of the sophisticates. But a careful study of casualty statistics had shown that the leading planes invariably got through in a raid, whereas the following streams suffered most from all causes.

So it was that, in August, 1942, a Pathfinder unit was designated in each Group, as a first move in this direction—a move due to which the whole bombing picture was to be changed for the rest of the war.

The idea was that skilled pathfinder aircraft, with the most efficient skippers and the most accurate of navigators and bomb-aimers could fly in first to find and light a target quickly. The rest of the mainly-inexperienced armada could then follow on in, with a minimum of difficulty or delay, and bomb where they saw the pathfinders' markers. Speed had become as important as accuracy. Many bombers had been lost in the five giant raids because it had taken up to two hours to pass all the planes through the heavily defended target areas. With efficient pathfinding this period could be cut to well under an hour.

So it was that some of the finest remaining crews in Bomber Command found themselves in line for 'promotion' to a body which was to have no equal anywhere in the world—in sheer brilliance of techniques and of courageous initiative.

The Pathfinders, becoming the key to the AOC-in-C's dramatic new plan for his Command, would make general bombing more accurate and more dreadful for the German people. They would also beget the incredible dambusters—the greatest fliers and back-up crewmen of all time.

Alas, as the old lags, and the new young 'aces' who had come to the fore, took up their specialist roles, so the rest of Bomber Command would inevitably lose much of its spirit, its colour and its individuality, diluted in quality as it was increased in quantity. For the chosen few, the great days of precision bombing were at hand. For the main mass of crews, there would be little to look forward to other than the nightmare routine of taking-off, flying inexorably to a target, and getting back perhaps once more . . . perhaps not. For the many, eighteen ops was now to be the statistical maximum, and nearly everyone not lacking in moral fibre was to be asked to exceed that number and accept the inevitable, awful consequences.

Chapter Thirteen

The vital and virile pathfinding plan was just part of the AOC-in-C's general re-thinking of his Command in the summer of 1942. A complete new deal was overdue and the time was right for setting it up and carrying it through while squadrons were being re-equipped with four-engined bombers and while re-training of crews was proceeding apace.

In a sense, Harris's re-thinking was actually a form of pioneering. The sort of bombing he had been working up to since he took command six months before, and which now had to be defined and scheduled, was something completely novel. It had never been attempted anywhere in the world before.

An impatient and irascible man, 'Bomber' Harris suffered fools not at all and could jump equally heavy on scientists, politicians and top service brass if they tried to waste his valuable time with impractical schemes or half-baked ideas. But he knew where his greatest fount of knowledge and fund of inspiration lay. Tirelessly he questioned crews personally on what was going wrong in raids and on what they felt were the remediable deficiencies in their equipment. It was a waste of time talking to staff officers about why bombs were missing targets, about why collisions were so frequent, or about the chances of rescue after dead-stick landings in the North Sea. Direct man-to-man communications with experienced crews were the basis for many of the notes he made in order to give yet more vitality to a still imperfect bombing force.

Nothing escaped his attention. One of the first of his many new orders (issued as personal directives in the blunt language that characterised his no-nonsense attitudes) was to the effect that in future no wives would be allowed to live within an hour's drive of a bomber base. Only those already living out were exempted temporarily from this rule. All-out war was all-out dedicated hard work, in Harris's view. There could no longer be any room for sentiment. The enemy had to be the target for everyone's thoughts and deeds every day and in every way. Womenfolk had to keep out of the way until the war was won. Men could drink and share experiences in man-talk. Discipline and purpose would thereby be tighter and stronger. It was a hard rule from a hard man, but Harris followed it himself by working faster, longer and with more dedication than anyone.

WAAFs were a different thing from wives. They were creatures in uniform. They could take it. They blended into the scene. More and more of them began to take over airmen's jobs, to release greater numbers of men for aircrew. They manned bowsers and crew transport. They took over stores and even did engineering maintenance work. None became aircrew, although plenty volunteered when it was heard (rightly or wrongly) in 1942 that Russia had an all-woman bomber squadron.

Harris approved of the orders permitting WAAFs to take on a wide range of duties. It suited his overall purpose. But no one around his monastic, hutted HQ would have believed that he actually *noticed* any of the 'beauty chorus' (as they were known) who were working in his vicinity.

But the greatest of Harris's concerns in mid-1942 was to get more and more bombs on the target area. He still had fewer than 500 first-line planes and crews available to him for any raid. Mass-bombing would come again next year. For now, if he could increase accuracy, he would increase power. Previously only a quarter of the bombs dropped on Germany had hit the targets. Any improvement in accuracy would be equivalent to an improvement in numbers. One hundred per cent accuracy would be equivalent to quadrupling his bomber strength. Such were the vital facts he hammered away at, day after day, in his modest hut at High Wycombe as those around him sweated blood to find the ways and means to achieve such miracles.

One of the earliest and simplest ideas for boosting information, and so providing a basis for detailed criticism and improvement, was an extension of the camera scheme. In recent months a number of planes had carried cameras on raids, and the photographic evidence had indicated just how far off the mark the aiming was. Now the order went out for all squadrons to become photograph-minded. More and more planes were to have cameras slung in the bomb-bays.

The result was that, when the bomb-aimer pressed the tit to release his load, the camera shutter opened and remained that way until a flash bomb went off at about 3,000 feet, just in time to light up the bursting bombs beneath. This would show within a few hundred yards the area bombed. It was a simple idea, which immediately cut out the bluffing and line-shooting some crews had previously indulged in. It had the effect of ensuring that more crews would try harder to press home their attacks. Where COs were tough with their men, the fear of a roasting was usually greater than the fear of facing up to flak over the target. Crews still came home with pictures of open fields, but fewer and fewer of them.

Additionally, a very English scheme was allied to the camera one. This was to award points to all whose photo-plots showed they had obtained bulls-eyes and on a decreasing scale to those claiming 'outers'. Ladders were drawn on walls of squadrons, groups and at Command HQ. Everyone, from the AOC-in-C downwards knew thereafter which were the top crews and which the top squadrons. It was very public school, and all that, but it worked.

Harris had the knack (which Montgomery also possessed) of making his men feel that they were very much part of his grand scheme and that what they said and thought mattered. Crews had been long troubled at having to fly on routes prepared by backroom boys with no recent experience of conditions in the Ruhr and in other heavily defended parts of German-occupied Europe. In addition to having to cross the twenty-mile wide belt of searchlights and guns the Reichswehr had set defensively across Europe, on the way out *and* on the way back, they were often asked to pass over stoutly defended cities on the way to their main target. The night fighter 'zones' had also become fairly well known to crews—the main ones being between the Ruhr and the Danish border—but apparently not equally well to the route-makers.

Active participation in raid planning by experienced squadron

commanders was an imaginative answer. Under Harris's new thinking, it was resolved, where there was time and opportunity, to allow
final routes and flight plans to be decided by the chaps in the
squadrons who had to do the jobs; conferences were in future
to be arranged on suitably scrambled telephones an hour or so
before briefings whenever possible. Altitudes and bombing
heights, according to knowledge of German defences, were also
to be a matter for such discussions. This way, crews would feel
themselves to be more in the picture and would be able to
approach their tasks in a happier frame of mind.

Improvisation, together with trial and error, inevitably had to
form part of the re-organisation of the bomber force. Manpower
shortages were difficult to deal with. The increases in crews,
from four to seven in the new bombers against the old, had to
be made up somehow or other, and there was an extreme
shortage in flight engineers in particular—a new crew position.
Suitable men were rounded up wherever they could be found.

Some suitable volunteers came from groundcrew, but not
many. The gap between the fliers and their support was widen-
ing all the time, as between natural leaders and bread-and-butter
workers. The air force was unique in this respect in that it was
the only fighting service where a tiny section of each unit did
the most dangerous job of the war, while the largest part did
one of the safest. It led to resentments and problems, but on
the whole relationships between aircrew and groundcrew were
good. In the main, the latter had their frustrations in the place
of dangers.

Another source of material lay in volunteers from other
services overseas. But as often as not these were the wrong
types altogether—disgruntled and complaining blokes who
imagined that by volunteering for aircrew they were going to
have a trip home *and* an easier life in the future.

At first, in conversion to heavy bombers, each squadron was
given a third flight, commanded by a 'rested' flier of experience,
but later separate conversion units were established. Crews had
to fit in periods of training in which they got in a dozen hours
or thereabouts on new types of aircraft and learned the more
complicated cockpit drills, becoming in a few weeks more or

less proficient in heavy bomber techniques. Keen types even volunteered to make up crews in jobs other than their own, and such were the shortages of trained men that it became nothing for a good man to fly a dozen trips with different crews and in different crew positions—as gunner, wireless-operator, engineer, or even navigator—knowing only some of the drills required.

Meanwhile, more airfields were also needed, and existing runways had to be lengthened and/or strengthened to take four-engined planes. Even harder work was put in hand at the bases: more paper work, armament preparation, fuel tanking, and general administration. Attempts were made to get everyone working flat out, from airfield contractors to ground crews.

Aircraft with new experimental devices aboard had to be guarded day and night, and the new RAF regiment was given this as an added task, their main job being the general defence of airfields. Security was one of Harris's pet topics. He subscribed to the poster theme, in use at the time, that 'careless talk costs lives'. It was not easy, with so many people involved in each bombing raid, from WAAFs in Ops Rooms to waiters in ante-rooms, to maintain absolute surprise and security on a mission, but, by God, Harris was determined to get it every time. One of the worries was drink. The AOC-in-C was in favour of his boys having plenty. He was no kill-joy. But they normally drank so much when not standing-by, that it just had to be noticed in public places that most crewmen laid off the hard stuff religiously before a 'big show', knowing and respecting the dangers of 'flying on the bottle'. So they would tend to sit there being polite and making their cans of beer last as long as possible, while strangers got to guessing that something important was afoot. A warning to keep away from hostelries, unless resting for a day or two at a time, was therefore issued.

The question of what to do if unlucky enough to be taken prisoner had also come up in conversations between the AOC-in-C and his skippers. So a series of *amusing* instructional films was made and shown around crew rooms. The humour was appreciated and got the messages over strongly. Punching the message by this means was a new departure in service education; alas, it was soon to be shelved. For the record, someone had had the brilliant idea of using Naunton Wayne as the typical Wing Commander and Anton Walbrook as the personification of the German officer. The interplay in the 'plot' was delicious, with the Germans trying to get the British crew drunk in the mess in order to pump them for information about aircraft and new scientific devices. But the serious points were put over strongly, with emphasis on the fact that the more senior the officer the tougher the interviewing techniques. There was much value in these warnings when it is remembered how many bomber crews became prisoners.

Various ideas for preventing crew and plane losses through collisions were discussed with flight captains on the one hand and scientists on the other. With even a few hundred miscellaneous bombers flying around a target area at different speeds and heights, maybe in conditions of cloud or mist, such disasters were inevitable (the more so when you consider that even nowadays a very few planes flying in open sky above airfields in daylight can have near-misses, controlled though they are by traffic controllers and computers).

The dangers were the greater now that the Germans were jamming radio communication and navigational boxes with ever-more success. In such circumstances, virtually anything could happen up there. Nothing new was offered to prevent collisions (or the other hazard of bombs from a plane above striking a friendly plane beneath) except ever-better disciplines and keener planning. Towards this, still more practice bombing flights were arranged, even for crews who thought themselves above such things, with the incentives again of points being awarded for flying and bombing. Sensibly, practice bombing was carried out from greater heights (as, for example, 18,000 feet in the case of Lancasters and Halifaxes) which was more like the real thing, as against the 5,000-10,000 feet that had been previously used in training. With bomb-sights still elderly and unsatisfactory until the new ones came forward later in the year, night aiming was still rough and ready, within accuracy of a quarter of a mile considered very good for the inexperienced.

Even more dangerously, a number of 'special' Lancaster squadrons began practising mass low-level formation attacks, aimed at outwitting German radar and generally achieving surprise. This technique was tried, first in squadrons, then in wings and finally at group strength. It was extremely hazardous, and led to many crashes, especially when the almost-wing-tip-to-wing-tip formation levelled out for the practice bomb-in. But such techniques were to be tried out ever more in the grim do-or-die years still to come.

To 'blood' new crews and ease them into their headaches more gradually, a programme of raids on less well-defended targets was arranged. These raids had the added useful effect of tending to confuse the enemy and dissipate his defences.

The old idea of bringing bombs back if the primary target could not be seen was now dropped completely. In the new all-out policy, crews were instructed to off-load on *any* heavily built-up area as an alternative to the chosen target. If the resultant explosion killed a few Germans, the trip had been worthwhile. Dummy 'raids' to confuse the German defences were much used.

One way and another, Bomber Command was helping to contain in Germany, France, Scandinavia, the Low Countries, and the Mediterranean, nearly half the total strength of the Luftwaffe (as well as about fifty divisions of troops, and 10,000 dual-purpose AA and Anti-Tank guns, with crews and ammunition), and Harris was determined to keep things that way. Churchill had recently flown from Cairo (where he was seeing for himself what could be done at Alamein) to Moscow, to tell Stalin firmly that there could be 'no second front until 1943', because of shortages of tanks and amphibious vessels; and because of the futility of going off half-cock on such a momentous adventure. The reception had been frigid, but by tough and eloquent talking he had thawed it a little. As he told Sir Arthur Harris after his return, Bomber Command's activities were an important card in his otherwise weak hand. He had told the Russian dictator that the strategic bomber offensive was now being fought over the Reich rather than England, and that this was the battle for supremacy on which future battles very much depended.

In one of his few cordial moments, Churchill recalled, Stalin had spoken with obvious admiration of the gallantry of the RAF, although he tended to play down and even disregard its strategic importance. The PM's generally encouraging words sent Harris back to his exhausting routine refreshed, and determined that more and more bombs would fall accurately. The German plan now was

to drive east both in Russia and North Africa, to link up somewhere in the Persian Gulf area. With stalemate the temporary
situation in the western desert, and Malta the only base available in
the Med, a great deal depended on Bomber Command's efforts over
Europe—the only means until 1943 of letting the German people
know there was a war on. Ever more furiously, the AOC-in-C set
about improving the skills and strengths of his bombing force.

New bombs were coming to the fore at long last, with better
explosives, and, as part of his new plan, Harris had given the green
light to a much-neglected inventor, Barnes Wallis, to produce
'specials' of several agreed types. There was also produced a 'pink
pansy.' This was a 250-pound incendiary which glowed in a fluor-
escent way for about fifteen minutes and could be seen through fog.
The idea was that leading planes should carry these if ground fog or
cloud was expected. But this was very much a period of bluff and
counter-bluff. In no time at all, the Germans would rumble this
device, and would 'plant' pink pansies in open spaces all over the
Ruhr ready to decoy the British bombers whenever an opportunity
presented itself.

An anti-capital-ship bomb had also come to hand which, it was
claimed, could knock out the biggest battleship in one go. Alas, its
ballistic behaviour left much to be desired. Unless it was dropped
from about 1,000 feet, it zig-zagged; at which height (as had been
shown all too recently in the Norwegian fjords) at least 50 per cent
losses could be expected to ship-borne flak. Dropped from comparatively safe altitudes, it would swing unpredictably off course. So,
back to the drawing-boards and the test ranges went the armaments
experts, to improve the turnip-like shape of their new baby. It was a
touchy business, the bombing of German battleships. No one had
forgotten (from Churchill down) how the *Scharnhorst* and
Gneisenau, or the 'Salmon and Gluckstein', as crews came to name
them, had been bombed for a year and had still escaped (admittedly
in bad weather) up the Channel, under everyone's noses, at a
moment chosen by them.

Mines were being dropped in shipping lanes in ever-increasing
numbers, so an improved technique was worked out for this also.
The drill was to fly low and fast (avoiding radar and fighter
interception) until the chosen area was reached and then pop up to

13—TLC * *

about 5,000 feet for a quick radio fix. This was achieved by switching on to transmit, counting one-to-ten, while three radio-fixer stations got bearings, being told the exact point to move to, and diving down again to sow the mines as instructed. It resulted in a dramatic cutting down of losses from these missions.

Better planning was very obviously the chief answer to many of the problems that had bedevilled Bomber Command in recent months. Short Stirlings, for instance, had been suffering heavier losses than other types because it had been necessary to send them in on raids in company with higher-flying Lancs and Halifaxes. Fully loaded (and their maximum load was *never* impressive) the Stirling often refused to climb much above 13,000 feet. The result, in difficult night and cloud conditions, had been hair-raising stories, told by lucky-to-survive crews at de-briefing, of bundles of 3-pounder and 50-pounder incendiaries spiking their way through Stirling wings or burning into the fuselage . . . apart altogether from disasters to neighbouring planes from HE bombs falling on them. Stirlings were also more vulnerable to flak and searchlights than were the other four-engined types. As a part-answer, Stirlings were allocated more suitable, less well-defended targets when possible, and they were chosen for flights to North Italy, to hit the Italians and help the struggle in the Middle East.

Better runway surfaces were also needed at Stirling bomber bases. Their take-offs were still slightly dodgy, with their high undercarriages and comparatively high gross weight, and they could swing alarmingly—a fault that could be fatally aggravated by grass and mud. But their manoeuvrability and robustness when flying were important pluses. Some had even returned safely from 1,000-bomber raids after colliding with one another in the clouds, or with whole sections of the fuselage torn away by flak.

Special-duty squadrons of Stirlings became part of Harris's new plan and, from the late summer of 1942, they were to fly from Tempsford (Beds) on very important missions, to which they were well-suited, dropping supplies, infiltrators and saboteurs into occupied territories. They were also to be sent on more and more mine-laying operations and on radio counter-measure flights in the hotting-up game of bluffing the Hun.

Twin-engined Manchesters, too, were suffering many crashes.

They were extremely difficult to fly if one motor was knocked out. It was now decided to phase them out completely to other tasks.

The vulnerable Bristol Blenheim, on which Bomber Command had had to depend almost exclusively in 1939-40, had already been taken out of service and the Mark V (known as the 'Bisley') was being used, with night-simulation filters fitted, for round-the-clock training at OTUs. The pretty tadpole shape of the Hampden (which had been involved in the five big raids of the spring and summer of 1942) was to be transferred to Coastal Command in September, in a torpedo-bomber role, and would also join the Russian air force in some numbers. After three years of almost continuous action, it was no longer wanted by Bomber Command. The 'flying barn doors', the Whitleys, which had been Britain's only night bomber specialist force in the early days of the war in 4 Group were also retired from bombing under the new plan, although they would continue in service for another year in leaflet dropping and as freighters. The ubiquitous Wellington, the most docile and distinguished of the 'twins', was to remain in first line service, and would continue to do so until October, 1943. Affectionately known as the 'Wimpy' (after Popeye's cartoon friend, the portly J. Wellington Wimpy) it would also have a temporary role to play for some months in pathfinding. The Wellington VIII had at this period been fitted with Leigh Light equipment (together with ASV Mark II radar) and was to do much useful new work, by means of these sophisticated aids, in finding and destroying U-boats by night.

Halifaxes and Lancasters were the all-important planes in the new scheme of things. The former, although not so elegant as the Lancs, were extremely versatile and reliable, to the point that four out of every ten bombers to be built from this time would be Halifaxes.

The Lancaster was to become everyone's favourite bomber, with its pleasing looks, its simplicity, and its rugged strength. Indeed, the AOC-in-C thought so highly of it, he was to describe it in his memoirs as 'the finest bomber of the war', adding significantly: 'Its efficiency was almost incredible, both in performance and in the way it could be saddled with ever-increasing loads without breaking the "camel's back". The Lancaster far surpassed all other types of heavy bomber. Not only was it easier to handle, and not only were there fewer accidents with this than with other types, the casualty rate was also consistently below that of all other types.'

'Bomber' Harris had found his ideal aeroplane with which to show the Germans that war did not pay. Although the Lancaster was now to be built in Canada and other parts of the Allied world, as well as in the UK, all too few were being produced at this particular period. But it was the perfect plane for most pathfinding tasks and it was to this vital purpose that the AOC-in-C was to put the Lancaster bomber for the rest of 1942.

Chapter Fourteen

The Pathfinder squadrons, under the command of a brilliant
ex-airline pilot, Group Captain D. C. T. Bennett, who had led
the raid on the *Tirpitz* at Aasen Fjord (and who had *walked* home
via Sweden, after being shot down), had been sent with Avro
Lancasters to new airfields, at the end of July, 1942, where they
were practising the new techniques that had been evolved about
the middle of August. 'Bomber' Harris, who had got Bennett his
appointment, has described him to me as 'the most efficient airman
ever and brave as a lion'.

Radio and allied technology was beginning to work in harness
with general aircraft development to produce devices to suit
particular types of plane and their functions. Whiz-kids from the
universities, who could think ahead imaginatively, and who
believed in the technical conquest of the air, had begun to make
their presence felt among the more elderly scientsts entrenched
at the Air Ministry as well as in the research and development
establishments. The arriving Americans were also putting bombs
under a few safe seats by questioning techniques at a high level
and criticising them, sometimes taking the infuriating line that
they were a breed of supermen talking to 'war weary Limeys'.
The lion had put up with having its tail twisted by its enemies
but when its friends did the same thing, it rose to its feet and
snarled. This was partly pride and partly a desire to impress and
keep up with our most important ally. There were fewer illusions
now. Thinking people realised that without America's manpower,
wealth and productivity, the war could not be speedily concluded. Some of the criticisms levelled by the tough-talking top
brass of the USAAF, who were now descending on Britain in
increasing numbers, was half-baked, but more than a little was

valid. The application of fresh eyes, ears and intellects to the bomber scene had an energising and almost effervescent effect in open-minded quarters.

American planes were good and bad, as ours were. But in the main they were gadget-packed limousines as against our somewhat spartan tin-lizzies. And they were alleged to have spot-on bomb-sights for precision aiming.

The Boeing B-17E Flying Fortresses which began arriving at English airfields allocated to 2nd USAAF groups on 1 August, 1942, were something of the order of Cadillacs in terms of their interior comforts and sophistications. They were also powerful air weapons, fairly heavily armed and substantially armoured, which could carry three tons of bombs, at an excellent operational height of 26,000 feet, but at a not-too-impressive maximum speed of 280 mph. British crews' attitudes to neighbouring Fortresses were a mixture of awe, mickey-taking and cynicism. How could they survive, these boastful bastards? It would be the slaughter of the know-all innocents. They didn't know what was ahead of them.

American policy was to bomb in daylight. The American Air Staff, under General H. H. Arnold, knew that they could not develop their full strength in Europe for another year; but they were determined to have a go, in their own fashion, on a small scale at the earliest possible date, thereby to show that the Eighth Air Force was no mere adjunct to Britain's Bomber Command, but a totally separate element in a military alliance.

It was to be proved to be fortuitous that UK and US strategists had pursued, according to their convictions, opposite bombing policies, in that this division of policy would lead in due course to round-the-clock bombing of the Reich which would do more to break the German spirit than a combined effort by night could ever have achieved. Not everyone could see this, and there was a certain bitterness in the working-up stages between British bombing strategists and their American opposite numbers (although no ill-feeling existed between commanders, who became the best of friends, and remain so today).

The more enlightened could already see that British and American aircraft types were complementary, rather than overlapping, and this, happily, would lead to an ad-mixture of combat planes neither country would have achieved alone. US production efforts had been concentrated on long-range day bombers plus patrol aircraft, transports and a considerable number of medium-to-light day bombers. They had already advanced the air transport situation for the Allies by undertaking the mass-production of virtually all the transport planes required for all Allied air forces. In 1942, indeed, nearly one-third of the total American productive effort was being devoted to the manufacture of such types.

Boeing B-17s had been tried out by Bomber Command some months previously. They had been rejected as night bombers partly because their roaring exhaust flames had given the game away to the disastrous detriment of the entire night forces with which they had flown. And in daylight, three RAF-manned B-17Cs (known to Bomber Command as Fortress Is) had all been destroyed by German fighters on a sortie to Norway. The remaining planes were relegated to Coastal Command and to the Middle East. Bomber Command did not think much of them.

The Boeing B-17E was an improved version in all respects, and the American strategic idea was that waves of Fortresses (which now possessed stronger armaments, affording the defensive cross-fire of hundreds of guns) should fly at very high altitudes, in close formation and with fighter support.

The first batch of 1,800 US 8th AF airmen and eighteen planes to arrive in Britain was commanded by Brigadier-General Ira C. Eaker, a hard man and an experienced professional flier. His ten-crew Fortresses had been flown in via Labrador, Greenland, Iceland, Northern Ireland and Prestwick, Scotland—a total distance of 4,000 miles. He quickly tough-talked himself into a 'blooding' mission for his crews, with RAF fighter support, and on 17 August—less than six months after the American bombing concept had first been committed to paper—he personally led twelve of his B-17Es, of 97 Bombardment Group, escorted by Spitfires, on the very first US bombing raid. Appropriately and characteristically, his own plane had the name Yankee Doodle emblazoned across its fuselage.

A short-range target had been chosen—the marshalling yards at Sotteville-les-Rouen on the left bank of the Seine, while another six flew on a diversionary sweep. All eighteen Fortresses returned safely having had moderate success in terms of accuracy. Ten further missions to nearby targets on the occupied coasts of Europe followed over a period of a few weeks, all with strong support from Britain's Fighter Command, and only two Fortresses were lost over that period. Inevitably the boys of Bomber Command sneered at these tentative and inconclusive efforts, as they got on with the job of hurting the Hun in his homelands.

The first Pathfinder-led British bombing raid was launched a few days after Eaker's baptism of fire. The second pilot in each Lancaster had been abolished. Specialised bomb-aimers had taken over the vacant place, allowing observer types to become specialist navigators. Each Pathfinder Lancaster therefore carried a pilot, the Captain, up front, with the engineer alongside him; plus a navigator, bomb-aimer, wireless operator, mid-upper gunner and rear gunner at their places in the fuselage and tail of the graceful, responsive aeroplane.

These 'leader' aircraft were adapted to carry a comparatively light load of incendiary flare bombs, plus cameras and extra fuel, and no heavy bombs at all. They therefore had greater speed, manoeuvrability and height than the bulk of the Lancs on a mission. The Pathfinders were split into 'finders' and 'illuminators'. The idea was for the leading squadron to fly on a course of extreme accuracy some time ahead of the main force. Until later in the year, when cockpit radar devices would become available, they had to use dead reckoning—on precisely worked out headings, ground-speeds and ETA's—to reach the target, so a great deal depended still on the skills of the navigators. Having spotted the target, the finders would retreat and drop a flare every thirty seconds, from a point ten miles nearer England. This would light the way clearly for the following streams. Meanwhile, the illuminators would have been hovering around above and they would now dump bunch upon bunch of flares (some suspended on parachutes) and incendiaries on the heart of the target itself, seeking to make it as bright as daylight, while the finders turned and flew across the line they had already laid, putting down an intersecting stream of flares, doubly showing by the crossing of the two lines the exact point at which the following bombers should aim. Such was the basic idea, although variations were introduced in the light of early experience. A marker back-up squadron followed the Pathfinders (leading in the first wave of bombers) in case the original markers were shot down, or failed in some way to light the target.

Inevitably, as with any new force, there were difficulties and disasters on some of the early Pathfinder-led raids.

The first mission went off well. It was launched on the night of 18-19 August and was directed against shipbuilding yards at Flensburg in Schleswig Holstein. The new techniques were proved to be infinitely better at lighting up the target and giving a clearer aiming point. A mixed force of 300 bombers was led through the target area in less than an hour with only 3 per cent losses and photographs showed that the harbour and naval base of the Baltic port had suffered considerable damage.

In bright moonlight on 1-2 September the Pathfinders set out for Saarbrucken, on the Franco-German frontier, with its important iron, steel and engineering industries. This time there was a straight boob in navigation by the leading planes, and the wrong target was 'found' and illuminated. The result was that 1,200 tons of bombs (including several 8,000 pounders, being carried for the very first time) completely flattened Saarlouis, a small town of no importance about ten miles from the city of Saarbrucken.

Incredibly, the same sort of thing happened seven days later when the Pathfinders lit up a satelite town instead of Frankfurt for a combined British-Canadian force. The error this time was smaller, and it led to an unplanned bonus when an Opel truck factory, which happened to be in the illuminated area, was plastered with bombs.

A bang-on-target success followed, on 10-11 September, when the Pathfinder Force led 250 bombers in a substantially-accurate attack on the industrial centre of Dusseldorf. But on 13-14 September there was again a disaster when the markers and their followers failed, for various reasons, to illuminate Bremen. The following waves of bombers lost their way, got scattered, dropped bombs over a wide area of the Ruhr and lost twenty-two of their number to flak, fighters and through mid-air collisions.

Six days later an attempted raid on Munich was equally disastrous. Cloud all the way to the target dispersed the Pathfinders as well as the main bomber force, resulting in heavy casualties. Weather was still a major enemy where a course depended on dead reckoning. The Germans were now jamming Gee to the point that it was virtually useless as an aid. Errors of navigation (which inevitably crept in, even with highly-skilled Pathfinder crews) when flying through cloud, could prove frighteningly hazardous for a mass bomber force, depending on its leaders, and this Munich raid was a depressing one for the AOC-in-C and his staff. And a subsequent failure at Flensburg, on 23-24 September, when heavy ground fog was the disrupting hazard and the attacking force was again scattered dismally, led to 'a pulling in of horns' until the promised navigational aids could be secured for the Pathfinders, probably in December.

Meanwhile a pathfinderless raid by a strong force of Lancasters had successfully attacked Mainz, in bright moonlight, from only 5,000 feet, and had devastated 135 acres of the fortified Rhine city with only 2 per cent losses. And a small force of Lancs had returned safely from the longest raid of the war so far, having flown 1,760 miles to attack shipyards at Danzig, Poland.

Although the British Air Staff were still as opposed to daylight raids as the Americans were committed to them, the Mosquito was still being used, when the opportunity presented itself, to hit the headlines with daring stings at the enemy's rump. The great virtue of the 'Mossie' as a bomber was that it could make pin-point attacks to a degree of accuracy not possessed by any other plane, and it could invariably get safely through any target at speed, by means of a technique of combining dive attacks with low level passes, to the confusion of the Reichswehr. This was the means used on 25 September for a daring attack by Mosquitoes of 105 Squadron on Gestapo HQ at Oslo, Norway. They damaged the building with dramatic accuracy, gave heart to the local 'underground' and returned safely to their base at Bourn, Cambridge, to the plaudits of the populace.

But by night it was mainly the same old story. Bravery (and the Pathfinders were outstandingly the possessors of this commodity) had little relation to the success or failure of mass-bombing raids. A dangerous mission could be carried out with skill, courage and minimal casualties. What should have been a simple, routine raid, over a lightly defended target, could suddenly turn into a nightmare filled with death and disaster. The weather was still the enemy of which no inspired planning could take reliable account. The scientific establishments again got the thick end of Harris's tongue, and the Pathfinder squadrons were committed to still more practice.

Weather forecasting, too, became the object for further frustrated criticism. Statistical examination of photographic evidence from the earlier mass-raid on Bremen had shown that the bulk of the bombs had been dropped around the Ruhr countryside to the south-west of the city for the simple reason that the wind had strengthened and changed direction after take-off and no one had told the crews. Too often the story was that when the weather was good, the raid was good; when the weather was bad, the raid was bad.

Not a few of the best Pathfinder pilots, bomb-aimers and navigators now undergoing rigorous training were Canadians, which was not surprising in view of the overall strength and quality of Royal Canadian Air Force units and independent RCAF crews in Britain. Harris was in no two minds about their abilities. 'We in Bomber Command,' he said simply, 'regard our Canadian group and Canadian crews outside the group as among the very best.'

The RCAF was already well on the way to becoming the fourth largest airforce for the Allied cause, and its largest overseas formation was about to be established as No. 6 Bomber Group, stationed around Yorkshire and held in much affection by the blunt Northerners with whom they mixed freely. They were as keen as they were tough and Bomber Command regarded the RCAF bomber squadrons as the equal of any in the country.

Canadian crews generally ranged from veteran bush pilots, who had pioneered the unrolling of the map of dominion in the 'thirties, to teenagers of equal spirit. The first RCAF bomber squadron, No. 405, had been flying in anger against the Reich since April, 1941, first with Wellingtons and then with Halifaxes. It had been commanded, since February, 1942, by J. E. Fauquier, a brilliant 33-year old flier who had logged 300,000 air miles as a bush-hopper in the wild Canadian west before joining up. He was to switch to Lancasters and lead his 'Vancouver' Squadron on many pathfinding raids in the course of becoming the only RCAF flier to win the triple DSO; and he would eventually take proud command of the part-Canadian Dambusters Squadron and he almost dropped the first ever 22,000-pound bomb. Unfortunately, his aircraft became u/s before take-off, and on attempting to take over that of Squadron Leader Jock Calder was thwarted when Calder, ignoring RT instructions, turned his tail towards the Canadian and left the latter standing there remonstrating vociferously through a cloud of dust. Fauquier was greatly respected by Arthur Harris and contributed many suggestions at this stage for the improvement of the Pathfinder Force.

The Canadian aspect of the re-named British Commonwealth Air Training Plan had by now contributed a number of ace fliers to the RAF, and one of the volunteer skippers of No. 35 'Pathfinder' Squadron, RAF, from the earliest days at Linton-on-Ouse, was a young Canadian, R. J. Lane, who had taken part in the Trondheim and Brest raids, and who had been awarded the DFC after the first of the 1,000-bomber raids. Lane was a 'natural,' who took to flying and pathfinding like Heifitz took to the violin, and Harris quickly earmarked him as an instructor of pathfinders in a new school that was to be established at Gransden Lodge.

The Commonwealth Air Training Plan had been set up at Camp Borden in May, 1940, and had spread to several hundred schools and ancillary units across the country, centred initially on airports built for Trans-Canada Airways, and already complete with hangars, meteorological facilities and radio aids. The scheme was now turning out nearly 2,000 graduates a month, trained to appreciably high standards by private fliers, World War I veterans and tested 'old lags' from Britain. Navigation schools were operated by civilian firms expert in such techniques. Recruiting standards were extremely high, as they could be in a country where every other young man wanted to fly and where increasing numbers of refugees from Europe also wanted to join up. Navigation was, if anything, superior to the best in Britain, largely as a result of the ease of identification, and bomb-aiming was an important part of the appropriate courses.

After they had won their Observer wing, graduates (one-third of whom were commissioned; two-thirds of sergeant rank) were sent to an Air Navigation school, where they were taught advanced navigational skills. Wireless operators had equally tough courses, taking in morse and lamp signalling as well as RT, and the Canadian gunnery ranges were among the most advanced in the world.

In response to pleas from Britain, in July, 1942, the Canadian Training Plan was extended (as a sort of Empire university of flying) with an increase from fifty-eight to sixty-seven training schools (including twenty-one double-sized ones), and ten advanced schools were added. The RCAF also assumed control of twenty-seven RAF units that had now been established in Canada, and these also became up-to-date training units. In addition, post-graduate training now came under the jurisdiction of the Empire Scheme, and a plan was implemented for giving different aircrew trades additional advanced training in their own specialities as well as together as complete crews. An extension of categories was also introduced at this time in view of the fact that most crewmen would be posted to squadrons with four-engined bombers when they reached England. The earlier training units had turned out pilots, observers and wireless operators/air gunners. The observer category was now abolished and replaced by four specialist grades—navigator; navigator 'B' (i.e. a navigator-cum-bomb-aimer); navigator 'W' (a navigator experienced also in radio); and straight bombardier. In addition specialist AGs (air gunners) were trained; and flight engineers, as a new trade, were turned out, mainly for the RCAF.

These improvements in the summer of 1942 were to result in their graduation of a further, invaluable 22,431 aircrew by the end of the war, plus several thousand trained in the United States. In all, from 1940-5, the BCATP would have been responsible for turning out 49,800 pilots; 15,870 navigators; 9,800 navigators 'B'; 4,300 navigators 'W'; 15,680 bomb-aimers; 18,500 wireless operator/gunners; 15,000 gunners; and about 2,000 flight engineers. The part Canada played in this way in stoking-up the Bomber Command manpower needs from 1942 on cannot be over-stressed. Together with young crews from Australia, South Africa, Rhodesia, New Zealand (with about fifty training schools between them) and other parts of the Commonwealth, they would show a spirit and courage that had never perhaps been welded into one purpose among men from so many countries before and certainly not since.

As was the case with the RAF itself, pathfinder volunteers from

Canadian and Empire squadrons were mainly 'old lags' and there was a problem here. This was that in 'specialist' squadrons, like the Pathfinder ones, promotion slowed down almost to a halt for talented leaders who would have forged ahead if they had remained with their own squadrons in a group. And it is worth recording that at this time many of the volunteers accepted this cheerfully, while others even took a lower rank 'to join in the fun'. It certainly was not for lack of enthusiasm or for lack of quality that the first Pathfinder-led raids boobed more than they scored.

After the first series of finding and marking sorties by the Force, rough rules and regulations were laid down for Pathfinder squadrons. It was thought that they could do a much longer tour without rest than ordinary bomber squadrons—perhaps as many as sixty trips. After ten trips as illuminators they would be registered as 'qualified Pathfinders' and would then be permitted to wear a special pair of gold wings underneath their medal ribbons. It was the glamour bit again, and the men involved loved it.

Inevitably there were jealousies, as with any corps d'elite or 'private army', and internal bleats about the best crews being creamed off, with a resultant lowering of standards all round and a loss of position on the photographic ladder. That this was mainly true did not help matters; undoubtedly morale in the best squadrons suffered in this period as a result of the coughing up of some crews for the founding and expansion of the Pathfinder Force.

Meanwhile, normal raids were being carried out by small forces of bombers without benefit of pathfinders. While the new Group's finders and illuminators were cutting their teeth on targets in the Ruhr at the end of August, 1942, a squadron of Lancasters was on its way in full moonlight to Gydnia, Poland (a 950-mile, ten-hour flight) where the new German *Graf Zeppelin* aircraft-carrier was being fitted out. The Lancs were truly showing their powers for the first time. Overloaded to the unheard-of all-up weight of 67,000 pounds (as against the 45,000-pounds of the first prototype), the twelve Lancasters were carrying one each of the new anti-capital ship bombs—which had proved heavy and uncertain in their behaviour on practice runs.

The plan was to drop these bombs from 6,000 feet, in careful run-ins over the target, in the hope that at least one of the twelve bombs would hit the carrier. But again the weather changed dramatically during the long flight. A strong south-westerly breeze had blown up and carried industrial smog from the Berlin area over Danzig and Gydnia, with the result that visibility was down to less than a mile when the Lancs got there. Although several large ships could vaguely be discerned in the harbour, the *Graf Zeppelin* could not be identified, although the crews bravely made a number of dummy runs over the well defended port. They did their best, after an exhausting flight, but photographs taken later showed no direct hits and little damage. They had carried unprecedentedly heavy loads over a risky distance and had nothing to show for it. Again guts had been beaten by the elements.

In the three months from the end of September, 1942, the magnificent defence of Stalingrad filled columns of news nearly every day, and raised the British people's morale aloft with their hopes. The sudden stemming of the Nazi tide had come none too soon; in the late summer Hitler's conquests had looked staggering on the map. Apart from Malta and Gibraltar, the Mediterranean had been an Axis lake; in effect, German jackboots had stood astride territory which stretched from northern Norway on the Arctic to Egypt in the Middle East, and from the Atlantic at Brest to the southern reaches of the Volga on the borders of Central Asia. Rommel's offensive at El Alamein in August had posed the likelihood of a further breakthrough to the Nile. Hitler had believed, and all too few had doubted it, that final victory was at last in his grasp.

Now, dramatically, the whole picture was changing. The long uphill road of defeat, disillusion and downright failure, which had been hell to climb, seemed suddenly less steep. The great and terrible Nazi dream of a Reich lasting a thousand years was beginning to go sour on the mad Fuehrer. His stomping and shouting was becoming wilder. The high tide of conquest was beginning to ebb—equally in Russia and in the Western Desert—and, God willing, could never flow back.

The tremendous news from Stalingrad and the improving situation in the Middle East—with Rommel held and the 8th Army building for attack—took the focus off Bomber Command for a time, to everyone's relief. Despite the best efforts of the persistent, fast-moving Harris, and the dedicated support of Winston Churchill, there had been no growth in the overall strength of Bomber Command as far as numbers of planes were concerned and the Conversion Units were taking longer than had hoped in switching squadrons to bigger and better bombers. Repairing and patching of damaged planes was as important as ever.

In October, low-level practice flights in close-formation by Lancasters of 5 Group, stationed around Nottinghamshire, reached fruition in two daring daylight raids.

Nobody in Bomber Command particularly liked day-raiding with heavy bombers but if 'twere to be done 'twere better done in mass-formation. Like migrating birds, instinctively flying in V-formations —as the simplest way of following a leader, keeping out of his slipstream and retaining good vision—eighty-eight Lancasters swept in over the French coast, south of Ile d' Yeu, and flew almost wing-tip to wing-tip over 200 miles of occupied territory to attack the Schneider Co. factory at Le Creusot, thirty-nine miles north-north-west of Macon in east-central France, more or less on the border between German-occupied and Vichy France. Le Creusot, a small town of only 30,000 people, featured at Schneider's one of the largest ironworks in Europe. It was the late afternoon of Saturday, 14 October, 1942, the weather was favourable and the formation kept below radar range for most of the way, climbing from a few hundred feet to about 4,000 as it reached the target area. As the outward flight had taken more than five hours, the sun was setting as they arrived at Le Creusot, but there was more than enough light for the leading planes to identify the industrial complex without delay. Together the large armada swept over Schneider's; almost together they dropped over 200 tons of HE and incendiary bombs, blanketing the town as well as the iron-steel works. Simultaneously with this raid, six Lancasters made diversionary sorties on an important power-station at Montchanin, in the same general area, in a low-level attack with bombs and guns. They succeeded in knocking out the transformers.

All ninety-four aircraft, having split up after their bombing runs, made their way home independently in the darkness, some damaged by flak, but all in high spirits. The newspapers of the free world subsequently made much of these two British daylight raids—and called for more. But conditions had been unusually good for 5

21. *Silhouetted against a background of fire and flak this Lancaster is over Hamburg. The place was photographed from another Lancaster when the ninety-fourth raid on Germany's largest port was at its height.*

22. *One of the most impressive things about the war in the air was the way in which crews went back time and time again despite their experiences. A flight-sergeant brought Lancaster J for Jig of 100 Squadron home minus 6 feet of wing sliced off in collision with a German fighter. Four nights after this picture was taken his plane failed to return from Schweinfurt. Only the wounded member of the crew in the picture, who had been left behind, remained.*

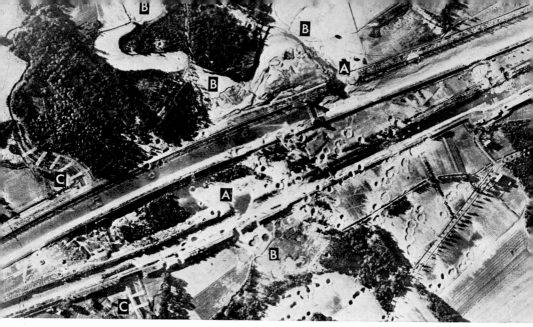

23. *A photographic reconnaissance aircraft brought back this picture, following the famous raid on the Dortmund-Ems Canal on the night of 23-24 September, 1944. It shows (a) two direct hits by 12,000-pounder bombs; (b) the water flowing over the broken embankments; and (c) the camouflaged River Glane.*

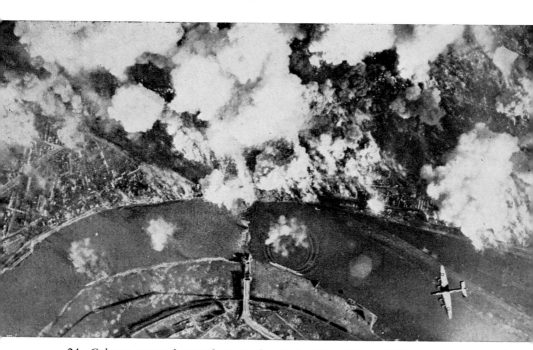

24. *Cologne, worst damaged city in the whole of the Ruhr and Rhineland, was given its heaviest attack of the war by RAF Bomber Command in the daylight attack of 28 October, 1944. Lancasters and Halifaxes dropped a great weight of high explosive and incendiary bombs on the railway and industrial city. The bombers were escorted by Spitfires and Mustangs. The picture shows the industrial and dock area of Mulheim in the North East of Cologne during the attack. A Lancaster aircraft is seen flying near the highway suspension-bridge, which was completely demolished.*

Group, in that no Luftwaffe fighters had appeared, before, during or after the raid.

The versatile and long-ranging Lancasters were then used, Pathfinder-led, sometimes by day and sometimes by night, in many successful raids by up to 100 bombers on the cities of northern Italy, between the end of October and the middle of December. Stirlings and Halifaxes also took part, despite icing troubles over the Alps. During these missions, 5 Group Lancasters experimented with early versions of a new Mark XIV bomb-sight. Although complicated and demanding to be fed with information on wind velocities, trail angles etc., it had the virtue that it still worked well even if the plane was flying at an angle, swerving to avoid flak, or diving. Tiny built-in gyros did most of the work and if the strength of the wind was correctly allowed for, the accuracy was greater than had been the case with any previous British sighting device. As these missions were mainly beyond the range of the German fighters in Europe, which were mainly disposed in the Pas de Calais and in Norway, the casualty rates, even by day, were comparatively low. Indeed there was much competition among bomber squadrons for these 'soft' raids, which were something of a holiday against raids on Germany and still counted towards a completed tour.

Not all of these 'thrashes' over northern Italy were easy. Hauling Stirlings over the Alps, Hannibal-like, could usually be managed if conditions were good. But there were occasions when the aircraft would not go above 12-13,000 feet which, with 15,000 feet peaks in the way, led to hair-raising, spine-chilling high jinks through the rarefied air of high mountain passes just prior to the dive down on Turin or Milan, to drop blockbusters where the pendant flares of the Lancaster pathfinders would be lighting the target. Petrol, too was never too plentiful on these trips and, even on a direct course home, there was never much left for taxi-ing after fighting the inevitable head-wind for much of the way. But mainly the crews favoured these 'bus-runs' over lightly defended France and graded them pretty cushy. Losses supported this. They were a mere fraction of 1 per cent over this period. Bombing was mainly very accurate, in proportion to the weakness of the Italian defences, and the dropping of the latest 8,000-pound 'cookies' by Lancasters towards the end of November did Mussolini's shaky prestige no good at all.

The Italian raids, mainly on Genoa, Turin, Milan (and later Naples) were designed to persuade Mussolini to keep his fighters and anti-aircraft units at home, and to bring the realities of war home to the wavering Italian people. These were timely and salutory raids, with the 8th Army about to break the Rommel legend; the Russians holding at Stalingrad; the Allied 1st Army assembling at Gibraltar for Operation Torch; and a second, and even more important eastern battle about to begin on the snowy steppes of southern Russia.

Chapter Fifteen

As the year 1942 ended, it seemed that the Allies were at last within reach of an all-important prize—the initiative Hitler had held since 1939. It was also ending with top-secret equipment of one sort and another being carefully fitted to selected planes in Pathfinder and other squadrons. As usual, these aids to navigation and bombing were all too few in number, but the quality was impressive. 'We had been in the dark for so long that it was like a blind man suddenly being given cats' eyes,' one master-bomber recalls. 'It really was as dramatic as that."

Disturbingly, although there were lots of the latest bombers in the pipeline, Harris's effective front-line strength at the turn of the year would be smaller in numbers than when he had taken over as AOC-in-C in February—an average availability of 339 planes Granted most of the obsolete and obsolescent types had been weeded out, and the proportions were now 261 four-engined 'heavies' to seventy-eight 'mediums'. Conversion to the larger bombers was still dragging a bit for various reasons, but among the 'twins' the versatile Mosquito was coming to the fore and exciting Harris ever more and more with its possibilities as a 'nuisance' raider, as a long-range fast bomber, and in an improved pathfinding function.

Mosquitoes as well as Lancasters had been chosen for early experiments with the new 'finding' devices and, in a more negative but important way, for 'spoiling' gadgets, which, it was hoped, would make life much more difficult for German air and ground crews. As always, each ploy had a counter-ploy and technical devices could be two-edged.

The sophisticated gadgetry of a science which was later to become known as avionics was suddenly exploding with ideas on both sides of the Channel. The crying need for help to see and work in conditions of bad weather and plain darkness, which had been known to crews from the first day of the war—but which had never had sufficient money nor high enough priorities allocated to it in the backrooms of planning and research—was now beginning to be satisfied.

If you saved aircraft you saved crews—automatically. Every crew was inexperienced when they began. If they flew more often they became more experienced—how else would they learn? If less-experienced men flew even more often and more safely—if the new devices saved aircraft—they would become more experienced, fly more ops. and reach the tour expired stage QED. Thus would more bomber crews see the war through.

But the war was not being fought with the ultimate aim of seeing more bomber crews through. It was being fought to defeat Germany through a bomber offensive. And an offensive is costly in lives and material. Bomber crews and aircraft were expendable—up to a certain limit—and this was acceptable if the effort was having some effect on the enemy. This is a principle of war—and the crews of Bomber Command knew it, accepted it and did not expect anything else. This is why the C-in-C was called 'Butch' Harris—a name they pronounced with a wry affection, not as a cry of desperation. The bomber boys knew they were fighting a tough war, but they believed they were the only force of the Allied services who were taking the reality of war to the Germans, literally taking it into his backyard—and they were proud of their efforts and they accepted the odds.

No matter what the losses, the rest clambered aboard and kept on flying—whatever the targets. There was some insulation, of course, for you didn't see the burned-out aircraft and the broken men—they were on the other side, hundreds of miles away. Even seeing a friendly aircraft explode and burn left a momentary impression only. Empty beds in a billet or empty chairs at the mess table were harrowing, but throughout the Air Force, life was lived as a member of a constantly moving population. Aircrew were being posted in or out whatever the station—and during training, at every station, death occasionally grabbed a comrade or two. They were young and very resilient—also very scared a lot of the time. But they had to live with that, too.

Of the new devices about to be introduced operationally, two were paramount. These were Oboe (an improvement on Gee, which had quickly been rendered useless by German counter-measures) and H2S, a completely new concept.

Oboe, which could only be used by a few aircraft at a time, was much more accurate and less-easily jammed than Gee had been. It was still dependent on ground radar stations, which transmitted a beam for the aircraft to fly along, direct to the target, or to a point on the way to the target chosen to confuse the enemy. Its range was proportionate to the height of the aircraft using it, so that Mossies could use it on longer flights than other bomb-leaders, but in general it was capable of ranging over most of the Ruhr. Oboe had its drawbacks, but it was certainly a long step forward from the crude AI (Airborne Interceptor) devices that had preceded Gee, which, working on short pulses of high intensity and measuring the time taken for the pulses to return, had given only a very rough indication of a target bearing.

H2S, even more sophisticated than Oboe, was a real advance in navigation *and* accurate bombing techniques, and the first of a family of such devices that would stretch into the 'fifties. All the equipment in this case was carried in the aircraft, making it independent of ground radar and giving it, in theory, an unlimited range.

The self-contained H2S box and screen produced a radar map in the cockpit of the changing terrain directly beneath the aircraft, showing clearly such features as coastlines, rivers and lakes, even from above thick cloud. It was supposed also to show towns and other large features, but, except in the case of land-water margins, it was at first rather difficult to read. With a wavelength of only ten centimetres, as compared with one-and-a-half metres of previous devices, it had the virtue of being less easy to detect from the ground or by interceptors.

In support of these advances, meteorological section techniques had meanwhile also been improved. More than ever, the third dimension of height—which had been relatively unimportant at the start of the war, when the latitudes, longitudes and land-sea areas had been the main concerns—and with it the volume and shape of the masses of air high above the earth, had become paramount.

Weather rooms, where pilots and navigators could get individual amplified perspectives on the atmosphere before taking off, were expanded. Pressure maps of isobars and fronts—a sort of balloon's view of the world they had to fly over—were issued together with a cross-section of the course, looked at horizontally from the side, with symbols in colour showing rain, snow or lightning (with the freezing level indicated as a dividing line) and figures for winds at different altitudes, together with temperatures, ceilings and visibilities, to help keep navigators out of trouble.

A realistic concept of weather to be faced was often clearly a matter of life and death for crews. But, too often, all these maps, charts and plans were academic rather than practical. They appeared real in the minds of the met men. But the true picture the fliers would see with their own eyes and a bird's perspective would often be different. With the whole sky more than half covered with ever-changing cloud formations at any given time, the whole picture could change at a speed with which no weather expert could cope. All too often, pressure ridges and troughs would have moved beyond the realities of the charts by the time the crews were airborne, or the wind would have radically changed course, giving conditions very different from those the forecasts had led the navigators to expect.

Other important advances at the turn of the year included bombs that were bigger and more varied, plus (and this was a vital plus) more efficient marker bombs, promising a clearer aiming point to follow up bombers when used by the specialist bombadiers of the Pathfinder Group.

The first Pathfinder-led raid using Oboe was aimed at the Krupps' works at Essen on 20 December, 1942. It was a small, experimental mission, with a main force of only twenty-five Lancasters. One of the reasons for this was that it had been decided to make the raid a really high-level one by four-engined bombers for the first time, with the pilots instructed to climb to about 23,000 feet at the earliest possible moment after leaving their bases, and then for the navigators to set an accurate course for the Ruhr city at this height and at a ground speed of 240 mph. Their orders, when nearing Essen, were to look out for two yellow flares laid by the finders at the start of the run-in. On flying straight through these, they would see two red flares and on passing between the reds they would see a cluster of greens laid by the illuminators at a few thousand feet above the Krupps factory. They would then bomb straight through these, while flying on a carefully-timed compass heading.

Punctuality by the Pathfinders and main bomber force was the secret weapon which would implement the accuracy offered by Oboe. The parachute-borne flares could drift away from the exact aiming point at as much as a mile a minute, so chronometers had to be synchronised that night with more than usual care. Careful timing would ensure that the entire force would pass through the fifteen mile straight run above the flares in a very few minutes, with less risk than previously, whence they would see a further group of flares ahead, marking the assembly point for a safety-in-numbers mass-flight home.

All went well initially, except that Essen turned out to be defended by an unprecedentedly-heavy steel wall of 88 mm flak, which had the range to reach the high-flying Lancs. Several blew up over the target, as the others followed instructions and kept on a straight course. The Pathfinders, thanks to Oboe, had marked the target well, and the timing was excellent, but because of a variety of new danger factors within the giant planes, only ten Lancs dropped their bombs through the flares, so that only a limited success was to be recorded.

The difficulties which had prevented the other fifteen Lancasters from reaching the aiming point had mainly been caused by the height at which the fairly-new bombers had been asked to fly. In the rarified, sixty degrees below zero air, engines had apparently failed, with subsequent crashes; there had been oxygen failures; guns had seized-up in the intense cold; and rear gunners had been frozen to the point that they had to be thawed out with rum.

It was a beginning rather than a success. The plan itself had been OK, but the crews were not used to flying so high and the Lancasters had shown their first weaknesses at this ceiling. Casualties had been an alarming 6 per cent overall on the raid, and post-mortems were necessary before anything similar could be attempted again. New radiator flaps were improvised, within the squadrons, against over-heating. Experiments were carried out at equivalent altitudes with guns wiped free of oil. De-icers were tested and re-tested. Electrically-heated flying suits were introduced to supplement the multiple underwear crews had been wearing. Above all, more Mosquitoes (with their superior high-flying capability) were hustled-up for Pathfinder squadrons and were used for special training with the new equipment and techniques. Mosquito IVs of No. 109 Squadron had already been experimenting with Oboe for some weeks, flying out of Huntingdon.

Lancaster pathfinders again led a force of four-engined bombers on the first operational raid with the new target-indicator bombs (TI for short) on the night of 15-16 January, 1943, when the target was Lorient, the fortified seaport and marine arsenal cum submarine base in north-west France. It was a clear night and a successful raid, with the new markers giving greater accuracy than any device tried out before. The new TI's were 250-pound missiles in light-weight casings which were fused to burst about 3,000 feet above the target, where-upon some hundreds of small coloured balls would descend on the aiming point, where they would burn for five or ten minutes.

These were the markers that were to put night bombing on the right course at last in terms of accuracy. They were used in harness with flares in the sky (in case smoke was used to obscure the ground beneath) and, unlike so many 'gimmicks' that had been tried, were a big success from the start. They possessed the additional virtue that the colour of the balls they spewed out could be changed, even when the pathfinders were airborne, so that the German dummy-target experts would have a thin time in attempting to duplicate TI's on the ground.

In turn, H2S had its baptism a few weeks later, on the night of 30-31 January, in a raid on Hamburg, and in conjunction with the other devices already introduced. This was a tentative and limited experiment, but the radar screens in the Lancaster cockpits of the leading planes using them worked fairly well, and the navigators were able to 'see' through the industrial smog of the German port as predicted. The map of Europe would come to life more and more on the compact H2S radar screens, and it was safe to say that from this date on H2S was itself on the map.

Meanwhile, a few hours before the Hamburg raid, Berliners had been dumbfounded at the sight of fast twin-engined bombers sweeping over the city, each in turn dropping one 4,000-pounder from nearly 30,000 feet, smack-bang in the centre of the capital. It was the first sign of things to come, the first use of the Mosquito as a long-range fast bomber, and the first ever daylight raid on Berlin.

The sleek Mosquitoes were from 105 Squadron at Bourn, Cambridgeshire, and their spectacular sortie hit all the front pages in the free world the next day. The raid had been timed to disrupt a parade, in celebration of ten years of National Socialism, addressed by none other than Reichsmarshall Hermann Goering and the fury of the Luftwaffe leader at this traumatic 'happening' was such that he immediately recalled his two best fighter pilots from Russia and instructed them to form Jagdgruppen 25 and 50, with specially modified interceptor planes, specifically to combat the Mosquito menace. But the Luftwaffe still had no plane of any sort in operation with the performance capability of the Mosquito. German fighters could only match its speed by diving from a great height, and they were seldom offered this opportunity. In fact, the special Jagdgruppen squadrons were to be disbanded towards the end of 1943, without ever recording one Mosquito kill.

The day raid on Berlin was to be the first of many from which Mossies would return unscathed. The German capital had also been attacked by night in January, for the first time since November, 1941, when 388 Lancasters had flown through fog and snow in an attempt to pulverise the city. This, alas, had been a much less successful raid in all respects. The Lancaster pathfinders had mistimed their marking; the main force had had to circle for a time, losing ten planes in the process; and most of the bombs had fallen at random in the suburbs. To attack the German capital, the Lancs had had to fly for more than four hours each way over heavily-defended territory, and had suffered serious losses. Bomber Command was patently not strong enough yet for such distant raids in force by the heavies. Even at this advanced point of time, only 515 bombers were available for any one raid.

Meanwhile, the American 8th Air Force, with 500 heavy bombers assembled in Britain (from an output to date of nearly 3,000), but not more than 100 available for any one raid, had been venturing further and further into France, escorted each time for the first 180 miles or so by limited-ranging Spitfires. And on 27 January they had made their first raid of the war on Germany itself, when General Eaker had dispatched a mixed force of ninety-one Fortresses and Liberators to attack U-boat targets at Wilhelmshaven. This time, Luftwaffe fighters were up in good time to intercept them, and had no difficulty in outmanoeuvring the escorting twin-boom American P-38 Lightning fighters. But the mission, and the battle that ensued, were equally inconclusive. The intercepting Focke-Wulf 190s were surprised by the fire power of the American bombers and did more harrying than killing. And as for the raid itself, while fifty-three bombers were credited with reaching the target (while two had attacked U-boat targets in Emden by mistake) the damage shown in reconnaissance photographs was negligible. Only three of the attacking force were lost and one of these, a B24 Liberator, had caught fire after suffering only superficial damage—a fault to which the ubiquitous and versatile Liberator was to be alarmingly prone for months to come.

But in a sense, this raid was a grim landmark for the German people, although they may not have been aware of it at the time. It foretold the crushing of the Reich, which was to have lasted 1,000 years, in that it indicated that General Eaker was getting under way with his daylight air offensive against Germany (albeit in the face of anticipated heavy losses) which would soon build into the terrible, retributive, round the clock programme (in harness with Bomber Command) which had been promised from the moment America came into the war.

Coincidentally, the moral brake had been taken off the wholesale destruction of German cities by pronouncements made at an historic meeting between Churchill and Roosevelt at Casablanca on 24 January. The mood was bouyant, as it had never been before, for the Germans and Italians had been more or less swept out of Africa. Invasions of their respective countries was imminent in the one case and inevitable in the other.

In a concluding press conference, Roosevelt had summed up the new all-out policies of the Allies. He had said bluntly that world peace could only be brought about by the unconditional surrender of Germany, Italy and Japan and he suggested that the conference at which he was speaking should be called 'The Unconditional Surrender Meeting'. This was the first public reference to such a policy. Just as importantly, decisions taken at the conference included (*a*) high-priority for operations against submarines; (*b*) the assembly of a powerful force without delay for the 'second front' invasion of Europe; (*c*) a major offensive against Japan as soon as Germany was breaking; (*d*) a heavy air offensive against the production and morale of Germany; (*e*) formation of a new Mediterranean-North African Air Command; (*f*) the occupation of Sicily; and (*g*) efforts to persuade Turkey to join the Allies.

The conference had, in fact, laid down, in some detail, the basic strategy for the combined British-American bomber offensive, which was to weaken the enemy's heart, with the primary objectives outlined as . . .

> . . . the progressive destruction and dislocation of the German military, industrial and economic system, and the undermining of the morale of the German people to a point where their capacity for armed resistance is fatally weakened.

Harris immediately interpreted the Casablanca directive as an instruction to proceed with the bombing saturation of every accessible German town of any size on every possible occasion. As he was later to put it in his book, *Bomber Offensive*, there were no two ways of looking at the matter. 'I was now required', he states bluntly, 'to proceed with a joint Anglo-American bombing offensive . . . which gave me a wide range of choice and allowed me to attack pretty well any German industrial city of 100,000 inhabitants and above . . .'

Harris, who still clung to the belief that area bombing should be enough in itself to bring about the collapse of Germany, lost no time in getting on with the job. On the night of 5-6 March, 1943, he began a long series of heavy raids, to be known collectively as the Battle of the Ruhr, in which high-flying Mosquitoes would play an ever-more-important role with the pathfinders. As the number of heavy bombers available was at long last increasing by about 100 per month, Harris was also able for the first time to implement his theory that ever-larger fleets of bombers, in concentrated formations, could swamp German air and ground defences around key cities and so contain the percentage of losses. Radio and radar counter-measures also began to be introduced on an ever-greater scale during the Battle of the Ruhr.

Simultaneously (to Harris's regret, because it diluted the numbers of bombers available to him on any one night) the continuing Battle of the Atlantic was making frequent calls on Bomber Command for sorties against Lorient, St. Nazaire and other U-boat bases—at which the Americans, too, were hammering away. These attacks, as well as being frustrating to the AOC-in-C, were largely useless. Germany had now built heavy concrete pens for her submarines, and no bombs available at this time could penetrate them.

Another frustrating difficulty, because it diverted valuable aircraft from the Ruhr, and tended to lead to unbearable losses per mission, was the need to spread out the German air defences by making spasmodic attacks on targets as widely spread as Pilsen, Stettin, Berlin, Munich, Nuremberg and Stuttgart.

On these long raids, beyond the range of Oboe, H2S was invariably used. Because it was a much more complex device, failures were much more frequent at this stage than was the case with ground-controlled Oboe. When H2S worked, it was very good; when it failed, the whole raid generally aborted, with bombers flying a long way to little purpose in terms of concentrated bombing. An example of this was on the night of 8-9 March when five finders and nine illuminators, all equipped with H2S, led a force of 333 aircraft to Nuremberg. Six of the fourteen H2S sets failed before the planes reached the target and two of the remaining leaders were shot down (fortunately an unusual happening among pathfinders, whose loss rate to date had been less than 2 per cent). Several of the finders, bereft of H2S, used visual sightings, which were off-target and merely confused the back-up planes. The overall result was that TI bombs were spread around far too wide an area, and the bombs dropped were equally scattered.

Although H2S was undoubtedly the device of the future, Oboe was to prove much more reliable from the start, and the pity was that its range restricted it more or less to the radius of the Ruhr.

Inevitably, Essen was, as ever, the prime target in the Ruhr, which is also why it was the best-defended one in Europe. Previous attacks on it had been at best inconclusive and at worst pin-pricking sorties. Now Harris was determined to blast Krupps as an hors d'oeuvre to the wholesale carpet bombing of the main Ruhr towns. On the night of 5-6 March, he used his new device to penetrate the smog that enveloped the Prussian city and plaster its industrial heart. Led by eight Oboe-equipped pathfinding Mosquitoes of 106 Squadron, 442 four-engined bombers set out early in the evening for Essen in good flying weather. This time the finding and illuminating were carried out in copybook fashion.

Four of the Mossies, operating entirely on Oboe indications, arrived dead on the 9 pm zero hour (the others having had technical failures en route) and dropped salvoes of red TI bombs through the murk for a period of thirty minutes. Twenty-two Lancaster illuminators followed the Mosquitoes in and slammed their green markers right on top of the Krupps works. The main force, flying in three waves, had no difficulty in finding the red lights and in bombing through the green ones. All the bombers dropped their loads, totalling about a thousand tons of incendiary and HE bombs, in the proportion of about two to one, within a period of only forty minutes. An unheard-of degree of accuracy was achieved, and only fourteen out of nearly 500 aircraft involved failed to return to their bases.

Daylight photographic reconnaissance, on 7 and 8 March, when examined in conjunction with bomb-flash pictures brought home by the bombers involved, showed that 153 crews had succeeded in dropping their bombs within three miles of the Krupps complex, which, in view of the fact that Essen was the most heavily defended target in Germany, was success indeed. The photographs also showed unusually severe damage in the target area.

The city itself had been devastated, with 160 acres flattened, and in an outer ring of about 450 acres, three-quarters of the buildings had been laid waste. The Krupps works appeared to have suffered about 50 per cent damage, by fire and explosion, to the point that when Gustav Krupp saw the devastation in the morning he collapsed in a fit.

It was the greatest raid of the war to date, and was to be followed by four other major attacks on Essen before the end of July, several with heavier losses, as part of the Battle of the Ruhr, together with major raids on Duisburg, Bochum, Oberhausen, Mulheim,

Gelsenkirchen, Wuppertal, Remcheid, Krefeld, Munchen-Gladbach, Munster, Aachen, Cologne and Dusseldorf—totalling nearly 20,000 sorties in all.

The scale of these Ruhr raids varied from nuisance and diversionary sorties by single Mosquitoes to near-1,000 bomber raids late on in the series. The losses, many of them to German night fighters, which had now been recalled wholesale from other fronts, from which they could be ill spared, to defend the German homeland— over the five-months' period were almost too terrible to contemplate. Fed to the public in small, underplayed doses, they seemed insignificant in relation to the retributive effort. But to the wives, sweethearts, families and friends of the men involved—and to the communities of the stations and villages from which they operated—it was the bleakest, blackest period of the war to date.

In all, between the beginning of March and the end of July the Ruhr raids resulted in an almost unthinkable failure to return of 872 aircraft and getting on for 6,000 crewmen. In addition, 2,126 heavy bombers were severely damaged or crash-landed in England.

Apart from the wholesale decimation of the flower of Bomber Command's young manhood, these losses in aircraft (which added up to 16 per cent overall, with 4.7 per cent of the bombers involved actually destroyed over the targets) were insupportable, even with the increase in deliveries of planes to squadrons. The daily prospect of sudden death was now paramount among the front-line crews.

Chapter Sixteen

Guy Gibson said, at about this time, that it was strange how the public deferred more to the fighter boys than to those of Bomber Command. In his opinion, this was wrong, because, it seemed to him, bomber aircrew led altogether tougher and more dangerous lives than their brothers of Fighter Command.

That Gibson's opinion was uniquely based on experience, no one could deny. In some ways he *was* the air war to date—at twenty-five, one of the few all-flying, all-thinking, all-caring veterans still alive. Not that he could hope to survive the war, of course, but he was still blessedly around at this stage.

As at March, 1943, Wing Commander Guy Gibson had completed two tours as a bomber skipper. These had totalled seventy-eight sorties. Thanks to a points system that had been introduced, the total could have been slightly different, and still have counted two tours. This was because, apart from the necessity to press home an attack to get points, some raids (as, for example, those to the Ruhr, Poland, etc.) counted more than did 'soft' sorties to the French coast.

Between his initial tour, which had lasted from the first day of war until November, 1941, and his second, from March, 1942, until 15 March, 1943, instead of accepting the usual six months' rest period, Gibson had sandwiched in 100 night fighter sorties, flying Beaufighters. So he knew only too well what life was like in the two Commands, and could judge between them.

Now he was due for a long leave, and was looking forward to it as he had never done before. But it was not to be. Of those who give most in this life most is asked.

When Harris had decided to back Barnes Wallis and his bombs some months before, he had known that a special squadron of 'old lags' would be necessary to carry out the specialised and extremely dangerous techniques needed to make full use of the ideas behind the 'super' mine-like, special-purpose bombs. So, on 15 March, 1943, he asked his much respected old friend, Air Vice Marshal the Hon. Ralph Cochrane, commander of 5 Group, to form an elite squadron and train it for a single raid on the Mohne and Eder dams.

The rest is history, and anyone who has not read Gibson's own account of these events in *Enemy Coast Ahead* has missed the best book to come out of the RAF in World War II.

Cochrane chose Gibson to form the special squadron, to be numbered 617; Gibson chose the twenty-one best crews ever assembled in one unit (while cheerfully forfeiting his leave as he would forfeit his life, too, in 1944); and training to achieve unparalleled accuracy was undertaken as never before.

The main thinking behind the dam-busting raid, and a parallel series of attacks shortly to be launched against two ballbearing plants at Schweinfurt, was that the downfall of Germany could be greatly speeded by accurate knock-out blows against key supplies.

The attack on the Mohne and Eder dams had been made possible because of the ingenious, rotating bomb Dr. Barnes Wallis had invented, and which only specially modified Lancasters could carry. The bomb could skip and skim across a stretch of water, in a series of diminishing leaps, like a flat stone thrown by a child. Upon meeting, as a spent force, the resistance of a barrier, it would sink to the bottom where its shock waves would cause the whole structure to crumble. That was the theory. As the bomb had a tendency to break up if dropped even from a few hundred feet, practice runs were eventually made in lone attacks at less than 100 feet, demanding flying skills of a high order and the use of give-away down-pointing spotlights to maintain the necessary level flight. The problems in rehearsal were endless, but one by one they were overcome.

Although he personally gave the go-ahead for the dam scheme, Harris was somewhat apprehensive that it might lead to a costly

25. *One of the many dangers facing British planes was the risk of being struck by bombs dropped from planes flying at a higher altitude. This is what happened to V for Victor, a Liberator of 37 Squadron, in a raid over Italy in March, 1945. Despite the damage the plane limped 300 miles to safety.*

26. *Bill Reid was a handsome young Lancaster pilot when he won his VC in 1943.*
27. *Group Captain Leonard Cheshire, VC, DSO and 2 bars, DFC.*

28. *Marshal of the RAF Sir Arthur Harris, Bart, GCB, OBE, AFC, LLB, in his studi*
with a silver model of the Lancaster bomber.

failure. But his worries were only to be half-realised. Costly it would be, but a failure, no.

Gibson and the nine finest bomber crews in Britain took off from Scampton, Lincs, at 9.30 p.m. on 16 May, 1943, under a full moon, while a diversionary force of five Lancs headed for a third dam, the Sorpe, and five others stood by to take-off later. Operation Chastise was under way.

The precision that would be required of the crews, while flying through almost horizontal flak at exactly the 'impossible' height for a Lanc of 60 feet, was almost too unbearably extreme to be contemplated. To be effective, the bomb had to be timed to do a specific number of skips—otherwise it would sink out of contact and be wasted, or, if delivered too late, would bounce over the wall. Height and timing had to be absolutely spot-on.

Gibson's nine were to attack all three dams in turn, if unwasted bombs allowed this. The second five were to go straight to Sorpe. The remaining five Lancs were to act as a mobile reserve, under the orders of 5 Group HQ.

One of Gibson's nine planes, piloted by Flight Lieutenant Bill Astell, was shot down on the way to the Mohne dam. The other eight flew steadily on, in formation, to circle the lake.

Gibson went in first at the prescribed level, and his bomb seemed to skip correctly, but left the dam intact. The second Lanc, under the command of Flight Lieutenant J. V. Hopgood, was hit, and exploded as it dropped its bomb. The ack-ack gunners had got the message and the range.

Flight Lieutenant 'Mickey' Martin went in third, escorted by Gibson to draw off the flak, and dropped his rotating bomb just twenty yards short, as his plane was hit by cannonfire. Martin, despite, heavy damage to his Lanc, then escorted the fourth plane, piloted by Squadron Leader H. M. Young, while Gibson made a dummy attack from the far side of the twin-towered parapet, his guns blazing at the flak batteries. Again the bomb bounced the required number of times without breaching the dam. The fifth Lancaster, flown by Flight Lieutenant D. J. H. Maltby, then dropped what looked like the third perfectly timed and placed bomb, with no immediate result, and Gibson was about to send in his sixth crew, when to their joy the circling seven saw the huge dam heave in agony, to collapse in a torrent of spray and flood.

A kind of cheer went up over the planes' VHF RT sets, and Gibson, using plain speech, called together the three Lancs which still had bombs aboard, and his mighty deputy-leader Californian-born 'Dinghy' Young, and led the way to the second dam, while Mickey Martin and David Maltby were ordered to fly home to Scampton.

Astonishingly, there was no flak over the Eder lake, but the surrounding hills made the level fly-in extremely difficult and fog was clinging to the water.

Flight Lieutenant D. J. Shannon took his heavy aircraft in first, but unable to hit the right course, he overshot. Squadron Leader H. E. Maudsley, who immediately followed, fractionally mis-timed his bomb-aiming signal, with the result that he destroyed his Lancaster in the explosion. Shannon then flew in again, diving between the overhanging, thousand-feet hills, and got it exactly right. But the dam did not collapse until the third and last mine-type bomb was dropped, by Pilot Officer L. G. Knight's bombardier.

The water foamed through the gap. It was two up and one to go. The news was flashed by morse, by Gibsons' radio operator to 5 Group HQ and thence to Washington and other centres of the free world to the almost unbelieving joy of the recipients.

Meanwhile, the diversionary force was faring less well. Two of its five Lancasters had been forced to turn back, and two more had been shot down en route to the Sorpe. This left only the leading aircraft, piloted by an American, Flight Lieutenant J. C. McCarthy; so, when this information had been received by morse at Group HQ at Grantham, Cochrane decided to dispatch the reserves.

McCarthy pressed on and reached the mist-enshrouded Sorpe long before the others. A dummy run over the target showed a hill at each end, making the dive before levelling-out incredibly difficult. On his third run, he got his bomb away exactly right and the third dam was damaged for about fifty feet in one go.

The five planes of the third formation had been pressing on

towards the Ruhr. Two had been lost on the way—one flown by a Canadian, Pilot Officer Burpee, and the other by Pilot Officer Ottley. No one ever knew the why or wherefore of their deaths. Lancaster 'F Freddy', commanded by another Canadian, Flight Sergeant K. W. Brown, was ordered to take a look at the Sorpe dam, as was Flight Sergeant Anderson, in 'Y Yorker'. Brown struck the wall near where McCarthy had knocked away fifty feet of concrete and added to the damage. By the time Anderson arrived, the mist had closed in completely and he had to turn back without bombing. The last man of the five, Flight Sergeant W. C. Townsend, was then diverted to an alternative target at Ennerpe, where he released his mine-bomb with apparent success.

Mosquito reconnaissance in the morning was to show the Mohne and Eder lakes empty, with 332 million tons of water (representing the main storage for the Ruhr basin) flooding through the towns and villages of the valleys of the western Ruhr for fifty miles. Coal mines had been drowned, electricity stations had been knocked out and factories demolished. Roads, railways, canal banks and bridges had disappeared. Communications had been disrupted. And, in the remaining attacks of the Ruhr raids, there would be desperate shortages of water to put out Bomber Command's fires. In all, about 500 Germans, together with over 700 'slave' and foreign workers, would be found to have lost their lives by drowning that night. But what of the dam-busters who had risked so much to pull off the most fantastic act of precision raiding of the war?

It was a sad, sad story. Of the nineteen Lancasters that had set off that night, ten flew home flat out a few feet above the deck, relieved of eight tons of bomb and petrol load. Somehow nine got through the flak and fighters that were by now awaiting them. The tenth, 'Dinghy' Youngs' 'A Apple', had been hit by flak over the Dutch coast and ditched in the sea. Young had got his nickname because he had paddled away from ditched aircraft twice before. This landing was third time unlucky. He and his crew were lost, presumed drowned.

In all, fifty-three young men—among them Gibson's few veteran buddies from the early days—were dead, from the total of 133 involved, and three were prisoners. The by-now-famous 'supermen' survivors went on seven days' leave. Guy Gibson, who was now to add a VC to his double DSO and double DFC, remained behind at Scampton to write fifty-six personal and individual letters by hand to the next-of-kin, as someone else would do for him sixteen short months later.

In Germany, Albert Speer was left to wonder at the destruction they had caused to his productive effort. But, more especially, he could not understand why so little had been attempted at the Sorpe dam. It, he was later to write, was far more important to Ruhr industry than the Eder.

Chapter Seventeen

While history was being made by the dam-busters at Mohne and Eder, and the glory of 617 Squadron was brushing off on the whole of Bomber Command in terms of prestige, in other parts of the Ruhr the mass-bombing series of raids was continuing, and with it the efforts to make general area bombing still more accurate.

But bulk was equally important, and even more so to some. Following a heavy raid on Dortmund, on 23-24 May, Air Chief Marshal Sir Arthur Harris was able to announce that Bomber Command had dropped a total weight of 100,000 tons of miscellaneous bombs on Germany. In a message of congratulation to his crews, recalling Goering's statement to the German people that 'if an enemy bomber reaches the Ruhr . . . you can call me Meier!' Harris offered congratulations on putting Goering's nose out of joint so many thousands of times.

A new way of hurting the Axis on its more remote flanks was devised at this time. This was by means of shuttle-bombing sorties, and the versatile Lancaster bomber had made it possible.

Lancs of 5 Group flew by night from England, made a successful raid on the former-Zeppelin works (now used to produce radar equipment) at Friedrichshafen, on the northern shore of Lake Constance, and then flew on to North Africa, now Allied-occupied. On the following night, having taken on another load of bombs, they headed back home, attacking the Italian naval base at Spezia on the way.

During short summer nights, raids like that on Friedrichshafen would not have been possible had not the shuttle-method been devised. It was to be used a number of times during the summer of

1943 to help increase the number of places the Germans might think needed night-fighter defences, but shuttle-bombing eventually became infrequent because of difficulties in servicing Lancasters and other heavy bombers away from their home bases.

On the night of 29-30 May, 1943, just two weeks after the breaching of the Ruhr dams, the whole weight of Bomber Command's front-line forces fell on the Rhine city of Wuppertal, thirty-five miles east of Dusseldorf, with its multiple manufacturing activities, taking in chemicals, rubber goods, armaments, paper machinery, glass and other war-vital materials, and its population of 400,000.

Over 700 bombers (by far the largest number since the scrambled 1,000 bomber raids) were so well led by Oboe-equipped Mosquito pathfinders that the follow-up heavies achieved the best yet degree of concentration.

Wuppertal is formed out of three cities—Barmen, Elberfield and Rousdorf—and the chosen aiming point was the centre of Wuppertal-Barmen. The industrial heart was razed to the ground and 2,500 people died in the holocaust. A second raid on the Wuppertal complex of cities a few weeks later devastated the Elberfield section and killed another 2,700 of the population.

At the subsequent mass funerals, Dr. Goebbels condemned the terrorism launched by 'the sick minds' of the West and referred to British war chiefs as 'plutocratic world-destroyers'.

Harris rejoiced at the speech for the very good reason that it showed we were hurting the Germans as never before. And he now prepared to play another ace the back-room boys had produced. This was Window, a counter-device of great promise. It consisted of thousands of strips of tinfoil-covered paper, cut to appropriate German wave-lengths, which when dumped at regular intervals in large quantities from the bomber stream, produced thousands of unwanted blips on the Reichswehr screens. It therefore had the exhilarating effect of interfering with all radar equipment in the area, from interception equipment to radar-laid flak and search-lights. Window had been available to Bomber Command for about fourteen months, but until now Harris had been forbidden to use it by the War Cabinet for fear that the Luftwaffe would use it in turn over Britain. He had had to write literally hundreds of memos and make countless personal representations before he was finally allowed to try out Window over Germany.

The 'coning' of blinding searchlights had become an ever-greater worry to waves of bombers attacking German cities. Quite simply, a small number of German radar-equipped lights would fix on the first stream of bombers over a target and, having lit them successfully, would move on to the next stream as soon as a cone of and so on. This was one ever-present fear for the crews that concentrated non-radar lights had taken over the first stream ... Window should be able to tackle for a time, it was thought. It should also be able to take care of radar direction of guns and fighter planes.

A really big raid on an important target was the obvious occasion on which to launch Window, now that Harris had permission to do so ... and what better than Germany's second city and the world's second greatest port, Hamburg? So it was that soon after midnight on the Saturday-Sunday of 24-25 July (the night of the downfall of Mussolini) pathfinders, using H2S, 'read' the winding Elbe river and the adjoining lakes to lead them to the centre of Germany's sea-gate and great maritime commercial city, with its $1\frac{3}{4}$ million population. Hamburg had been destroyed by fire in 1842. Harris was determined to use Window to raze it to the ground again in 1943.

Most of the TI bombs and marker flares fell plumb in the centre of Hamburg at the right moment, as thousands of metallised strips fluttered groundwards, and Operation Gomorrah was under way.

Harris was not only launching Window at Hamburg. Using a front-line strength which still was not much more than 800 aircraft, he was trying out the 'ultimate' air weapon, as Douhet had conceived it, in its most terrifying form, thereby perhaps to silence his critics once and for all.

Gomorrah was to be a quadruple-raid on Hamburg, involving 3,000 bombers, over four nights, and using up 10,000 tons of bombs, half of them of the incendiary type. The dates chosen, in addition to 24-25 July, were to be 27-28 July, 29-30 July, and 2-3 August.

There had never been anything like the Hamburg raids. On the first night, the bulk of the damage was done, when 2,396 tons of HE and incendiary bombs were dropped on the dockyards and the city. It was history's first man-made firestorm. Nearly 750 bombers had followed the H2S-guided pathfinders and quickly found the correct markers, to the point that all the vast armada passed through the target area in about forty minutes. H2S had been outstandingly accurate because of the special position and characteristics of Hamburg, with its clear land-water patterns. And Window had done its stuff rewardingly well. It had disorganised the radar-directed searchlights, making gunfire inaccurate, and the German ground-controllers had been unable to direct their night fighters to their boxes in the sky. The result was that only twelve British bombers were lost on this raid, out of 748, an astonishingly low figure of less than 2 per cent of the force dispatched.

As the streams of bombers made for home, the second German city was nothing short of an inferno of flame. Such heat had been whipped up by the concentration of HE and incendiaries—the former blowing the latter into ever-greater fires—that the individual conflagrations linked and spread into a vast blaze, one-and-a-half miles in diameter. By the early hours of Sunday morning, the fire had become a man-made storm-centre, a tornado of heat, in which the sparks were flying, as in the devils' whirlpool, to a height of more than two-and-a-half miles.

The principal police officer in Hamburg was later to describe it as 'a great and terrible meteorological phenomenon . . . but with the difference that, if it had been a weather storm, the temperatures involved would have been 20 to 30 degrees centigrade . . . whereas, over the city, they were in the order of 600 to 1,000 degrees centigrade . . . which explained the colossal force of the firestorm winds'. And these terrible, uncontrollable fires were to burn for over twenty-four hours, in 'an intensity such as was never before witnessed and against which every human resistance was useless.

As Harris had predicted, the fire and rescue services were swamped—this despite the fact that Hamburg claimed to have the most efficient system of civil defence in Germany. In the centre of the city everything that would burn burned, and most of the rest melted in the heat; people and objects were sucked into the inferno, to fly in pieces thousands of feet up in the writhing heart of the volcano of heat, in roasting winds which exceeded 150 mph. Nothing survived in the fire area. Even in the air-raid shelters, citizens were suffocated by carbon-monoxide poisoning, and their bodies were reduced to ashes, as in a crematorium, which is what the shelters had become. It was a fate of biblically hellish proportions, and the awesome inspiration of naming the series Gomorrah was all-too-real in its fulfilment.

The other three raids (interspersed with nuisance sorties by Mosquitoes and minor attacks by American heavies) at two or three nightly intervals, effectively finished the job. The second attack featured 705 aircraft, of which twenty-six were lost. And the third, again by over 700 aircraft, which dropped 3,000 tons of bombs, led to a million people fleeing their stricken homes. The final Bomber Command attack, on 2-3 August, encountered bad weather (contrary to forecasts) with resultant collisions and widely scattered bombing, But there was little left to bomb in any case. In the words of the official report, the city's condition was 'beyond all human imagination'.

Over the series of raids that made up the Battle of Hamburg, about 50,000 Hamburgers had been killed and another 40,000 seriously injured. More than half the homes and factory buildings (280,000 houses and 191 factories) had been destroyed; all the port installations had also been seriously damaged; 180,000 tons of shipping had been sunk in the harbour; and the water, gas and electricity supplies had by now failed entirely.

Colonel Adolf Galland, perhaps Germany's greatest flier, wrote this about the Hamburg holocaust:

A wave of terror radiated from the suffering city and spread throughout Germany. Appalling details of the great fires were recounted, and their glow could be seen for days from a distance of a hundred and twenty miles. A stream of haggard, terrified refugees flowed into the neighbouring provinces. In every large town people said, 'What happened to Hamburg yesterday can happen to us tomorrow.' Berlin was evacuated with signs of panic. In spite of the strictest reticence in the official communiques, the Terror of Hamburg spread rapidly to the remotest villages of the Reich.

Psychologically the war at that moment had perhaps reached its most critical point. Stalingrad had been worse, but Hamburg was not hundreds of miles away on the Volga, but on the Elbe, right in the heart of Germany.

After Hamburg in the wide circle of the political and military command could be heard the words: 'The war is lost.'

Against all this, Bomber Command's losses had been much lighter than in the Battle of the Ruhr, thanks largely to the success of Window. Nearly 3,100 sorties had led to only eighty-seven aircraft (or 2.8 per cent) being lost over the target for one reason or another in the four raids, and, although another 174 bombers had been damaged or had crash landed, the overall casualty rate of 8.4 per cent compared favourably with the 16.2 per cent in the Ruhr series, and even more so with the 19.9 per cent of the five Essen raids within that series.

Window continued to confuse and frustrate German defences for most of the rest of 1943, and it was one of the tragedies of the war that it had not been used earlier—particularly in view of the fact that Germany still had no heavy bombers and therefore could not have used it as effectively against British cities. But members of the War Cabinet had deemed it more important to save British civilians than to save British bomber crews, and had hog-tied Harris's hands until now.

The truth was that, in the four raids on Germany's greatest port, Hamburg had suffered more devastation and slaughter than the total the UK was to endure from Luftwaffe raids throughout the entire war, and the truth also was that expected reprisal raids against England had been delayed by the trouncing the Luftwaffe had been suffering above the coasts and hills of Sicily.

The Reich was in such a state of alarm as a result of Bomber Command's terror raids, and was so incapable of any positive retaliation, that Goebbels had been drawn to admit in his diary that: 'The Fuehrer is exceedingly impatient and angry about the lack of preparedness on the part of our Luftwaffe ... We must try to develop counter-measures as fast as possible, especially reprisal attacks. Otherwise, sooner or later, the war in the air will become unbearable for us ... The London public fears that a German air blitzkrieg will suddenly break out again overnight. Would to God that we were in a position to do it!' And he had added, significantly

'. . . letters addressed to me keep asking why Hitler does not visit the bombed areas, and why Goering is nowhere to be seen . . . One worry after another piles on us, and we hardly know how to meet them . . .'

It was 'backs to the wall' for the now-on-the-defensive Nazis. Makeshift reconstruction of factories vital to war production was undertaken in eastern and southern districts, out of the reach of Bomber Command, or in underground bunker fashion in the Ruhr. Owing to the almost-unopposed way in which Germany had over-run western Europe, her war economy had never been stretched, as Britain's had, and there was still plenty of slack to be taken up. With nearly 7 million slave workers to draw on, her manpower resources were fluid and enviable. There were severe shortages of raw materials, bad communications, and over-extended defence lines, but the scope for improvisation in industrial rearrangement was great enough to prove endlessly frustrating to Harris.

On the home front, too, Hitler ordered his frightened but still obedient followers to extemporise and endure. 'Those who are not needed in the cities must get out', was his order. 'Small peoples' houses will be built in very larger numbers. They will have a bedroom for the parents, another for the children, with double-decker bunks, and a place for cooking. Nothing more is necessary.'

The fury of Hitler's counter-blasts of words continued to have their effects on the 300 million German and serf workers he controlled and hypnotised. Despite Bomber Command's devastating raids, in the summer and autumn of 1943 an immense increase in German arms production took place. The output of field, anti-tank and anti-aircraft guns more than doubled, to 27,000 tons, as did production of self-propelled guns. Giant submarines were put in hand in considerable numbers, and a momentous order was given by the Fuehrer for pilotless, jet-propelled flying-bombs and long-range stratospheric-rockets (successfully tested in Poland) to be put into large-scale production for use against the UK.

Meanwhile, the Battle of Hamburg was leading to the Battle on the Road to Berlin in the months to November, 1943. During this period, although the Germans were extemporising in a way that only their ruthless, highly-organised regime could do, and were fighting back against Window by talking their night fighters into contact with the bomber streams, Bomber Command's casualties were held down to something around 4.1 per cent 'missing' rate, and 10.7 overall. Window, indeed, allowed Harris to maintain his offensive, while actually building up the numerical strength of his command—although there was no hope of it reaching more than a quarter of the 4,000 bombers that had been scheduled for 1943.

Nemesis was beginning to overtake Germany. Alas, for a whole variety of reasons, including pressures from Russia—angry because the second front was again to be delayed—expressed in demands via Winston Churchill, that he should widen the range of his raids, Harris failed to follow through and flatten six more German cities as he had flattened Hamburg. Had he done so, the Germans might possibly have capitulated. Immediately after the Battle of Hamburg, Albert Speer (an organisational genius, who had been put in complete charge of Germany's war efforts a few months before) was forced to tell his Fuehrer bluntly that six more attacks on such a scale would cripple the will of the populace to sustain armament production, and would bring a rapid end to the war. Unfortunately, not only were the six more attacks not attempted at this vital moment of the war, but Germany was to be spared any comparable disaster until February, 1945, at Dresden.

As the weeks went on and the nights grew longer, three bombings were made on Berlin, over a period of ten days, involving a total of 1,647 aircraft. But, when no more great Hamburg-scale raids were mounted, Goebbels and Speer regained their confidence and turned respectively to the promotion and production of the secret rocket weapons with which Hitler had promised to raze London to the ground if his minions would hold on until Christmas.

Rumours about reprisal-weapon experiments at the research station on the Baltic island of Peenemunde, had reached Britain through the Polish underground movement earlier in 1943 and Mosquitoes had brought back pictures of the installations. Churchill's son-in-law, Duncan Sandys, had already headed a committee to investigate the facts and had concluded that a new threat (in the form of flying bombs and of a rocket weighing eighty tons, which had a ten-ton explosive warhead) was under way which should be tackled at the earliest possible date, whereupon the Prime Minister at once urged Harris to 'knock out' the island.

In fact Peenemunde was no longer a secret, in general terms.

Since the destruction of Hamburg, Hitler, who had at one time blown hot and cold about missile warfare, had been hysterically demanding mass-production of V-weapons; and Goebbels had seized on the idea of throwing out heavy hints in his propaganda (as virtually the only morale-booster still available to him) that new 'miracle' weapons were coming up fast which would win the war, while exacting a just and terrible retribution on Britain.

Churchill's urgent request had its expression in a brilliant feat of air arms on the night of 17-18 August, when 597 heavy bombers made the very long flight and attacked on timed runs from a small island off Mecklenburg, in bright moonlight. This raid had to be precision rather than carpet bombing, and three specific aiming points were allocated to the pathfinders, all of them segments of the scientific experiment base. The finders and illuminators were led by a highly-experienced master-pilot, Group Captain J. H. Searby, commander of 83 (Pathfinder) Squadron, whose persistence in remaining over the target, after he had seen the three parts of it accurately 'marked', in the most difficult conditions, was one of the greatest acts of individual bravery of the war.

The full moonlight, which had helped the leading planes greatly, was also a boon to the German night fighters, which rose in force and pressed home numerous attacks during and after the raid. Searby, ignoring the dangers, circled for over an hour, switching successive waves of bombers from one section to another of the target as more and more buildings were knocked out, giving them advice and encouragement over his radio telephone.

The flak was inconsiderable and, of the forty-one bombers that fell from the skies over Peenemunde, at least thirty were the victims of single and twin-engined night fighters, while several others had collisions in the congested air lanes and crashed. In addition, thirty-two bombers were extensively damaged and several were written off on return to base. It was an extremely heavy (if not unexpected) toll. But the raid itself had been a dramatic success in terms of accuracy as well as of destruction.

Huge fires swept the entire scientific complex by the time the last Halifax turned for home, mingling with a defensive smoke-screen the Germans had got going too late to do any good; the main aiming points, which were the assembly works, the drawing offices and the administrative block, were blitzed and well alight; the housing settlement for the rocket engineers was almost completely destroyed; and among the 735 people killed were many experts, including Professor Walter Thiel, a propulsion specialist, and Peenemunde's chief engineer, Herr Walther. Christmas was now out for Hitler's promised V1 and V2 attacks on London. Indeed, the rocket programme had been set back by several months.

Praise was heaped on Bomber Command for the accuracy achieved in this raid but, while he accepted it on behalf of his crews, Harris was not too happy about the demands for more and more precision-bombing of selected war-vital targets. He knew how resourceful the Germans were at redeploying such plants and he still favoured the wholesale destruction of large cities on the Hamburg scale.

As Harris's direct boss, Sir Charles Portal, who had issued the original order for indiscriminate bombing, now favoured precision bombing, it was inevitable that Bomber Command should gain have to be many things to many people. Its tasks included a programme of regular attacks (requiring incredible accuracy) on V-weapon launching sites on the coast of France.

Nor was the business of having to bend both ways the only frustration for Harris, as he struggled to achieve a period of single-mindedness in which to mount knock-out blows against the largest German cities. Window had thrown the German defences into such panic that they had been forced to reorganise completely. And, as always, they set about doing the job with diabolical thoroughness. Old ideas went out of the window and new equipment came in through the door. Even the central command (with the splendid Teutonic name of Nachtjagdfliegerkorps XII) was to be disbanded.

As far as the night fighters were concerned, there had to be first a stage of improvisation, while the planners and scientists cleared the decks. In addition to Window, Harris had largely neutralised the effectiveness of night-fighting 'zones', by swamping them with large formations of bombers passed swiftly through the target. So the zones and boxes were now abandoned, and single-seater 'Wild Boar' fighters were given the freedom of the skies, to 'kill' where they could. Radar being temporarily out, the fighter pilots mainly did their own plane-spotting, looking out for bomber shapes in the lights of the fires, the flares they themselves dropped, the marker flares, and the searchlights' glare, their planes having been fitted with anti-dazzle screens and exhaust-shrouds. But these freelance activities were incredibly hazardous, and resulted in unbearably large numbers of fighters being destroyed by their own flak, or in shooting down one another, or in becoming hopelessly lost and crashing. The period of improvisation had to be short, and control had to be re-established quickly, or there would be too few planes left to reorganise.

The Luftwaffe still had no true night fighter, the specialised Heinkel 219 having been delayed by a policy of quantity rather than quality, and the adaptable, powerful Messerschmitt 262 jet-fighter having been held up for a whole year while it was modified, on Hitler's orders, into a Mosquito-type fighter-bomber. These had been incredibly stupid decisions, which had changed the course of the air war in our favour at a critical period. But the Luftwaffe, well used to making the best of what was to hand, now set about modifying the adaptable Junkers 88s and the less attractive Messerschmitt 100s into 'search and destroy' night fighters, bristling with new built-in devices.

Included in special equipment within the planes was a compact Lichtenstein radar set which could pick up radiation from the H.2.S. beams in the British bombers. Using such signals, the technique was that the German fighters would infiltrate a stream of homeward-bound bombers, and either shoot some down over the North Sea or pounce as they began their landing approach. These new dangers and stresses to crews exhausted from long flights tended to catch them off-guard and at the lowest ebb of their strength, when bacon, eggs and coffee were in their minds rather than small dark shadows in the night. Casualties from this technique were therefore heavy.

The Germans also set up monitoring posts to record all radio transmissions from Bomber Command aircraft and to feed up-to-the-minute information to fighter-controllers, who were now using a technique of running commentary instead of radar to guide their pilots towards the bomber streams. Although the total number of Luftwaffe night fighting planes that could be mustered at this period was never more than 350, it seemed to Bomber Command that there were thousands lurking in the sky. Concentration was achieved by efficient and flexible deployment. Single and twin-engined fighters were combined into divisions for specific regions, but they could also be switched around to new areas and fresh tasks at the shortest notice. If controllers found the focus changing, they could scramble northern units and switch them to the south, and vice versa, dozens of satellite airstrips having been cleared for them to refuel and rearm wherever suited their circumstances.

Thanks to this greatly-increased efficiency, Bomber Command's losses were again creeping well past the 5 per cent figure which was then the 'bearable' one. And Harris still had no long-range night fighters available to him to counter this new threat. The few elderly Beaufighters (never more than one squadron at best) which sometimes escorted bomber streams on the first part of their route out, and sometimes met them coming back, were of but little help.

Alarmed at the numbers of planes being gunned down, the AOC-in-C furiously demanded the help of several squadrons of the latest Mosquito night fighters, which had a greater range and more sophisticated 'searching' aids than the Beaufighters; but his demands were turned down flat, on the grounds that the limited numbers of Mossies available were required for home defence and that their equipment should not be hazarded away from British shores, lest it fell into enemy hands. It was the 'Window' story all over again. Bomber crews were obviously regarded as expendable dross in certain quarters, at high level.

Spoof raids (as when a squadron of Mosquito bombers had been sent up to make a feint attack on Berlin on the night of the Peenemunde mission); deception in planning the route chosen to the target; and the jamming of German radio and radar . . . these were the main alternatives open to Harris, but though he made full use of them, losses to German night fighters continued to increase.

All too slowly, as 1943 drew to a close, new techniques to counter those of the Germans were introduced on the British side. A new group (No. 100) was formed under a radar expert, Air Vice Marshal E. B. Addison. Equipped with specially prepared Halifaxes and Stirlings, armed normally and scientifically to 'confound and destroy' the enemy by jamming as well as fighting, it was unable to be of much help until 1944.

A high-power transmitter, to be known as Jostle, was built, on the south-east coast, which could emit a raucous, warbling note, rather like bagpipe music. When this was beamed to overlay the Luftwaffe's night-fighter transmissions it could cut them off from control. Alternately, the transmitter was also used, by German-speaking Intelligence officers, to put out false orders to enemy night-fighters. This technique became so highly developed during 1943 that when, in the middle of a raid on the Ruhr, the Germans tried to counter the deception by introducing a woman controller, the RAF took only three minutes to bring in a German-speaking WAAF officer to renew the verbal confusion.

Powerful new devices, known as Mandrel and Pipecrack, were used in conjunction with Window, to interfere with German air and ground radar respectively. To help with these drills a fresh squadron (No. 192), stationed at Feltwell, was established and given the 'special' role of ferreting out signals and wavelengths from any new German radar or radio equipment. It did this by cunningly using a mixed bag of Mosquitoes, Wellingtons, Ansons and Halifaxes.

A trio of remarkable devices, known as Serrate, Perfectos, and Monica, fitted to night fighting, home-based Mosquitoes, enabled them respectively to home on emissions from any German night fighters that ventured to penetrate British skies; to trigger-off the identification signals fitted to the latter; and to defend the tails of their Mossies against attacks from the rear. Later when Mosquitoes carrying these secret gadgets were finally allowed to venture over the North Sea and into Germany, they were to prove of enormous help to Bomber Command and a grave threat to the Luftwaffe. But that would not be until 1944. In 1943, the night fighter menace to RAF bombers grew ever more effective to the understandable depression of morale.

Inevitably, when their radio and radar were jammed, the Luftwaffe's night fighters had to improvise individually in seeking and killing bombers. One way was to employ filters to pick up bomber exhausts. Another used on moonlit nights, was to fly fairly low over the ground and peer upwards to where the bombers were silhouetted against the lighter sky.

A favourite trick, which worked very well, after a bomber had been spotted, was for the two-man night fighter to fly a little ahead

16—TLC • •

of the quarry, throttle back and climb until the bomber made a perfect sitting target in the observer's gun-sight. The only answer to this Bomber Command pilots found (and it could only work if they saw the fighter in time) was to go into an immediate corkscrew manoeuvre.

The corkscrew was from then on widely practised in squadrons. It not only made the plane difficult to hit in darkness; it also allowed the bomber's gunners to fire at the fighter with reasonable chances of success, as the huge plane spun down and up twisting, turning, and altering speed all the time. This was a rare and welcome indulgence for British air gunners and did their bile no harm. Normally their .303 machine guns were constantly out-ranged by Luftwaffe cannon. They had to endure fire, while holding their own, for precious dangerous seconds before the attacking 'bandit' was close enough to be hit.

This apart, corkscrewing was a technique which was to save many lives over the remaining years of the war, particularly in the case of Lancasters, which could be corkscrewed with tremendous style in violent fashion, but such evasive action was only possible if the bomber's crew spotted the night fighter at an early stage in the proceedings. And the more successful of the Luftwaffe's night fighter pilots claimed that once they had moved on to a bomber, the chances of it taking evasive corkscrew action in time were about eight to one against.

Some German night fighters also armed themselves with signal pistols and short-range flares, which they would fire into a bomber stream to attract their searching colleagues; and towards the end of 1943, a technique was developed for dropping lanes of bright flares over a bomber formation, turning night into day and allowing single-seater intruders to have a field-day in sequences of ahead, quarter and astern attacks. So serious did these various Luftwaffe counter-measures become that, by the spring of 1944, Harris was to be forced once more to reduce the range of his bombing raids mainly to near-home targets in Germany and the occupied countries.

Before this happened, however, the series of Road to Berlin and Battle of Berlin raids had been proceeding, despite increasingly heavy losses. Between the firestorm at Hamburg and the last of the sixteen winter raids on Berlin, in March, 1944, there were to be thirty-three major attacks on German cities. The greatest of these were on Hanover and Kassel, and the others included Essen, Dusseldorf, Remscheid and Bochum (in the Ruhr); Bremen, Frankfurt, Mannheim and Stuttgart (in the central area); and Munich, Leipzig and Nuremberg (in the east and south).

The long mission to Nuremberg which was the last target in the total series, was so shattering for the already-badly-mauled Bomber Command that it quickly forced disengagement from remoter parts of Germany until fighter support could be ensured—a bitter pill this for the proud AOC-in-C, but one which he just had to swallow in the face of unsustainable slaughter and sagging morale.

Nearly 800 heavy bombers flew all the way across Germany to the rich manufacturing city of Nuremberg deep in Bavaria. With plenty of time to get into position to intercept this vast armada before, during and after attack, the Luftwaffe had one of its greatest nights of the war. To the distress of all who were told the true figures, ninety-four bombers failed to return to Britain, twelve crashed in England and fifty-nine were badly damaged. This was a missing rate of 11.8 per cent and a total casualty rate of 20.8 per cent. The gloom in Bomber Command HQ that week could be cut with a knife.

The October to March raids on Berlin had been bad enough, with an average of over 5 per cent fatalities, but this Nuremberg slaughter meant no more heavy blows at the heart of the Reich for months and months. The command had known its 'Black Friday'.

Germany was by now in fairly desperate straits, but would not admit it. She had lost at least a million men in Africa, Russia and Sicily. Having lost her principal ally, Italy, she was having to shore up 3,000 miles of coastline against invasion in the south—this in addition to the 3,000 miles of western European coast which was having to be held against invasion by half the German army and two-thirds of her air force. It was an ever-worsening nightmare, but everyone in Germany thought that Hitler was infallible and had his secret weapons yet to play . . . or so Goebbels would have the world believe.

Little precision had been used in any of the Bomber Command raids from October to March. Mainly they had featured blind saturation of the target area. The Battle of Berlin, conducted on sixteen nights, had been typical. In all, it had embraced 9,111 sorties—7,256 of them by Lancasters, 1,643 by Halifaxes, 162 by Mosquitoes and fifty by Stirlings. A total of 492 bombers had failed to return, ninety-five had been destroyed in crash-landings and 859 had been fairly severely damaged. 3,500 young men, all of them volunteers, were the victims.

It was bus route bombing at its most primitive. Several of the attacks had caused fairly massive damage, and Field-Marshal Milch, Hitler's Chief of Aircraft Production, had told his staff, in February, 1944, that Berlin could not hold out much longer . . . But disengagement for Bomber Command came, alas, before Berlin or any other of the more remote German cities could be Hamburged. Bombing policy went too far at this time, while it also did not go far enough.

Harris had believed that Berlin was the new key to the whole strategic air offensive, and had sent out his fleets to hammer away at it, mostly in almost unbearable conditions of hardship for the crews. In his book, *Bomber Offensive,* he was later to explain: 'The whole Battle (of Berlin) was fought in appalling weather, and in conditions resembling those of no other campaign in the history of warfare. Thousands upon thousands of tons of bombs were aimed at the Pathfinders' pyrotechnic sky markers and fell through unbroken cloud which concealed everything below it except the confused glare of fires . . . ' But at the time he had willingly accepted the difficulties, and had told Churchill: 'We can wreck Berlin from end to end if the USAAF will come in on it. It will cost between 400-500 aircraft. It will cost Germany the war.' Again, he might have been right (as he probably would have been had he been allowed to 'Hamburg' six more cities), except that he had obviously underestimated the potential casualty rate. But the matter could not be resolved. The Americans would not 'come in on it'. They lacked the equipment, the experienced crews and the faith to undertake long-range night operations, and so they declined to attack Berlin in any fashion until well into 1944, when the opportunity to make Milch's words come true had gone forever.

Their attitude was more easy to understand when viewed against the sort of traumatic bombing experiences the 8th Air Force had been going through. So bad had things been for them that there were doubts, early in 1944, about whether they could survive any longer in daylight over Germany. Everything hinged for them on the success or failure of a new fighter, the Mustang, which had been planned to fly as far as the day bombers and defend them. Fortunately, the Mustang, in its P-51B form, with Packard built, 1,520 hp Rolls-Royce engine, was a winner from the off, and round-the-clock bombing was saved. Indeed, when it first appeared over Hanover, Goering at first refused to believe the reporting centre and told off its staff for 'seeing things'. Then, when he finally saw the Mustang with his own eyes, he cried out in anguish and simply exclaimed: 'We have lost the war.'

The new Mustang—featuring cleverly-engineered capacious fuel tanks, and a top speed of 440 mph at 35,000 feet—had arrived only just in time. It had been a hellish year for the 8th AAF. In April, 1943, when General Eaker and his flying army had really got under way with his precision bombing daylight campaign, only 153 heavy bombers had been fully operational at any one time, which meant that the 8th AAFs raids were very small in relation to those of Bomber Command. They were also mainly near-at-hand missions, taking in such 'soft' targets as Emden, Wilhelmshaven, Vegesak, Flensburg, Bremen and Kiel.

Reinforcements in the rest of the year had arrived but slowly in relation to the exceptionally-heavy losses the unsupported American heavies were sustaining daily even on short flights across the North Sea and back.

Bereft of fighter support after the first 180 miles or so, the American heavies felt duty bound not only to beat down the highly-skilled German fighters but also to attempt to cut down their numbers at source. This would involve flying much further afield and bombing the widely dispersed factories of the German aircraft industry.

By September, the 8th AAF had been able to step up their available daily raiding strength to about 300, but in raids on fighter factories they were losing as much as 16 per cent of the bomber forces they were dispatching. It just could not go on. So, in October, the decision had been taken to implement the twin idea that had been put forward when Gibson's Lancasters had knocked out the Ruhr dams, and hit at the war-vital ballbearing factory at Schweinfurt. It was thought that destruction of the vast plants there would deal German aircraft production a crippling blow. So on 14 October, 1943, 291 Flying Fortresses had been dispatched to the Bavarian city, supported to the limit of their range by P-47 Thunderbolt fighters (which, even with extra fuel tanks, could not be further than Aachen): Spitfires were simultaneously sent off to carry out sweeps and draw off German fighters.

The Luftwaffe had been listening in on the not-too-security-conscious American wavelengths for some time, and on this occasion, wisely chose to wait until the Thunderbolts had to turn for home before attacking the Fortresses. Thence to the target and back the two waves of American bombers had had to endure attacks on a scale never experienced before by any bomber force. Sixty of the 228 Fortresses that had not turned back by this time were shot down over Germany and, of the remainder, only thirty got home undamaged.

In all, 198 of the original 291 giant planes had been lost or damaged. It was by far the worst-ever disaster in the history of air bombing, and would be known for ever as Black Thursday.

The raid had only been a moderate success. Within a matter of days Speer's teams of 'flying squad' experts were able to re-start production at Schweinfurt and at other *pre-arranged* alternative centres; and simultaneously, stocks were topped up simply by stepping-up imports from Sweden, where trade with the Nazis was at its height.

As was their wont, too, returning American crews had created a false picture by greatly exaggerating the number of kills by German fighters they chose to claim at de-briefing. They swore they had shot down 186; the true number was about thirty-five.

Whatever the results of the raid, however, it was obvious that day missions into the heart of Germany just were not on any more—at least until the spring when the Mustang would have proved itself a success.

Not that the Americans reduced the scale of their attacks. Reinforcements were now coming forward in impressive numbers (added to the fact that the 9th AAF had joined the 8th in Britain) and ever larger fleets were able to attack targets on the Continent daily in the early months of 1944. But these were mainly within a radius of about 500 miles, with escort from P-47 Thunderbolts with specially fitted drop-tanks to give them range, and it was only when the Mustangs arrived in sufficient quantity that the 8th Air Force began really to pulverise the German heartlands.

The catastrophic Schweinfurt idea, which had all but finished off the 8th AAF, had originally been placed on Harris's desk, but the wily old warrior had opposed it wholeheartedly, largely on the grounds of forecasts of what had now happened to the more foolhardy Yanks. But Portal, the Chief of Air Staff, who was ultimately responsible for the round-the-clock bombing polices of the Allies, now leant heavily on his bomber AOC-in-C and almost incredibly ordered him to pull the American chestnuts out of the fire by carrying out a follow-up raid on Schweinfurt, explaining that if ballbearing supplies could be cut, the impending invasion of Normandy would be that much easier.

Much against his better judgement, Harris had agreed to follow through with a major raid on the ballbearing factories. It took place on the night of 24-25 February, and was disastrously unsuccessful. More than 700 heavy bombers were sent to Schweinfurt. Only twenty-two of them found the target area, which was almost impossible to pin-point in the dark. In any event, Speer had already done his stuff and there was nothing important there to bomb any more.

March came and went and Harris licked his wounds, as he cried out for night-fighting Mosquitoes 'on a substantial scale'. Not for the first time, Bomber Command had had to pause on the brink of a precipice too terrible even for its brave crews to face. In the operations between 18 November, 1943, and 31 March, 1944, 20,224 sorties had been carried out; from these, the incredibly depressing total of 1,047 bombers had failed to return and another 1,682 had been damaged.

It should have been the high-point of Britain's war-long bombing offensive. In many ways it was the low-point of the war for Bomber Command. In November, 1943, the average number of aircraft available for all operations during a given month had reached the all-time high of 864, and supplies were at last reaching the squadrons with regularity and in quantity. But so heavy had the casualties been over the four-and-a-half month period that the average in March, 1944, was still only 974. In effect, Bomber Command had wiped itself out completely over the period . . . and then some. Not only did this add up to a complete turnover of planes it also meant that nearly all the squadrons had lost the bulk of their semi-experienced crews, and that those that remained were very frightened. But bombing policies were there to be followed and there was the ever-present dilemma, as Harris has stated it to me, that 'you cannot make omelettes without breaking eggs.'

Chapter Eighteen

The Allied round-the-clock strategic bombing offensive had lasted a full year, but now, in April, 1944, much to the relief of the heavily-mauled squadrons of Britain's Bomber Command, but to the chagrin of its AOC-in-C, who still had not had his big chance to strike a series of knock-out blows, it had to be abandoned for the time being to allow the invasion of Normandy to take priority over all else.

This switch of policy was to give German industry a lull of six months to repair some of the ravages of the previous twelve.

Speer made full use of this time to move essential production as far as possible from the areas favoured by Allied bombing. But there were some essential goods and services no one could move, among which were transport and oil, both of which had been the subject of many shelved plans during the shifts and changes of strategic opinion over the years at the Air Ministry, since they were first spelled out in parts WA4 and WA5 of the famous thirteen Western Air Plans in December, 1937. These too were about to be dusted and looked at afresh.

Operation Overlord was the subject of everyone's thoughts, hopes and prayers. At last we would be breaking out and hitting back. Thoughts of land and sea battles ahead had at last taken the harsh spotlights off Bomber Command. Dwight D. Eisenhower had been appointed Supreme Commander of the Allied Expeditionary Forces, with Montgomery commanding the assault forces on the ground; Admiral Ramsay was to command the naval forces; and Air Chief Marshal Sir Trafford Leigh-Mallory had been appointed Commander-in-Chief of the Allied Expeditionary Air Forces.

There were squabbles and quarrels about the role of air power in the invasion, although everyone was agreed that if command of the air was not held, Overlord could fail.

As far as bombing was concerned, the Allies had a formidable daily total of 1,119 planes, on average, available each day from mid-April. Harris was at this time anxiously re-thinking ways in which his bombers could be saved from the terrible beating they had been taking from the infiltration of the Luftwaffe night fighters into their midst, so that he could get on with the job as before. On 15 April he warned the Air Staff that 'remedial action' was immediately necessary by the direct support of night fighters 'on a substantial scale'. His Command would otherwise suffer a casualty rate beyond which they could not go on.

Harris was gloomier at this stage than perhaps he had ever been. Nuremberg, Leipzig—when ninety-six aircraft had been lost—and the Battle of Berlin had been bad for morale as well as being grim in terms of losses. The jitters were rather widespread in the ranks. Perfectly understandably, everyone was now flying in fear, whether they admitted it or not. The proportion of pilots reporting things wrong with their aircraft (with Mag. drop faults a favourite let-out) and aborting from a raid, had risen alarmingly. The aircrew detention centre at Sheffield, for flying men judged to be short of guts— or 'lacking in moral fibre', in the official phrase—was by now heavily inhabited, with an average of something like 2,000 unhappy souls in convict-like residence by the spring of 1944. This was bad enough. But the condition of LMF was difficult to prove. And even one bad apple in a squadron—the one man at whom everyone began looking sideways—could also do a great deal of harm to morale in a short time. There just had to be a change of tactics to restore the hearts and spirits of aircrew. But it was not easy to find.

It must have seemed to the AOC-in-C that all the years of apparent steady improvement in planes, equipment and techniques had led to a big let-down. There were no new gadgets in the pipeline to which hopes could be pinned of saving the RAF night bombers from the Luftwaffe night fighters. H2S was slightly improved; Oboe was still the more reliable, but limited in range; the Mark XIV bombsight could only be used after intensive training; all the heavies could fly a bit faster and a bit farther. But these factors bore little relation to the sabre-versus-bludgeon battles that had been decimating his forces.

Nothing had changed very much and yet everything had changed. By sheer cunning rather than increased numbers, the Luftwaffe had won the initiative again in the sky at night. Once they had penetrated a bomber stream (as they were able to do on nearly every mission now) the fight was unequal, with the bombers not only outclassed as far as in-fighting was concerned, but prone to burst into flame all too quickly and easily, thanks to their explosive cargoes of bombs, oxygen, 100 octane fuel, and other inflammable materials.

Spare pathfinders had been used where possible to draw off and deceive German night fighters, by marking a false target to which the bombers were apparently routed, and some success had been achieved for a time by cutting in on Luftwaffe wavelengths and broadcasting false instructions to enemy fighters. But on the whole, the night fighters had turned the tables, with a vengeance, for Bomber Command.

Harris, who, in Tedder's words, supported the invasion plans 'loyally', still wanted to blast German cities to kingdom come, as a means of shortening the war. The chances of ever doing so decisively were now dim, Nuremberg and the Battle of Berlin having produced a costly and tragic climax of the war for his brave legions. Fortunately, Harris was trusted and admired by his Chief of Air Staff, Portal, who was doing more towards winning the war than all the other members of the Chiefs of Staff Committee put together, and whose single-minded view was, that the Army must be given everything to go in with whenever it was feasible to go in. Almost alone, Portal healed the disputes between the three Services.

The basic problems all the British and American air chiefs were facing at this time was that it was absolutely vital that the Allies should be in a dominant position in the air, night and day, by D-day. During embarkation, disembarkation, and when they sought to link up with their equipment and supplies, the invasion armies would be wide open to German bombing and strafing. A similar situation, potentially disastrous, would also prevail afterwards, when the ground forces were ready to break out of their beachheads. At all costs, the air over the Channel and the Normandy coast had to be firmly controlled by the Allies. And as a prelude, all the appropriate Continental transport systems would have to be put out of action, as far as possible, to prevent the German land forces concentrating quickly.

Leigh-Mallory's Expeditionary Air Forces (which had mainly light bombers, plus fighters and transport planes) would be inadequate to ensure this. Authentic heavy bombing would also be required, and the C-in-C looked to Harris and to Lieutenant General Carl A. Spaatz (in charge of all American strategic bombers in Europe and the Mediterranean, with the famous American flier, James H. Doolittle, now in command of the 8th AAF) to satisfy this need.

Neither Spaatz not Harris was keen to get deeply involved in military operations. Harris felt his Command was still incapable of the sort of accuracy that bombing of transport and army-support would involve, the more so as Churchill was adamant that no French civilians were to be killed on any future raids! With Mustang fighter support, Spaatz had fewer worries than Harris and was already achieving daytime dominance in the air. He therefore wanted to continue with the ascendency he was achieving in day blitz raids. Neither of the bomber chiefs was particularly keen on Leigh-Mallory, who had been a fighter man throughout the war and was thought not to understand their problems.

Inevitably, those hardy annuals, the Oil Plan and the Railway Plan, came up for consideration again. In the former case, the theory was that, if the Reich's synthetic oil plants could be knocked out, the resultant shortages of fuel would quickly affect transport, industry, and ultimately the armed forces themselves (including the Luftwaffe). Spaatz was inclined to favour striking at oil, rather than at road and rail transport. Harris agreed, but wanted more information than was available before committing his planes and crews. Also, he was still not getting the fighters he needed, and the consequent troubles and tribulations were still very much with him; but he felt that if he could get enough Mosquitoes and Mustangs, as fighting escorts, and could be allowed to continue with what he considered to be the true heavy bombing role—the strategic attacking of the cities in the heart of Germany—the Luftwaffe could be drawn off, engaged and weakened to the benefit of the invading forces.

The arguments came to a head around the middle of April, with Portal suggesting that Harris should try out the Railway Plan experimentally, not by cutting isolated railway tracks, but by hitting hard at the nerve centres and repair facilities of the systems. Road junctions, bridges and aerodromes were also to be bombed.

Harris volunteered immediately to begin a series of attacks, mainly on French marshalling yards, using Halifaxes, Lancasters and Mosquitoes. The results were very much better than anyone could have hoped; and the Railway Plan was given full priority at Bomber Command.

A new air expert had appeared on the British scene at this time—new in the sense that he had been engaged elsewhere for some years, but a man old enough in experience and wisdom to be able to play an important part in decision-making. Sir Arthur Tedder, uniquely experienced in bombing from the early days of the war, when bombs and aircraft had all too briefly been his main concern, and fresh from his recent tremendous successes in the Middle East, Sicily and Italy, had become Deputy Supreme Allied Commander. Tedder had rapidly become convinced that the Railway Plan and the Oil Plan, in that order, could first help greatly with the invasion and secondly shorten the war. With Tedder as well as Portal firmly supporting these changes of policy, no argument could hold them back.

Although most of the raiding in the Railway Plan (March to June) fell into Harris's lap, something over one-third of the transport targets, in the pre-invasion phase, received the attentions of the 8th and 9th AAFs in daylight to bolster Bomber Commands' massive efforts by night. Similarly, later, the Oil Plan (May to December) would be pursued vigorously by Harris to the point that Bomber Command dropped 63,000 tons of bombs to Spaatz's 43,000 tons.

When it came to the bit, the Railway Plan was shown to be a stunning success—the most immediately profitable sustained bombing programme of the war to date—and worked to the benefit of the invasion forces, as had been predicted at the top.

In due course, when the Americans in Britain began their systematic blitz on the whole spectrum of oil production in Germany (and also resumed their attacks on Reich cities, in conditions of weather unfavourable to oil targets), the 15th AAF in Italy joined in. They were able to batter away at oil plants, aircraft factories and cities in areas which were difficult for British-based bombers to reach—mainly in south and east Europe, and the Balkans.

Part of the reason for the success of the so-called Railway Plan was that the 'old lags' of 617 Squadron participated in it. After the historic dambusting raid, in May, 1943, some members of the War Cabinet and some of the Air Council wanted to have the brave but decimated squadron stood down. Indeed, for a time, the survivors themselves thought they were going to end up as a joke 'one operation' outfit. But Harris had had faith in the continuing idea of a super unit standing by for highly-specialised jobs, and his point of view was eventually accepted.

After the dams had been ruptured, there had been a negative period in which '617' had been given new aircraft in which they were able to do a lot of flying training, at high and low level, but no ops. Then they had been moved from Scampton to Coningsby, another Lincolnshire airfield where the runways were of bitumen instead of grass. This cheered up the bored and 'hand-picked' crews somewhat, as it seemed to indicate that there might be some truth in rumours that really heavy 'special' bombs were to be allocated to them.

Guy Gibson had been taken off flying, on the personal orders of the Prime Minister, and Squadron Leader George Holden, DSO, DFC, had arrived to take his place. The first resumed operations for the squadron under his leadership were 'soft' ones against power stations in northern Italy, on shuttle-services via Algiers, and a few weeks later '617' was somewhat ignominiously involved in leaflet-dropping on Milan.

Then, on 14 September, 1943, the surviving dambusters had been called upon to show and use their unique skills for a second time against a comparable target, the Dortmund Ems Canal—the freight link which carried vast tonnages between the Ruhr, central and eastern Germany, and the North Sea. Eight crews were involved, skippered by Holden, Maltby, Knight, Shannon, Wilson, Allsebrook, Rice and Divall. Of these, Maltby, Knight and Shannon were survivors of Gibson's nine first-line dambusters, and Rice had been in the McCarthy back-up formation of five that had suffered so grievously on the way to the target.

Like the Moehne and Eder dams, the canal was a narrow, difficult target to pin-point, and it was equally susceptible to Ruhr fogs. When the eight Lancasters were half-way to the target, a weather plane had radioed that the target was obscured, whereupon the planes were recalled and turned back, flying low over the North Sea. Somehow David Maltby (one of the last of the originals) made a miscalculation, easy to do when carrying six tons of bombs at just above the dark waters. His Lancaster cartwheeled into the sea and he and his crew of six were never seen again.

The next night, the raid was on again, with fellow dambuster, Mickey Martin, taking David Maltby's place. This time a Mosquito radioed that the weather was clear over the target and the big Lancs flew in towards it at about fifty feet, each carrying a 12,000-pound blast bomb in a light-weight case—the first time bombs of this size had been carried on an op by any aircraft in the world.

The moon was up as they crossed Holland towards Germany. Over the Dutch town of Nordhoorn, an ack-ack gun opened up suddenly, and George Holden, in the leading plane, was hit at once and crashed in a terrible explosion (his blast bomb having been primed) which all but sucked down the other two planes in his vic formation. Lost with Holden were Guy Gibson's hand-picked crew of Spafford, Taerum, Pulford, Hutchison, Deering and Trevor-Roper, who had refused to be rested with Gibson.

At once, Mickey Martin took over the leadership. He had led the survivors safely to within a few miles of the canal, when, with typical but dramatic suddenness, a curtain of fog rose up and enveloped them. The canal was completely invisible until they were right over it, flying very low in swirling mist. Immediately light flak came up at them, in tremendous density, from lock gates along the waterway.

As the laden Lancasters flew around, trying to get a good enough sighting to bomb accurately, Allsebrook was the first of the remaining seven to fall to flak. Wilson crashed and his bomb exploded only seconds later, and Divall apparently crashed at the same time. Knight was hit, lost two engines, dropped his bomb and crashed in flames on the way home. Rice tried, over and over again, to pin-point the canal, was hit several times, jettisoned his bomb and somehow got back to base. Shannon circled for over an hour and finally, catching a glimpse of water, succeeded in bombing the towpath, just failing to breach the wall. Martin was the last to bomb, having flown around at between 100-300 feet for ninety minutes, trying desperately to give his bomb-aimer a reasonable sight of the canal banks. On their thirteenth run in, although hit several times, they apparently managed to get their bomb into the water, but somehow the banks held and Martin turned for Coningsby, cursing his luck on the intercom of the heavily-holed Lanc.

Only three planes got home out of eight—those of Martin, Shannon and Rice, all dambusting 'originals'. It was to be regarded forever after as the blackest night in the many to be endured by the legendary '617'. At this date the squadron had recorded only two 'special' ops and had lost all but six of the original twenty-one crews.

Next day, Martin was made a squadron leader, and deservedly put in temporary command of '617'. New crews were mustered, some fresh-faced 'teenagers', others weather-beaten 'old lags'. There were not over-many volunteers now for what had become known as the 'Suicide Squadron'. Harris was deeply disturbed at the losses, and took '617' off general ops completely, defining their role, within 5 Group under Cochrane's command, as 'special duties only'. They then switched from low to high-level practice, using the modified SABS bombsight, which was incredibly accurate in the right circumstances (and especially when a straight ten-mile run-in to the target was possible) but which could also be temperamental. As soon as possible, the dambusters tried it out on the real thing—a viaduct, near Cannes in the French Riviera. Over the target, they circled like Red Indians, until conditions were right, and then swooped in to bomb, twenty at a time, from two miles short of the target and about 18,800 feet. The viaduct was pitted and, although it still stood, the experience was good and only one Lanc was lost—that of Ted Youseman, shot down over the Atlantic on the way home.

At this stage, a permanent replacement for Holden was brought in by Cochrane, with Martin remaining in the squadron as second-in-command. The new man was the brilliant and eccentric Leonard Cheshire, who, at twenty-five, was the youngest Group

Captain in the RAF, and who had asked to be dropped a rank to Wing Commander to join '617'. He had completed two tours at this time (a rarity in itself) and wore the ribbons of the DSO and bar and the DFC.

Wallis had meanwhile been working on his greatest dream-child, a ten-ton bomb, towards the time when '617' would be ready for it, but even the improved Lancaster was not yet capable of carrying it, so a scaled-down version of six tons was being prepared for the 'special' squadron to use. Both bombs had been designed to be dropped from a great height to be effective, so the SABS bombsight was thought to be ideal for the purpose.

The so-called ski-sites which were being built in northern France, in the form of substantial ski-shaped buildings, with rails for launching buzz-bombs, for Hitler's V-weapon blitz on London, had been receiving the attention of Bomber Command by day for some weeks, with heavy losses to fighters the main result. Even with specialised Pathfinder marking, the targets had proved much too small to be hit.

Cochrane now asked Harris for permission for 617 Squadron to try to pin-point the ski-sites, in conjunction with the Group's Pathfinders, and this was agreed.

On the first attempt, Cheshire led a formation of nine Lancasters while an Oboe-directed Pathfinder Mosquito went in first to light the target. The follow-up force bombed away, using the 12,000-lb blast bombs first tried out on Dortmund Ems. Although the most accurate night bombing of the war was achieved, with an average error of only ninety yards, the ski-sites still stood. Tragically, the TI markers had fallen on the incendiaries all right, but these illuminating precursors, dropped by the Pathfinders, had been 350 yards out.

A few nights later, the same planes flew to mark and bomb an armament factory at Liege but had to return because of the density of the cloud over the target. German night fighters were up in force and on the way back, with their bombs, '617' was again nibbled at by the Reaper, when three Focke Wulfs shot down a Lancaster. Tragically it was that of Geoff Rice, one of the last six of the original dambusters, and who was due to be rested within a few days.

A month later, in January, 1944, the squadron had another go at

17—TLC * *

the ski-sites, dispensing with the pathfinders, with Cheshire and Martin 'illegally' marking the target from a few hundred feet (low-level bombing having been banned by Cochrane after the canal disaster). This time the ski-site was damaged. It was something, but it was not quite good enough for the two perfectionist leaders.

About this time, '617' was moved again, to a one-squadron station at Woodhall Spa, about ten miles from Coningsby. This was to give then a greater measure of security from any prying eyes that might be around. And, as they waited for the expected arrival of Barnes's six-tonner, which had been codenamed Tallboy, Cheshire and Martin continued their target-marking experiments.

Suddenly, almost by accident, Martin hit on the answer to the problem of how to achieve even greater accuracy. By dive-bombing his Lancaster at a target, without using the bombsight, he found he could pin-point it every time. In going forward, he was also going backward. This was mainly a casting back to the techniques the Germans had used in Spain in the late 'thirties. The elaborate gyro-protected super-bombsight was good in some circumstances, but the professional judgement of a dead-eyed pilot was still superior to any manufactured device.

Dive-bombing was to be the new drill for releasing markers.

At once, more attacks were logged on the ski-sites and each time the bullseye was hit. Cochrane, when he realised what had been happening behind his back, as it were, remonstrated with Cheshire and Martin, but the two veteran fliers were able to persuade him that it was actually safer to mark in a fast dive.

To prove the new accuracy, a twelve-bomber raid was then attempted, with the 'dive-bombers' leading to plant incendiaries and markers respectively, on an aero-engine factory at Limoges, in south-west France. So well marked was the plant that the squadron was able to plaster it accurately from 10,000 feet, levelling it to the ground more thoroughly than any factory had been levelled by a small force before. Precision bombing had come to mean just that, at long last.

After a couple more missions to southern France, Micky Martin, against his will, was 'rested' and posted to 100 Group HQ, where, characteristically (and subconsciously following the Guy Gibson pattern) he soon wangled himself into intruder ops by night, in

Mosquitoes. In a tribute, Leonard Cheshire described Martin as the greatest operational pilot the RAF had ever produced. As he was by then one of the greatest in the world himself, this was praise indeed.

After Martin left, Cheshire re-formed '617' into three flights, for easier administration, and he appointed the only three original dambusters still with the squadron, Munro, McCarthy and Shannon, to lead them. This created an appropriate international situation. Cheshire was as English as they come, and the other three were a New Zealander, an American and an Australian respectively.

After five successful raids with the three-flight squadron—to an aircraft factory at Albert, a ballbearing plant near Lyons, a rubber factory at Clermont Ferraud, and two explosives factories at Bergerac and Angouleme—Cheshire came to the conclusion that he could improve his master-bombing accuracy still further, especially where the targets were heavily defended, if he marked with a Mosquito instead of a Lancaster. Harris thereupon *lent* the squadron two Mosquitoes, which had to be returned if they did not improve performance. Cheshire in fact made his point so strongly, in two more outstandingly successful raids (on factories at Toulouse and St. Cyr) that in mid-April, 1944, four more Mosquitoes were *given* to 617's most experienced fliers, McCarthy, Shannon, Kearns and Fawke, who thenceforward flew nothing else. Sophistication was being added to sophistication, and accuracy was continuing to move towards perfection, albeit within a small scale of one dedicated 'special' unit.

With their Mossies proudly leading the way, '617' marked for 5 Group, with flares and TI bombs, on the night of 18 April, 1944, in a Railway Plan raid on the Juvisy marshalling yards, eleven miles south of Paris. So accurate was the target-finding by Cheshire's 'cats' that the 200 Lancs, which quickly followed them in, plastered the yards with 1,000 *overlapping* craters. In fact, the damage was such that Juvisy was to be out of action for the rest of the war and would not be reconstructed until 1947. This was the sort of success (albeit against comparatively-undefended targets) the Air Staff had been dreaming of since 1937. It was better late than never.

The next night the target for the same force was the equivalent set-up of marshalling yards at La Chappelle, on the other side of Paris, but nearer the city. As there was a serious risk of French casualties (which Churchill had forbidden, more or less on penalty of the rack for any fliers who disobeyed) even greater marking care had to be taken. Again the raid was successful.

La Chappelle was the perfect example of how crazy Churchill's notion was. The sidings were close to the Gate du Nord and were surrounded by French homes. Despite the most stringent warnings and disciplines, several Lancaster-borne bombs fell on a block of flats alongside the marshalling yard and demolished it. There were rockets all round, in memo form, when recce-pictures revealed this 'horrific' fact. For a few days the Railway Plan was in jeopardy, and was only allowed to continue after further warnings had been issued about saving French lives at all costs. The pay-off came after the war when records unearthed in Paris showed that the tenement had been occupied at the time by a Reichswehr flak battalion.

By various cloak-and-dagger subterfuges, Hitler had to be persuaded to guess wrong about the Allied invasion of Europe. And a major contribution to his lack of intuition at this vital time was made by 617 Squadron in Operation Taxable. After intensive preparation, night and day for a month, sixteen of their Lancasters, in two groups of eight, pulled off one of the best thought-out bluffs of the war. This was for the aircraft to impersonate, for eight long hours, a massive fleet of ships moving towards the French coast at Cap d'Antifer and Calais on the night of D-day, 5-6 June, 1944.

The drill was to fly over the Channel, from dark to dawn, on short back-tracking courses, dropping Window at regular intervals on eighteen small British ships which were towing balloons towards France at a steady seven knots. The effect of Window, added to the 'images' of the real ships and balloons, would, it was hoped, give the picture on German radar screens of a big convoy, fourteen miles wide and several columns deep, moving towards the Pas de Calais. Hopefully this would tie up large German forces on the wrong side of the Seine, while other Bomber Command units prepared to blow up the bridges in between, just before the true landings took place in Normandy.

It was an incredibly tricky manoeuvre. If one bomber had been fifty feet out in height, or three seconds out in ETA timing, the game might have been given away. To achieve absolute efficiency, perfectionist Cheshire had manned each Lanc with twelve crewmen for the mission—an extra pilot and an extra navigator to double-check every reading, plus three men with stopwatches to time the jettisoning of the bundles of Window. Everyone had been locked up in their quarters, at Woodhall Spa, for twenty-four hours, to prevent any chance of a leak of information, although only Cheshire knew exactly what it was all about.

The first wave of eight Lancasters set off at 11 pm and flew at exactly 200 mph over the little ships, from the Kent coast onward, in wide formation (invisible to one another) at exactly 3,000 feet, following the drill to perfection—forward for thirty-two seconds, turn, back for thirty seconds, turn, forward for thirty-two seconds and so on, heaving out Window at precise intervals to coincide with blip-intervals on German radar screens. Everything went exactly as planned—with the big guns of the coastal batteries on the Calais coast blasting away at nothing, or next to nothing—the only tricky bit being the change-over by the second wave of eight Lancs at 3 am. Indeed, the Germans were fooled to the point that the main forces up the Channel were to be saved the many casualties reinforcements from the Pas de Calais area would have caused them. It was another demonstration of how discipline and precision could be used, even among heavy bombers, to achieve a success out of all proportion to the strength of the forces used.

By now the measure of air superiority the Allies had gained over the Luftwaffe at this decisive moment of the war was all too apparent. The selected invasion coastline had been largely isolated by the Railway Plan and its destruction of road bridges, airfields and marshalling yards. And it seemed as if the Luftwaffe was also being contained as never before. In the course of 200,000 sorties in which 300,000 tons of bombs had been dropped, in the two months prior to D-day, the Allies had lost only one aircraft per thousand sorties. On D-day itself, 14,674 sorties had been flown in twenty-four hours (5,656 of them British) for a loss of only 113 aircraft.

Despite more than two years of round-the-clock bombing, however, during which about 30,000 acres of forty-seven cities had been razed, German production of fighters was at least twice as high at invasion time as it had been a year before, so there would be much bitter air fighting to come, when the Luftwaffe had adjusted to the new situations and had found answers to them.

Nor had the Germans ever given up the idea of bombing Britain. In the 'little Blitz' which had petered out just before D-day, 550 aircraft of Fliegerkorps IX, using Pathfinders on the Harris pattern (but not, repeat not—contrary to predictions—making much use of Window) had caused some hardship and casualties in southern England. These raids, however, had been pin-pricks compared to what Bomber Command had been able to achieve in Germany. The Luftwaffe still had few bombers of any type and no true 'heavies'. Proportions of bombers to other planes had been miscalculated for five years. And now, with German production running at its highest-ever rate in June, 1944 (but due to decline steadily from July), fighters were actually accounting for 78 per cent of all production and bombers for only 11 per cent, thanks, undoubtedly, to Harris's blitzes on Germany.

Two days after D-day, the specialists of 617 Squadron, unharried by the Luftwaffe, were again used to great effect when they dropped the first six-ton Tallboy 'earthquake' bombs on the Saumur tunnel, to prevent a Panzer division moving by rail to Normandy.

Tallboy was to prove itself a truly great Barnes Wallis invention. A formidable, 12,030-pound, scaled-down version of the 10-ton Grand Slam weapon he was planning, it could only be carried by Lancasters and (as each bomb was individually made) had to be used only for very important and suitable targets. The greater the height from which Tallboy was dropped, the greater the penetration of the target. At the Saumur tunnel, using the new, incredibly accurate, but frighteningly sophisticated, high-level SABS gyro-stabilised bombsight again, Cheshire and his crews dropped their precious loads from a maximum 20,000 feet, and watched the Wallis monster-weapons spear into the railway embankments with disappointing little puffs and flashes of light. But, contrary to appearances, this was no anti-climax. Tallboys did the work almost invisibly. Burrowing at least ninety feet deep into the ground, they triggered their earthquakes. The tunnel quietly collapsed, buried in 10,000 tons of earth and chalk. The Panzers never got through, and the tunnel still had not been put back when the Allies eventually over-ran the area. Wallis had certainly done it again. The pity was

that no one had listened to him when he first offered to create
'earthquake' bombs four years before.

In the weeks that followed the Saumur triumph, although the big
bombs were scarcer than Rembrandts, 133 troublesome E-boats
were sunk in Le Havre and Boulogne, provoking Harris to say, in
his message of congratulation to Cheshire: 'If the Navy had done
what you have done, it would go into the history books as a major
naval victory . . .'

The very next day, after the E-boat attacks, Hitler's 'secret
weapons' began landing on London and southern England in the
form of the first of 7,547 V1s which would buzz their erratic ways
across the Channel from bunkers on the coasts of northern France
and later from aircraft and from mobile Vergeltungswaffe-units
elsewhere in Europe. At once, 617 Squadron was sent on a new
series of missions to attack the ski-sites, and the blockhouses from
which other V-weapons were to be fired, using all the penetrating
Tallboys that could be mustered. For these raids, the Mosquito-led
Lancasters flew in daylight, using their own 'gaggle' formations,
which differed radically in technique from the wing-to-wing style of
the 8th AAF. Cheshire had characteristically chosen the word
'gaggle' to describe the method he had devised, which was for the
bombers to fly 200 yards apart in lines of five abreast, each line 300
yards away from the next, and each at a different height. This had
to be very carefully worked out and practised, so that bombs did
not drop from the topmost planes on to those beneath; but it was
brilliantly successful, in the context of precision bombing, in that
the formation offered a well-dispersed target to flak, and in that,
finally, it allowed the aircraft to converge when necessary and bomb
almost as one plane.

Thanks to Cheshire's disciplines, and his intelligent leadership,
casualties to his 'suicide' squadron had been nil for some weeks,
although they were inevitably to creep up again in the even-more
difficult sorties of the summer to come. His latest idea, at the time of
the anti-V-weapon campaign, was typical of his imaginative approach
to the ever-present demands for greater accuracy with safety.

He reasoned that if a medium-sized Mosquito was better than a
big Lancaster for fast, accurate marking of targets, an even smaller
fighter-type plane would get him in and out more quickly and

safely, while affording at least an equal degree of precision. So, knowing that it would waste valuable time to go through the usual channels, and might not meet with success in the end anyway, he went to see a friend at the 8th AAF, explained his theory and was immediately given a Mustang. This was typical of American quick thinking generosity. No strings were attached. The valuable plane was his to do what he liked with. He did not even have to sign a chitty for it.

Never one to waste a moment, Cheshire incredibly made his very first flight in the very different American fighter as marker-leader on an operation against an important rocket site at Siracout, learning how to fly the single-engined plane on the way to the target. The new, faster Mustang was an immediate success, providing an even more nimble target for German ack-ack batteries, and allowing equally accurate marking in the course of dramatic dives to 100 feet or less. Cheshire was delighted and employed the Mustang on subsequent raids against reserves of rockets and buzz-bombs, in mushroom caves at St. Lieu d'Esserent, near Paris, when Tallboys caved in and sealed the hill under which they were stored and assembled, killing 800 German workers in the process. He also led in the Mustang when '617' attacked a little-known rocket site at Mimoyecques, where the value of the complete success that was again registered was not fully appreciated until after the war.

British Intelligence knew that something important was going on in extensive diggings near the French village, but exactly what they did not know until 1945. The truth was that slave workers were creating vast underground tunnels in which were to be installed V3 weapons (one of Hitler's few aces which we knew absolutely nothing about). The V3 was a 'big Bertha' type gun with a barrel several hundred feet long, hidden in the ground under many tons of concrete, and capable of firing 400 tons of shells a day into the heart of London. The V3 never fired once. Cheshire's Mustang, backed up by 617's Lancasters, and their Tallboys, saw to that.

This had been Leonard Cheshire's 100th trip. Statistically, he ought to have thrown away six or seven lives. Enough was enough. Harris insisted that he had to be rested, forcibly if necessary, and with him his brilliant flight commanders, McCarthy, Shannon and Munro. There were all-too-few such men still alive to tell the tale.

In his place, Cochrane called in Wing Commander Willie Tait, a dour, pipe-smoking Welshman, with a double-DSO and a DFC. Fawke took over one of the three flights and Tait brought in two very experienced pals to command the other two, in the shape of Squadron Leaders J. V. Cockshott and T. C. Iveson.

At first, Tait used a Mosquito for marking, but soon he took over the Mustang, and was 'accepted' by the toughies of 617 Squadron as a worthy successor to Gibson, Martin and Cheshire, when he led his Lancasters on a difficult raid on V-weapon blockhouses at Watten. Smoke had been used by the Germans to obscure the target, and the marker bombs could not be seen. So Tait dived again towards the dimly-discernible concrete structures, calling on his radio-telephone for the high-flying Lancs to bomb at him. In the end, it was a very effective raid and Harris sent special congratulations.

By the end of July, after raids on V1 storage dumps in railway tunnels, the battle of the rocket sites was brought to a very successful conclusion, with the Allied ground forces bursting through to the Pas de Calais. As they did so, their commanders were astonished to discover that 617's earthquake bombs had achieved fantastic accuracy in all cases. This was all the more remarkable when it is considered their tasks, in flying at 200 mph, and 20,000 feet up, and aiming from several miles back, had been equivalent to hitting a pin in a haystack with a peashooter from 200 yards.

At this point in time, it was announced that Group Captain Cheshire had been awarded the Victoria Cross—not for any single act of gallantry, but for a sequence of persistently brave activities over a period of four years—which was by far the hardest and most deserving way in which to win the most coveted of all medals.

Now that 617 Squadron had lost its priority V-weapon targets, something new, of special importance, was sought for its skills and its Tallboys. Cochrane had been keen to prove that the six-ton earthquake bomb could be used on water, as well as it could on land, so a new sequence of raids, at two-day intervals, was made on U-boats and U-boat pens at Lorient, Brest and La Pallice. Tallboys were still very hard to come by and in one raid, on La Pallice, only seven could be mustered. But true to its fantastic tradition for accuracy, 617's Lancaster bomb-aimers succeeded in lobbing six of the seven earthquake bombs into the mouths of the pens, resulting in a cryptic message from Cochrane: 'All goal-scoring records broken in this raid'. And as a direct result of this series of attacks, scores of U-boats were forced to head for Arctic waters.

Alas, a number of 'old lags', including Duffy, were lost in these extremely hazardous operations, in which ship and shore flak was at its heaviest. Tragedy could never be far away amid such risks.

Equally dramatically, at this time, '617' succeeded in sinking the cruiser *Gueydon* in Brest harbour, thus preventing its intended use as a blockship to stem the entrance against use by the Allies.

This inevitably led to fresh thoughts about the *Tirpitz*, lurking in Alten Fjord, at the extreme northern end of the long Norwegian coast. Its presence had long been a frustration to Harris, who was constantly being asked to do something about the threat to shipping it posed from the convenience of this Norwegian Arctic inlet . . . the more so as Britain was having to hold a battleship fleet ready to engage her, which could be profitably deployed elsewhere.

Obviously, the best chance of sinking the *Tirpitz* lay with '617' and its Tallboys. The trouble was that the fjord was beyond the range even of the versatile and greatly-improved Lancaster, especially carrying a bomb weight of 12,030 pounds. Then the idea of a shuttle raid was revived, with the amendment that the bombing would be additional to the shuttling. So it was that, early in September, 1944, two waves of Lancasters, of 617 and No. 9 Squadrons (9 Squadron, with its Mark IV bombsights, being regarded as the second most accurate squadron in the force) set off on the dauntingly difficult 12-hour journey from Scotland to Russia. They were to refuel at Yagodnik, an island airfield, 25 miles from Archangel, and bomb the *Tirpitz* from there. Accompanying the two squadrons of thirty-eight Lancs were two Liberators, packed to the wings with skilled ground-crews and their equipment; a weather reconnaissance Mosquito; and a spare Lancaster, equipped to film the project.

Inevitably individual planes got separated from the main forces en route, with the magnetic compass, plus icy blasts of air, adding new tricks to their troubles as they got nearer the North Pole. In the event, after one plane had accidentally dropped its bomb in the sea and returned home, thirteen of the thirty-seven remaining Lancs failed to find the tiny island in the Dvina River that was their destination. Lost and nearly out of petrol the thirteen had to land wherever they could, which added up to an area of about 100 square miles. In the case of Iveson and Knilans, this meant a small tree-lined field where they put down together, their petrol gauges showing zero and their noses all but poking into the trees. Incredibly both were able to take off again later from the muddy grass (when the helpful Russians got some fuel to them) by cropping some of the tree tops as they powered upwards at full throttle.

There were no casualties in either squadron, and only six aircraft (four them from 9 Squadron) were written off where they lay in marshy ground. After three days of heavy sleet and rain had delayed the return, the remaining thirty-one sound (and patched up) aircraft set sail for Norway in the west, on 15 September, the Film Unit Lancaster tailing along behind.

The weather plane had reported that the skies were clear over the fjord, but, by the time the Lancs got there, smoke-pots had been lit by the Germans, and the huge battleship could scarcely be seen for black billows of chemical smoke. Unable to take satisfactory pictures, the film Lanc flew directly back to Waddington, while the others circled the target area.

Using the SABS and Mark XIV bombsights respectively, the bomb-aimers of 617 and 9 Squadrons did their best, but they had lost their aiming marks completely in the drifting smoke. Despite heavy flak, half the planes dropped their Tallboys, and some smaller 'Johnnie Walker' anti-shipping bombs they were carrying, some after several runs over the target, before returning to Russia. One of the bomb-aimers thought he had seen Tait's Tallboy (the first to drop) hit the *Tirpitz*, but there was no confirmation from any of the others, and the Russians showed their displeasure at the apparent failure by cutting the hospitality short, and charging the squadrons 9,239 roubles for their previous entertainment. Disconsolately, the crews (six of them now doubled up because of the planes written-off) returned to Scotland. On the way, one of the best of 617's experienced crews (an all-Jewish one, skippered by Rhodesian-born Flying Officer Levy) was lost in the mountains of Norway, and with them the crew of another Lancaster.

The others returned safely, but low in spirits. It appeared to them to be 617s' first serious failure for many, many months, and it hurt.

[In fact, Tait's bomb *had* hit the *Tirpitz* (although reconnaissance failed to show this) and *had* knocked it out completely . . . but this was not to be known until after the war. On 12 November, 1944, the two squadrons would be greeted by an RAF band with the tune 'See the Conquering Heroes . . .' when they would return from restoring their honour by finally sinking the *Tirpitz* from 12,000 feet. The big battleship would have by then been moved to Tromso—just within 'hotted up' Lancaster range from Lossiemouth. What they would not know was that she had been towed to Tromso because Tait had in September rendered her useless for anything other than the immobile role of an ack-ack fortress.]

On the night of 19-20 September, four nights after the Russian shuttle, Guy Gibson was killed in operations against Munchen-Gladbach. He had been in America with Winston Churchill, who had personally coined the name for him of 'dambuster'. He had agreed to be put up for nomination as prospective Conservative candidate for Macclesfield. He had also written his book, and had quickly tired of the desk job he had been given at the Air Ministry.

'Gibbo', as he was known, had been absolutely determined to get back into flying almost from the day he was rested, but no one would authorise it. More and more, he felt he was being denied his whole reason for existence.

At last, in desperation, young Guy Gibson had turned to the one man he knew could understand *and* help—'Bomber' Harris, the AOC-in-C, who had been Gibsons' group commander in his first four of operations in Whitleys in 1939-40. Harris, quite wrongly in his own subsequent admission, but understandably nonetheless, had eventually given in, and agreed that his old friend could fly on 'just one more sortie'. It was left to Cochrane to decide which one.

Tragically, the medium-strength raid by 220 Lancasters on railway targets at Munchen-Gladbach and its sister town of Rheydt, near the west German border, was the one decided upon. Gibson was to fly a Mosquito (a new plane to him) as master-bomber. It would be his first operational flight since May, 1943.

The raid in itself was completed successfully, and the raiders were heading for home when Gibson's low-flying Mosquito was unexpectedly hit by random flak, and crashed, a blazing wreck, at Steenbergen, Holland.

Gibson and his navigator, Squadron Leader J. B. Warwick, had been thrown out on impact. Their bodies were mutilated and almost unrecognisable. They were buried, by the villagers, in one coffin in one grave, with only Warwick's name on the simple white cross. Wing Commander Guy Gibson, VC, had carried no identity documents.

One of the greatest pilots of all time was, perhaps appropriately, an 'unknown soldier' until Steenbergen had been liberated and his identity established some months later.

On the night of 23-24 September, 617 Squadron led 5 Group in an attack on the Dortmund Ems canal, the scene of the squadron's biggest tragedy of a year before. This time they made no mistake. There was no fog and quickly the waterway was breached. Furious at the cheek of the raid, Hitler called in his slaves and had the canal patched up within two months. So 5 Group promptly knocked it down again, within two hours of the lock gates being reopened. And this time the strategically important waterway stayed closed until after the end of the war.

Shortly after this, Tait (who now had four DSOs and two DFCs—a record) was persuaded to have a rest from flying, and another veteran pilot, Canadian John Fauquier, dropped a rank to take over. Fauquier was much older than the rest of the squadron, but he was a toughie and a first rate master-bomber. On the last day of the year, he led '617' successfully against convoys in Norwegian waters, and in January the squadron went back to Bergen to attack U-boats, alas with heavy casualties from fighter attacks. Meanwhile, the first of the Grand Slam 10-ton-bombs was ready at last and Fauquier was determined to be one who would drop it on the bloody Nazis.

While precision raiding was being carried out with commendable accuracy by the select few of '617' and by a couple of other exceptionally talented squadrons, the many fliers of the lost command had been continuing to do their duty, as best they could, in conditions that had continued to be disheartening and depressing.

Halifax crews had learned to drop newly-devised para-mines from 15,000 feet (as against the previously suicidal height of

600-800 feet) and their anti-shipping activities before and after D-day had played an important part in that operation. In Montgomery's break-out from the beach-head after the invasion, Bomber Command had dramatically laid a carpet of 2,363 tons of bombs north of Caen, where the Wehrmacht were heavily dug in, with the result that Field Marshal von Kluge, who commanded the area, was forced to write to Hitler in despair: 'There is no way by which, in the face of the enemy air forces' complete command of the air, we can discover a form of strategy which will counterbalance its annihilating effect, unless we withdraw from the battlefield.'

In suitable circumstances, army-support bombing, in blanket form as distinct from precision, was proving itself extremely valuable in dazing the German troops and rendering them that much easier to over-run and capture. Fighter-bombers of the TAF were able to follow the heavy bombers, on this and other similar occasions, and create a rout (by knocking out vehicles and tanks with its rockets) . . . a rout that soon became a massacre.

Later, as Montgomery sought to end the war by Christmas, and by-passed a group of strongly-held enemy fortresses, including Le Havre, Boulogne and Calais, Bomber Command 'captured' these by subjecting them to a few days of very heavy bombing. It was not all success, however, and Monty's failure in attempting to cross the lower Rhine at Arnhem, and so outflank the Siegfried Line on the north (although again Bomber Command gave prodigious support) was to condemn the Allies to fight well into 1945.

Many new types of bombs were now coming forward and napalm incendiaries (wing tanks containing specially prepared petrol mixtures) began to be dropped on suitable targets, including fuel depots.

Thanks to the ground work and examples of Cheshire, Martin and other dambusters, British Pathfinder-led night bombing generally had become more accurate, on average, than American daylight bombing, which relied on the excellent Norden bombsight.

This had considerable bearing on the Oil Plan, in which the Americans were scheduled to carry out many more sorties than the British. It was soon found that Bomber Command's contributions to it were achieving closer accuracy. There was also the advantage that British bombers could carry and drop much greater weights of bombs than their American opposite numbers. For example, in July and August, 1944—the peak months of the Oil Plan—Bomber Command dropped 128,000 tons of bombs, which was more than three times the tonnage they had been able to let loose on Germany in the same two months of 1943; and in the same period, the 8th AAF (although it now had more aircraft available than Bomber Command) achieved a total of only 85,000 tons.

Alas, even with fighter support, the British night formations were still suffering much heavier losses than those of the 8th AAF by day.

In successful attacks by 935 Liberators and Fortresses on synthetic oil plants at Zwickan, Brux, Luetzkendorf and Bohlen, during which a severe air action had developed, the Americans had lost the largest numbers for some months—a total of forty-six bombers—bad enough, but not disastrous. In these raids, by the way, a 'plus' was unwittingly scored that was at least as important as the one recorded by '617' in knocking out the V3 weapons. This was when bombs landed and knocked out a building near Merseburg-Leuna where Germany (unknown to the Allies) was experimenting with heavy-water towards the manufacture of an atom bomb.

By contrast, from 832 heavy bomber night sorties despatched by Bomber Command against oil installations at Gelsenkirchen, Wesseling, Sterkrade and Scholven, the alarming total of ninety-three Lancasters and Halifaxes had failed to return—a rate of loss more than twice that of the Americans' worst raid, detailed above. The supporting long-range Mosquitoes (and modified Beaufighters with drop-tanks) were proving less successful in beating off German night fighters than had been hoped—despite the ever-more-elaborate radar devices they carried . . . and few Luftwaffe night fighters were being shot down, whereas the Americans were downing day fighters in impressive numbers.

Gradually, however, as the Allies built and occupied airfields on the Continent, in the wake of the advancing ground forces, Spitfires were able to join in with the Mosquitoes and Mustangs, by night and day, in supporting bomber forces further and further into Germany, and losses began to drop again. There was also the fact that Oboe could now be directed from France, with subsequent range advantages.

By the same process, German night fighters lost their forward bases and a lot of their radar assistance, which increasingly restricted their activities. Indeed, by the end of the main Oil Plan, Bomber Command's losses (which had been a frightening 11 per cent at the start) dropped to something of the order of 3.5 per cent. And British daylight raids, which had again been introduced by this time, recorded even lower loss-rates, thanks to increasing and improving fighter cover.

Eventually, the oil offensive was to be extended, on a lesser scale, to the end of the war, and it is worthy of note that, in the total period, the Allied bombing fleets would make no fewer than 555 major attacks on 135 targets, taking in every known synthetic-fuel plant and major refinery in Axis-Europe. And the overall effect on German oil production was dramatic in the extreme. By the end of 1944 (when they had lost most of their alternative natural fuel sources in Poland and Rumania) synthetic supplies were cut in half; by March, 1945, output would have been reduced, in less than a year, from 662,000 tons to a mere 80,000 tons. This was undoubtedly the greatest bombing success of the war, which it certainly shortened. Unlike the abortive raids on ballbearings and other such 'vital' supplies, the Oil Plan really bit harder and harder. It also saved bomber crews from heavier losses, when the production of aviation gasoline went down from 170,000 tons per month in mid-1944 to 25,000 tons by the late autumn, with reserve stocks virtually exhausted. This was an important bonus for Bomber Command. Over the winter of 1944-5, a large number of Luftwaffe night fighters were grounded simply through the drying-up of fuel supplies.

Speer paid a remarkable tribute to Britain's Pathfinder-led night-bombing forces at this point when, in a depressing secret report to Hitler, he particularly stressed that the heavier bombs being dropped by the Lancasters 'were falling with ever greater accuracy and were doing much more permanent damage than the American ones'. This was praise indeed, if Bomber Command could have been aware of it.

Sir Arthur Harris was still hell-bent on having a further crack at flattening more German cities—continuing to believe that the Nazis would capitulate if he hit them hard and often enough. He favoured a plan, which had been drawn up earlier in 1944, known as 'Thunderclap'. This was based on the theory that one massive 24-hour coup de grace on Berlin, or some other city or cities, could conclude the war overnight.

As the Oil Plan's demands lessened, and as the winter weather worsened, medium-strength attacks on German cities were encouraged. In the last quarter of 1944, Bomber Command dropped (despite indifferent weather conditions) the staggering total of 165,000 tons of bombs on the Reich, more than half of them on the city centres. This was a fourfold increase on the tonnages dropped a year before, and twenty times as much as two years before. In particular, in day and night raids on Duisburg, by 2,000 Lancasters and Halifaxes (escorted by about 300 miscellaneous fighters), on 14 October, and the night of 14-15 October, Bomber Command had dropped a greater tonnage in twenty-four hours than the Luftwaffe had dropped on London in five years. Nor were losses heavy. In all, from these two giant raids, only twenty bombers were lost. Eisenhower had been very impressed with Harris and with Bomber Command's recent efforts. On hearing that they were proposing to fly in any weather short of the impossible, he is said to have replied: 'God-dammit, they've already achieved the impossible.'

Nor had specialist precision bombing been left out of account. In October, 1944, splendidly accurate raids were made in daylight on dykes at Walcheren, Flushing and Veere, causing considerable flooding on a wide scale to the considerable assistance of the advancing Allied armies; and, in December, V2 rocket sites in Holland were attacked with such accuracy and ferocity that the Germans were forced to switch to firing their rockets at night. Attacks on transport targets, particularly in the Ruhr, were also continuing with considerable precision. In all, between October and December, about 60,000 tons of bombs were dropped on the Ruhr, causing some 50,000 slave workers to have to be diverted from trench digging to repairing rail and road transport, communications links, and essential supplies, while another 30,000 had to

18—TLC • •

be taken from working in armaments factories to clear up the general damage done to cities by the bombing.

Despite bad weather, Bomber Command alone contrived to give assistance when the German Army's last offensive of the war was launched by Field Marshal von Runstedt in the Ardennes on 16 December, 1944—the unexpected and highly dramatic event which became known as 'the battle of the bulge'.

The very fact that the Germans were able to mount a counter-offensive, at a time when almost everyone had expected the war to be over, inevitably brought frustration and depression in high places in the Allied commands. The war seemed to be dragging on endlessly and dangerously.

There were fears at the top that Hitler *might* have developed an atom bomb and, if so, would use it soon. No one knew for sure, but not knowing was even worse than knowing. Equally depressingly, the stratospheric V2 weapons were becoming increasingly frightening, particularly because (unlike the buzz-bombs) no way had been found of shooting them down. Large U-boats, with schnorkels, were renewing the Atlantic war.

And then there was the jet-plane menace, which had been building up over the past few months. It had been experienced first by Allied fighters; then by Mosquito bombers (previously immune to attack, thanks to their speed and their high-flying capability); and, more recently, by Allied heavy-bomber formations. Messerschmitt 262 twin-jet fighters were the main cause of these alarms, but other advanced jet and turbo-jet planes were also reaching Luftwaffe squadrons, and no one quite knew the impending strength of them.

Germany had been playing around with jet propulsion before the war, more or less simultaneously with Whittle, and their first prototype jet plane had flown in 1941. Now Goebbels began boasting that '1,000 jet planes' were in the pipeline and would turn the air war in Germany's favour within months.

Certainly, the Luftwaffe was being presented with some truly remarkable jets and other advanced planes. Together with the Me 262 jet fighter, there had come to hand, in reasonable numbers, the Messerschmitt 163 rocket fighter; the Junkers 448 and 287 bombers; the Dornier 335 and 635 fighters; and the Arado 234 turbo-jet bomber. Dornier 217s were also being used to fire PC 1,400 FX and HS 293 radio-controlled bombs against Allied shipping.

There is a misguided impression in Britain that we invented and led in jet engines. The truth is, as Mosquito and other Allied pilots were to learn to their cost in the closing months of the war, Germany's jets were well ahead of any British (or American) ones, including the few Meteor 3s which were to be introduced into the battle from a Belgian base and which, with their poor climb and modest range, were to be shown to be unsuitable for combat. Although, towards the end of the war, more powerful Meteors would carry out some ground-strafing, they were never a match for their German equivalents and would not destroy a single enemy aircraft over Europe.

By contrast, German jets were not only highly successful in combat (and a growing threat to Bomber Command) but they also played an important part in a spectacular raid, by nearly 1,000 Luftwaffe planes, on Allied airfields on the Continent on New Year's Day, 1945, when 144 British planes were destroyed on the ground.

The very advanced, twin-engined Arado had been developed as a Mosquito-style multi-purpose plane, with recce and bombing thought to be its two main functions. Hitler had called it 'the blitz bomber' and intended that it should be used mainly in that role. But there were too many fingers in the air pie at this stage and the first Arados were spread too thin on the ground and asked to fulfil several difficult roles instead of being used the way Britain's Mosquitoes were.

Of all the new types, the Me 262 was so far ahead of its time that it might well have saved the Luftwaffe from ultimate defeat. With their superior speed and rate of climb, and with their four 30 mm cannon, the first squadrons of them began at once destroying the high-flying Mosquitoes which had long roamed free over the Reich. But Hitler wanted bombers to attack Britain, and half the 262s produced had to be converted to this role. Not for the first time, the Fuehrer bungled an air weapon and played into the Allies' hands. Notwithstanding this, by using air-to-air rockets, as well as their powerful cannon, the fighter version of the 262 achieved a sequence of notable successes against Bomber

Command formations, but they were just too late to turn the tide of the air offensive.

Jets, atom bombs, stratospheric rockets and U-boats that could remain submerged for long periods—these were some of the new imponderables that were examined nervously in the depressing period of Hitler's Ardennes counter-offensive. Indeed, the astonishing resilience Germany was still showing, led to such despondency on Allied councils that not a few normally optimistic individuals were now forecasting that the Nazis might survive 1945, with what eventual outcome no one could say.

Fortunately, the do-or-die Russians chose this moment to resume their advance towards the eastern borders of Germany, and the Western Allies quickly refound the strength of purpose that had temporarily been quenched.

On the bomber front, it was decided that specific attacks would have to be resumed on German fighter production and on U-boat targets; that every effort should be made from the air to help Russia; that missions should continue against oil and transport targets; and that something dramatic, but unspecified, should be attempted by the entire British and American bomber armadas as a morale-booster for services' and civilian hearts alike. As the total Allied bomber strength available at any moment had now topped the 4,000 mark, it seemed as if Operation Thunderclap (Harris's dream of a coup de grace) might well provide the desired boost to morale.

Bomber accuracy was beginning to improve by day as well as by night. The 8th AAF in Britain and the 15th in Italy were much troubled still by European climatic conditions in winter, and were mainly attacking from above cloud on radar indications, but they had brought their target radius of accuracy down to just under two miles, which was good for them, but poor by British standards.

Although the main aids issued to Bomber Command crews when they had resumed day bombing in the autumn had been sun-glasses, a new radar daylight device, GH, was now being installed in leading planes, so that precision aiming was the drill, by day as by night, rather than American-style pattern-bombing, with TI bombs seldom more than a couple of hundred yards out in their aim.

Lancs and Halifaxes alike were by now able to carry upwards of 8,000 pounds of bombs on an average mission, which was more than twice the amount the Fortresses and Liberators could lift. All in all Bomber Command was the most powerful and efficient force of its kind the world had ever seen.

'Thunderclap' *did* come up for consideration at this stage, but there was considerable argument and confusion over which city should be used to jolt both the Nazi leaders and the German people into a frame of mind in which they might make an organised surrender, as against months or even years of 'underground' resistance to a forced peace.

Berlin, Chemnitz, Leipzig and Dresden were among the cities discussed—all of them rapidly becoming congested with hundreds of thousands of Germans fleeing before the Russian advance, and all of them important links in the German communications network in the east of the country. Harris favoured wiping Berlin off the face of the Reich and simultaneously knocking out several other cities for good measure. Portal, the Chief of Air Staff; Bottomley his deputy; Sir Archibald Sinclair, the Secretary of State for Air; and Spaatz, the American air commander, were all involved in various two, three, four and five-handed discussions on the matter, which became even more frantically confused because Yalta was looming. Churchill wanted to be able to tell Stalin something positive, at the Conference of the Grand Alliance, which the Russians were convening at Yalta, about how Western bombing policy would immediately help the advancing Eastern Allies.

On 26 January, Portal (who had been at Churchill's side at Yalta) came out against a really massive attack being made on Berlin, on the grounds that it was too big to be knocked out completely and that casualties to crews would be unwarrantably heavy. He wanted the highest priority for the continuing oil campaign, plus watered-down but moderately heavy attacks on Berlin and the other cities Harris had mentioned, or any others considered suitable.

Sinclair, on the same day, addressed a memo to the Prime Minister in which he also favoured the stepping up of the attacks on oil, with the bombing of cities a lesser priority, to be taken up at random when the weather was unsuitable for the oil offensive. Perversely, he kept his foot in the door on Thunderclap, without in any way endorsing it, by saying that this was still 'under consideration'.

Churchill was far from pleased by the apparent vagueness being shown in the matter and demanded to know within twenty-four hours whether Berlin and other large cities in east Germany were going to be major targets in the immediate future. This brought matters to a head, and on 27 January Bottomley formally directed Harris to make 'one big attack on Berlin and related attacks on Dresden, Leipzig and Chemnitz . . . and or related cities'. Churchill was at once informed of this and a tentative date was pencilled in (weather permitting) of 4 February, when the moon would be on the wane. Again, however, there was a certain amount of confusion over priorities, and when Spaatz was called in on the plan, he was also told that oil was still top priority, with some form of Thunderclap second priority.

Characteristically, Europe's wayward weather now proceeded to blow the politicians' plans about a bit. February opened with excellent day-bombing conditions and atrocious nights. So it came about that, within hours of the opening of the Yalta conference, the 8th AAF was able to institute an impressive series of fighter-escorted heavy bomber raids on Berlin, Leipzig, Magdeburg and Chemitz, while Bomber Command's range was restricted to important but less dramatic attacks on oil, transport, shipping and rocket-sites around the North Sea coasts. Only a limited number of day-flying Mosquitoes were able to keep the flag flying for Churchill (as he pursued his arguments with Stalin) in attacks on Eastern Front targets.

Indeed, it was not until the night of 13-14 February that the skies opened up for a major raid in the east, and by this time Dresden was the only 'unmarked' city open to Harris from the list prepared by Bottomley.

As he prepared to press the button for an all-out blitz on Dresden, the AOC-in-C must have known that even this raid would be too little and too late in relation to the promise of Thunderclap. British and American bombing policies had been thrown out of step by the weather at a vital time. The Yanks were now tasting blood too often for them to be brought to heel, as it were, for a combined raid by more than 4,000 bombers. Harris's belief—inherited from Douhet via Trenchard—that one massive blow from the air, delivered at the right point, could instantly finish a war, would never now be put to the test in Europe. Only the atom-bombing of Japan in due course would seem to bear out the validity of his theory.

The bombing of Dresden that night was nevertheless an act of deliberate fury, aimed at shortening the war. The Germans considered the rococo city safe because of its beauty, and had made it an important communications centre for the Russian front. To Harris it was important also as the largest Reich city still intact. He 'gave it stick' as never before, with firestorms, devastation and death the agony of its fate.

The world was stunned by the magnitude of Bomber Command's attack on Dresden, the more so as the city had proved to be undefended. Even the A-bombs, shortly to fall on the Japanese, would not equal the devastation nor surpass the death-roll achieved in this one 'conventional' raid. But equally Harris and his beloved aircrews, who had so efficiently razed a once-beautiful city, felt no guilt over Dresden, as the Americans would apparently feel guilt over Hiroshima and Nagasaki.

The millions who had died in the concentration camps or who had been enslaved by their German conquerors would have raised instant and heartfelt hosannas to the night's work of Bomber Command and its Old Testament-style leader had they known of it.

The Nazis had 'sown the wind' (in Harris's phrase) when they were all-powerful. Now they were reaping the whirlwind. After Dresden the point was reached where there were all-too-few worthwhile targets remaining to the RAF's retributive force. But the command, which had suffered so long and so grievously at German hands, went on hitting and hating. They had somehow endured the longest continuous battle of the war; they had suffered fears, hardships and slaughter on a scale never before endured by any force of their size; and they who remained considered themselves bloody lucky to be alive at all. Over the years Bomber Command had embraced the sweet flower of a generation of natural leaders. Most had died terrible deaths, slamming their young bodies against the Nazi fortresses of Europe. Now that they had the upper hand, the survivors went about their business in the later stages of the war with a great gulp of fury. Precision came to Bomber Command all too late, but it allowed the last volunteers of the lost command to pick off their targets, in the spring of 1945, like trebles on a darts' board, relishing each strike as a blow for a lost friend.

Those—and this is the view of the official history—who claim that Bomber Command's contribution to the war was less than decisive are factually in error.

That was how it was.

Index